Spoon River America

P written before
2016? is small
town Midwest
really Sone?
irrelevant!

4 appreciated Not
significant

6 history q The
book and its
impact

9 "shepherded"

Spoon River America

Edgar Lee Masters and the
Myth of the American Small Town

JASON STACY

**UNIVERSITY OF
ILLINOIS PRESS**
Urbana, Chicago, and Springfield

Library of Congress Cataloging-in-Publication Data
Names: Stacy, Jason, 1970– author.
Title: Spoon River America: Edgar Lee Masters and the myth
    of the American small town / Jason Stacy.
Description: Urbana: University of Illinois Press, [2021] |
    Includes bibliographical references and index
Identifiers: LCCN 2020051237 (print) | LCCN 2020051238
    (ebook) | ISBN 9780252043833 (cloth; acid-free paper) |
    ISBN 9780252085826 (paperback; acid-free paper) | ISBN
    9780252052736 (ebook)
Subjects: LCSH: Masters, Edgar Lee, 1868–1950. Spoon River
    anthology. | City and town life in literature. | National
    characteristics, American, in literature. | American
    poetry—Middle West—History and criticism. | Middle
    West—In literature.
Classification: LCC PS3525.A83 S547 2021 (print) | LCC PS3525.A83
    (ebook) | DDC 811/.52—dc23
LC record available at https://lccn.loc.gov/2020051237
LC ebook record available at https://lccn.loc.gov/2020051238

For Diane Stacy,
who taught *Spoon River Anthology*

Contents

Acknowledgments

This book owes much to many people.

Diane Stacy introduced me to *Spoon River Anthology* many years ago. Ian Hunt, Chief of Acquisitions at the Abraham Lincoln Presidential Library, alerted me to a recently acquired collection of Masters's papers that rejuvenated my interest in the poet. The St. Louis Mercantile Library's collection of periodicals, especially *Reedy's Mirror*, proved to be essential to sections of this book. My colleagues at Southern Illinois University Edwardsville, especially Erik Alexander, Jessica DeSpain, Laura Fowler, Jeff Manuel, and Robert Paulett, provided invaluable feedback and recommendations. Michele Bigham and Deirdre Johnson at Lovejoy Library cheerfully fielded my many pleas for assistance. Southern Illinois University Edwardsville granted me a sabbatical that was vital to completing the book. The College of Arts and Sciences supported the project with the Going Award in 2017. Herbert Russell kindly met with me to discuss his excellent biography of Masters. The three reviewers of the manuscript, Marcia Noe, William Barillas, and the anonymous third reviewer, offered indispensable suggestions that strengthened the book's arguments and shored up its weaknesses. James Engelhardt of the University of Illinois Press saw promise in the idea; Alison Syring and Jennifer Argo helped bring it to fruition. Nancy Albright's expert copyediting helped turn the manuscript into print.

And Michelle, Abigail, and Margaret Stacy make me glad every day.

Spoon River America

Introduction

Good friends, let's to the fields . . .
After a little walk, and by your pardon
I think I'll sleep. There is no sweeter thing
Nor fate more blessed than to sleep.
I am a dream out of a blessed sleep—
Let's walk and hear the lark.

—Edgar Lee Masters, Epitaph
Oakland Cemetery, Petersburg, Illinois
From "To-morrow Is My Birthday,"
Toward the Gulf (1918)

The words engraved on Edgar Lee Masters's gravestone read nothing like the epitaphs he wrote for the citizens of the fictional town of Spoon River, Illinois. While the dead of Spoon River tell secrets, express doubts, offer justifications, and settle scores, Masters's gravestone hides more than it reveals. His ambivalent childhood, two marriages, four children, scores of books (one very famous) and, finally, his death in the middle of a century in which he was not born are veiled behind three simple requests: to walk, to listen, and to sleep. It is a very ordinary epitaph.

But Masters's *Spoon River Anthology* (1915) proved to be an extraordinary book in its subject, form, and effect. Ostensibly a collection of fictional epitaphs, it captured a regional idea of small-town life and disseminated it so widely that

Overclaim?

it helped shape the way many Americans conceived of rural communities for much of the twentieth century. Ultimately, *Spoon River Anthology* contributed to making the Midwestern small town, for a time, a mythological symbol of the nation itself.

The myth of the American small town developed in two phases. Between the 1830s and the 1890s, popular culture mythologized the New England village in reaction to social anxieties over the growth of large cities like New York. In this first myth, a romantic sensibility, coupled with an ambivalence about the economic and social changes wrought by the early phases of the Industrial Revolution, fostered a nostalgic vision of life in the countryside where small communities served as repositories of unaffected, unchanging American ways. While cities fostered affectation, pretense, chaos, and vice, the countryside preserved essential truths about nature and the founding of the republic. In the countryside one could, in Henry David Thoreau's words, live "deliberately."[1]

But a newer myth transformed this ideal of rural life. Starting in the Midwest in the late nineteenth century, the small town became a place where a pleasant surface fostered a hypocritical underbelly. This second myth of the American small town arose in tandem with debates over changes in the American economy and culture during the later phases of the Industrial Revolution and was shaped by multiple factors: the rise of new industrial centers, especially Chicago, along with conceptions of the "closing" of the frontier, the stabilization of a middle class in Midwestern towns in the aftermath of the Populist movement, and the popularization of modernist sensibilities in the early twentieth century. *Spoon River Anthology* portrayed the effect of these changes in a collection of poems by the dead citizens of a fictional Illinois town and unwittingly helped redefine the American small town in Midwestern terms.

Spoon River Anthology is a voyeuristic work of titillating and tragic tales about a place that appeared quiet and staid on the surface. Masters based his poems on childhood memories of two Illinois towns, Petersburg and Lewistown, and wrote them in a creative rush under the pseudonym "Webster Ford" from spring 1914 to early 1915 for the St. Louis periodical *Reedy's Mirror*. He was inspired by his reading of J. W. Mackail's *Greek Anthology* (1906), Ezra Pound's theories of imagistic verse, the fiction of Theodore Dreiser, and the poetry of Carl Sandburg, among other texts and authors.[2]

Despite *Spoon River Anthology*'s classical overtones and appeal to timeless human dilemmas, the book's emphasis on psychological, morally ambiguous themes, along with its free verse form, marked it as a work of modernist literature. But within this modernist package were familiar literary types who fueled the book's popularity: the materialistic, hypocritical elite; the soil-bound, exploited populist; and the skeptical community exile who understood the

New psychic space

town from an insider-outsider perspective. The postmortem divulgence of secrets by these small-town types proved a compelling formula for American readers throughout the early twentieth century.

Spoon River Anthology was astoundingly popular for a book of poetry—it sold, supposedly, 80,000 copies in its first year alone—and it engendered critical debates on its merits that eventually included the upper echelon of the American literati.[3] But more significantly, the book created a new psychic space for Americans to debate their contemporary values: the Midwestern small town. The popularity of Masters's iconoclastic graveyard confessionals established a modern myth of small-town life in America that elicited popular nostalgia for the seemingly eternal values of "Main Street" and a general ambivalence about the authenticity of those values in effect. Thus, the popularity of Masters's Spoon River inspired a genre that framed small-town America in both nostalgic and ambivalent terms.

ossified?

The Great Depression, the Second World War, and shifts in American living patterns toward the suburban ossified the twentieth century's myth of small-town life. Throughout much of the twentieth century, the drama of traditional values and their veracity played out against Main Street's idealized backdrop, even as fundamental changes in American residency choices depopulated the small towns of the Midwest. Ultimately, the mythology apparent in *Spoon River Anthology* was subsumed by changes in the way many Americans lived—both the depopulation of small towns and the rise of suburbia—though its poetry found a second life in American classrooms and on the stage even as the towns Masters fictionalized faded in popular memory as proper grounds for debating the nature of the American republic.

?

Edgar Lee Masters generated some interest among literary critics in the last third of the twentieth century, largely as an early modernist, a regional poet, and a representative of the Midwest in the years before the First World War. Many Americans perhaps recall reading Masters in their high school or college anthologies of American literature. Five of the two-hundred-odd poems of *Spoon River Anthology* are included in the *Norton Anthology of American Literature* ninth edition (2017), compared with Carl Sandburg's four poems; H. D.'s, Amy Lowell's, and Marianne Moore's six each; T. S. Eliot's seven; Ezra Pound's twelve; and Robert Frost's twenty-one.[4] If the *Norton Anthology* is a rough indicator of a poet's place in the general education curriculum of college-educated Americans, Masters casts a short shadow among leading lights. When I queried colleagues on Masters's status among literary critics, one said he had "certainly fallen to the byways and backwaters" of modern scholarship but added, "I love his poems." This is a reaction common among readers who know Masters by name or remember reading a selection of his strange poems

Our town?

in *Spoon River Anthology*: they recall a passing fascination with his confessing characters but don't acknowledge him with the grave recognition reserved for poets one ought to know. Masters is appreciated rather than significant for only one book, which continues to sell well. Trade publishers like Penguin still market *Spoon River Anthology*, and even the University of Illinois Press's 1993 scholarly edition of the book, with an extended introduction by John E. Hallwas and annotations throughout, continues to be "a perennial bestseller for us" according to an editor at the press.[5] The other twenty-nine books of poetry Masters published receive little attention, however.[6] *Spoon River Anthology* was, it seems, a one-off.

A few critics have tried to explain *Spoon River Anthology*'s origins and influence. All note that Masters grew up in two small Illinois towns and that his household was torn by the conflicting personalities of his father's easygoing free thinking and his mother's strong-willed religiosity. They repeat Masters's interpretation of his life as divided between the more "Virginian" culture of Petersburg, where he lived his first decade of life, and the "Calvinism" of Lewistown, where his family moved and his father waged a low-grade culture war against the town's elites before being accepted into their society.[7] Critics recount Masters's boyhood reading of classics, romantics, and contemporary authors with a few sympathetic schoolteachers and fellow students; his misbegotten year at college; his begrudging acquiescence to his father's desire that he study the law; and his move to Chicago, partnership with Clarence Darrow, unhappy marriage, and ongoing attempts to fit writing into a busy life. Then, in middle age, he published *Spoon River Anthology*.

In their attempt to explicate Masters's book, some critics try to reveal the real people behind his characters. Charles Burgess, for example, sees Masters's twenty-four years as a lawyer before *Spoon River Anthology* as the origin of the book's "variety, realism and . . . message."[8] Burgess likewise traces the significance of Masters's paternal grandmother, Lucinda Masters, who appeared in *Spoon River Anthology* as "Lucinda Matlock"[9] and finds the poet's celebration of "pioneer virtues" as his means to critique "American imperialistic adventurism in the early twentieth century."[10] For Burgess, the village politics of *Spoon River Anthology* echo the "experience of the Masters family," which the poet used to "show political motives and actions typical of many eras and settings."[11] Accordingly, the significance of *Spoon River Anthology* lies in Masters's ability to find the universal in personal experience and express through the little town of Spoon River a microcosm of eternal human dilemmas. In this interpretation, an illumination of *Spoon River Anthology* requires a careful biography of its author.

Other critics look for the intellectual origins of *Spoon River Anthology* and see Masters as an amalgam of long-standing European and American literary traditions. According to John Hallwas, Masters was a "literary naturalist" whose "struggle for self-realization" drove his peripatetic readings, writings, and relationships. Hallwas carefully reveals the influence on Masters of Spinoza, Whitman, and Dreiser and concludes that the poet was "both a traditionalist and a modernist," with roots in Jeffersonian and Emersonian ideals but with a skepticism that places him in the company of T. S. Eliot and Ezra Pound.[12] Ronald Primeau also finds in *Spoon River Anthology* a long foreground of European and American sources that reflect the poet's varied reading, from the ancient Greeks to Goethe, Emerson, Shelley, Whitman, and Browning, all of which ultimately "occup[y] a central place in the shaping of his own themes and style." Cognizant of his debt to great Western literature, Masters, according to Primeau, "made room for himself in that [American literary] tradition."[13]

Herbert K. Russell, in his magisterial biography of Masters, sums up the poet's legacy in similar terms:

> The lacunae in Masters's life have been literature's loss, for his biography has all the ingredients of a good story, that of a boy from the country who, against great odds, dreams, struggles and succeeds in his quest to be recognized as a world-class writer, only to be brought down by weaknesses inherent in his own being. Shakespeare and the Greek Tragedians recognized this type of person and left dramas concerning figures who exemplified it.[14]

Russell's summation of the poet's life itself reads like a Masterian epitaph, full of irony and tragedy about a character who only dimly understands himself, but who the author and the reader see in the round. It is as if Masters's compact and compelling epitaphs incline critics to a similar interpretation of their creator.

Masters has garnered some critical attention in the twenty-first century. Martín Espada extends interest in the biographical Masters and traces his poignant portrayals of the dead to his advocacy of the living. For Espada, "These persona poems were clearly written by a practicing lawyer. The language is often similar to that of an affidavit: written in the first person, direct and clear, telling a story, attempting to persuade."[15] Other critics are interested in Masters's influence. Jim McCue wonders whether T. S. Eliot's famous first line—"Webster was much possessed by death"—was a nod to Masters's pseudonym.[16] Still others have begun to think of the poet in terms related to the study of sexuality and gender. Scott Herring, for example, argues that *Spoon River Anthology* upholds heteronormativity by framing sexual deviancy in solely heterosexual terms.[17] And some transatlantic and international scholars see Masters as a

In print fa our 100 year

still-relevant subject. Julianne VanWagenen notes that *Spoon River Anthology* is remembered only in a piecemeal fashion in the United States but read as a cohesive whole in Italy. VanWagenen traces the difference to the legacy of Italian "literary isolation" and, later, a homegrown interest in Masters.[18] Romanian scholar Dragoș Avădanei connects Masters to Thornton Wilder and claims that in both "when the living talk about the dead, what we receive is remembered history; when the dead 'talk' about the living, the outcome is myth."[19]

Among modern critics, Masters is neither quite a leading light nor a forgotten poet. He is generally remembered and, therefore, never really rediscovered. In one sense, *Spoon River Anthology* is an interesting literary artifact: Midwestern, a work confined to its time and place in the literary canon. And yet, it has remained in print for over one hundred years; its poems have been, and continue to be, reconceived as drama and taught in classrooms and, according to Herbert Russell, poets like Sylvia Plath and Robert Lowell owe a debt to it.[20]

Instead of arguing for *Spoon River Anthology*'s literary merits, this book argues that the significance of Masters's one famous book lies in the way it gathered historical trends from the Midwest of the second half of the nineteenth century and repackaged them in a compelling style and format that, for a time, helped make the Midwestern small town a synecdoche for the United States. In effect, *Spoon River Anthology* captured a set of regional anxieties, expressed them through a collection of verse by fictional dead people who had no more reason to hide their inner lives, and disseminated them so widely that it helped shift the mythology of small-town America from a romanticized New England to a modernist Midwest. In this regard, I do not exclusively explore the origins of *Spoon River Anthology* and I do not seek a revision of its place in the American literary canon. Instead, this book is an analysis of the historical atmosphere into which *Spoon River Anthology* was born and the environments in which it thrived, even beyond the life and legacy of its author. This is the history of a book and its impact.

This history of *Spoon River Anthology* owes a debt to scholars of print culture, especially those who understand that books have histories of their own. Martin Barker and Roger Sabin, in *The Lasting of the Mohicans: History of an American Myth* (1995), note how little attention literary critics have paid to James Fenimore Cooper's *The Last of the Mohicans* (1826) in spite of its reprinting and adaptations throughout the nineteenth and twentieth centuries. For Barker and Sabin, it is "important to delve back into those lost histories [of books like *The Last of the Mohicans*]," but it is equally necessary to "examine those tales that continue to resonate" beyond the boundaries of high aestheticism and ongoing critical interpretation. According to Barker and Sabin, *The Last of the Mohicans* encapsulated and spread a long-standing mythology of the noble and disappearing American Indian by which Americans understood the displacement of native peoples during the nineteenth century.[21] Likewise, Sarah Meer, in *Uncle Tom Mania: Slavery, Minstrelsy and Transatlantic Culture in the 1850s* (2005), traces the transatlantic life of Harriet Beecher Stowe's *Uncle Tom's Cabin* (1852) as "meanings accru[ed] to [the] novel partly because of the ways in which it has been read. . . . [S]ome of the idea of '*Uncle Tom's Cabin*' was created by those who reviewed it, dramatized it, or borrowed its name or imagery to construct something else."[22] In both cases, these critics treat books like historical agents in their own right, whose words are textually stable, but meaningfully malleable in the context in which they are read.

While this book uncovers the milieu in which *Spoon River Anthology* was created, it also explores the way in which segments of American culture embraced, debated, and transformed Masters's interpretation of rural America into a new mythology of small-town life. Ultimately, *Spoon River Anthology* encapsulated a contemporary discourse about human nature, morals, and society in a format that made one suspect the romantic myth of rural living itself. For many Americans, Masters's exposure of the contradictions between the surface of Main Street and its dark underbelly felt real, or at least realistic.

There are four kinds of chapters in this book. The first type offers the broadest cultural focus and analyzes the myth of small towns before and after *Spoon River Anthology*. In this regard, chapters 1 and 7 frame the transformation of this myth over the course of the nineteenth and twentieth centuries. Chapter 1 traces the myth's origins to a romanticized New England village, follows it through the print culture of the generation after the Civil War, and concentrates on the nineteenth-century reading public, primarily the urban middle-class consumers of popular print, and the ways in which they romanticized the New England village in the face of urban growth and flux. Chapter 7 explores popular portrayals of small towns and suburbs in the twentieth century and includes film and television manifestations of the Main Street myth. The sources change in these chapters as the media consumed by Americans changed. Likewise, in flux during these years was the mythological location and nature of the American small town itself, which, I argue, shifted from New England to the Midwest and from a divide between the nostalgic countryside and the ambivalent city to the mingling of nostalgia and ambivalence within small communities themselves. Chapters 1 and 7, then, serve as beginning and ending points for the transformation of the myth of the American small town.

The second type of chapter in this book focuses on the historical elements that fostered this transformation. In chapters 2 and 3, I argue that *Spoon River Anthology* captured contemporary social, cultural, political, and economic trends in the Midwest, forged them into a popular and easily digestible format, and disseminated them widely enough to help foster a reconception of small-town America. In this regard, chapters 2 and 3 are narrowly focused and biographical. However, the biographical focus here is historically contextual, specifically in regards to the way in which Masters proved to be a product of central Illinois and Chicago in the late nineteenth and early twentieth centuries. This approach is inspired by biographies like David Reynolds's *Walt Whitman's America* (1995), where instead of re-creating a subject as he moved through and reacted to events, I seek to illuminate the way in which context shaped Masters and his creation. In other words, these chapters reconstruct Masters's habitat during the generation of *Spoon River Anthology* and analyze the way in which it shaped the book's sensibilities and inclinations. For example, it will not particularly matter whether Masters actually heard Frederick Jackson Turner speak about the closing of the frontier at the World's Fair in 1893; it was in the "air" the summer he arrived in Chicago and reflected a sense of identity among Midwesterners that had been gestating for two generations. Likewise, these chapters explore Masters's transformation from an author of the Populist-reformer type to an early (and unwilling) modernist and the cultural forces that came together in Masters's poetry during this period: the World's Fair, Populism, Turnerian ideology, bourgeois libertinism, muckraking reform literature, and nascent modernism.

Chapters 5 and 6 concentrate on the reception of *Spoon River Anthology* by both highbrow critics and popular audiences. These chapters seek to contextualize the short-term legacy of the book in terms Carl Van Doren called a "revolt from the village." Instead of a traditional literary history of this reception, however, my review investigates the literary and popular debate about what was "true" in *Spoon River Anthology*. The debate over the truthfulness of the book is what interests me most because it began a debate about small towns themselves. These chapters allow the reader to watch contemporary culture forge *Spoon River Anthology* and its literary inheritors into a twentieth-century myth of American small towns that struggled with a nostalgia for their promise and an ambivalence about their integrity.

The heart of this book, chapter 4, unpacks three character types in *Spoon River Anthology*: elite, populist, and exile. These individuals ultimately became flexible archetypes for defining sympathetic and nefarious characters in the twentieth century. It is this chapter, for example, that allows me to connect Masters's characters to twentieth-century "types" in chapter 7, say, the banker Thomas Rhodes to Henry Potter in *It's a Wonderful Life* (1946). In this regard, *Spoon River Anthology* helped frame the way in which Americans mythologized small-town types for much of the twentieth century.

In his book *Life* (2010), Keith Richards described the origins of the album *Exile on Main Street* like this, "When we first came up with the title it worked in American terms because everybody's got a Main Street."[23] Richards's Main Street is ubiquitous enough to elicit ready images for most Americans. Main Street is lined with nineteenth-century buildings that house a few essential, but indistinct, shops. Perhaps there is a grocery store, a barbershop, or a bank. There is likely a school on one of the side streets. Around the corner are one or two churches. Main Street might end in a courthouse or a field of corn. Main Street might be within sight of a park with a gazebo or a monument from a distant war.

Richards's Main Street is a place of middle-class satiety, of indistinct midcentury clothing or the rural garb of a farmer in town for the day. Its people are driving American-made automobiles or strolling and chatting with each other. All are likely white. When Walt Disney designed "Main Street, U.S.A." in the 1950s, the contours of the simulacrum were already drawn. When Barack Obama spoke of "Main Street" versus "Wall Street" in the aftermath of the Recession of 2008, he knew his audience.[24]

Keith Richards could just have easily noted how familiar the idea of an exile on Main Street is for Americans. The exile is in and out of small-town society; someone who knows the town but has been socially exiled from its company. Fellow citizens might look away when the exile passes; her presence is apparent, but not always recognized. Her ostracism lends shape to the town's idea of itself. From her vantage on Main Street, the exile sees its illusions; she is privy to its pettiness and fear, its ugliness and wrath. She knows its hypocrisy firsthand. The exile is Main Street's quiet arbiter and referee; she is both in and out of the game.[25]

But Richards's universal Main Street is not an eternal myth. It is, in fact, a relatively modern one, lined with nineteenth-century buildings and a straight, level thoroughfare, thereby hinting at a region only settled during the nineteenth century; the topography of Main Street is Midwestern. Edgar Lee Masters's *Spoon River Anthology* shepherded a regional and contemporary critique of the Midwestern small town into a myth familiar to Americans born far away from central Illinois's Spoon River. What are the origins of this myth and the processes of its dissemination? What avenues did it take through American culture so that it could come back to Americans in the title of an album by a British rock band? This book traces how a collection of epitaphs by fictional Midwesterners became part of America's conception of itself.

CHAPTER 1

Origin Stories

Where yonder stream divides the fertile plain,
Made fertile by the labours of the swain;
And hills and woods high tow'ring o'er the rest,
Behold a village with fair plenty blest:
Each year tall harvests crown the happy field;
Each year the meads their stores of fragrance yield,
And ev'ry joy and ev'ry bliss is there,
And healthful labor crowns the flowing year.

To yonder village then will I descend,
There spend my days, and there my ev'nings spend;
Sweet haunt of peace whose mud' wall'd sides delight,
The rural mind beyond the city bright . . .

—Philip Freneau, "The American Village" (1772)

When Philip Freneau published "The American Village" on the eve of the American Revolution, he perpetuated a long-standing dichotomy between urban and rural communities that stretched back generations.[1] Over the next century, in the midst of economic and social flux in the northeastern United States, anxious middle-class readers, especially those in cities shaped by changes in the market economy, adapted pastoral visions like Freneau's to soothe more pressing concerns by imagining a regional Elysium, the New England village, that preserved American ideals in the midst of troubling change. Freneau's celebration of the unchanging rhythms of the village, with its agricultural cycles following natural ones to produce a happy and prosperous population, expressed a broad ambivalence toward the "bright" city, and offered, instead, a rural community where "joy" and "bliss" sprang from the fertile fields. Throughout the nineteenth century, idylls like Freneau's resonated in new and compelling ways for the reading public in the fast-changing society of the Northeast.[2]

In the two generations before the settlement of the Midwest, New England supplied a now largely forgotten myth of rural life in the United States. Shaped by anxiety over growing urban centers like New York City, which were perceived to be dens of hypocrisy and vice, the small New England municipality offered a mental refuge for nineteenth-century urban dwellers, where unaffectedly natural citizens preserved the original goodness of the republic. This myth was at first largely perpetuated by those who feared their own sons and daughters would lose themselves in the American city.

The myth of the small New England municipality made little distinction between the terms "village" and "town." And while the term "village" called up more pastoral images, the nearest distinction that urban readers made between each was that the village was a smaller version of the town, though both served as a foil to the growing Northeastern cities of the era. Noah Webster's dictionary from 1841 exhibits the fuzziness of the distinction between the two during this period. A village was a "small assemblage of houses, less than a town or city, and inhabited chiefly by farmers and other laboring people." A town, on the other hand, was "any collection of houses larger than a village" while a city was a "large town."[3] Webster's definitions are helpful, however, in capturing the perceived connection between the village and agricultural labor, which provided a ready distinction between the countryside and the city: while the New England village remained tied to natural rhythms, the city proved to be an aberration that disconnected residents from all that was original and unchanging.

New York City's growth during the first half of the nineteenth century appeared to many Americans to augur a dangerous future. Manhattan itself exploded from around 124,000 residents in 1820 to 313,000 less than a generation later, and during the same period, New York City surpassed Philadelphia and Mexico City to become the largest city in the Western Hemisphere.[4] The infrastructure of the city could not keep pace with its growing population. Notorious regions like the Five Points, which housed much of the city's poorest populations, including thousands of Irish immigrants escaping famine and poverty at home, traded mud for dust during New York's changing seasons. With no organized police force until 1845, the city utilized a night-watchmen system of law enforcement that had been in effect since the eighteenth century and did little to control the rise of organized gangs, pickpockets, confidence men, and prostitutes.[5]

During the 1830s and 1840s, the urban middle class built a system of precise social rituals that, they hoped, allowed them to recognize con men and cutpurses on the streets and, if necessary, in their homes. The parlor, for example, arose in this era as the liminal space between the street and a home's interior. Within this public-private room, where guests displayed their social graces and tacitly assured hosts of their trustworthiness and honesty, the middle class created a space where the dangers of the street could be easily identified before they made their way into the more intimate interiors of the home.[6] The parlor was a polite stage upon which performers displayed their belonging to good society. It also expressed a certain siege mentality on the part of the urban middle class.[7]

But many of the newcomers to New York City were themselves middle class. Young men arriving from the countryside—most of whom sought positions as accountants, bookkeepers, cashiers, or secretaries—drove the haphazard growth of New York.[8] These young clerks often lived in one of the hundreds of boarding houses that sprung up during these years and fueled the reputation of the city as a locus of iniquity and vice. The murder of the prostitute Helen Jewett in 1836 revealed a thriving brothel culture that depended upon the excess earnings of young middle-class men.[9] Throughout the summer of 1836, James Gordon Bennett's *New York Herald* followed the case of Jewett, who had migrated from Maine, and the trial of her lover and john, the nineteen-year-old clerk Richard P. Robinson, originally of Durham, Connecticut.[10] The press debated Jewett's origins as a way to explain her descent into prostitution. According to Benjamin Day's *New York Sun*, Jewett came from the respectable family of "Major General Spaulding" of Augusta, Maine, and was seduced "whilst at boarding school" and pulled into a "degraded course of life" by the act of a "heartless" paramour,[11] thereby creating a narrative from moral error in New England to tragic end in New York City. On the other hand, four days later, the *York Gazette* (York, Pennsylvania), quoting the *Boston Morning Post*, claimed that Jewett was in fact from a poor family, was taken in by a local judge and, though "every effort was made to instil [*sic*] into her mind those high moral principles which could alone secure her happiness and respectability," nevertheless "betrayed . . . an obtuseness of moral perception" and "left the family that had so long protected her and was soon degraded." Thereafter, Jewett relocated to New York to find employment in houses of "ill repute," where she met her untimely end.[12] Whichever story proved ultimately true, both began within the moral safety of Jewett's New England hinterland and ended in the moral turpitude of New York City.

Richard Robinson, the accused, though ultimately acquitted of Jewett's murder, was himself a transplant from New England. Robinson exhibited an easy nonchalance throughout the trial, presented himself in fashionable attire, and, most troubling for many readers, became a temporary celebrity among a swath of young men who rejected their parents' and bosses' morality in favor of the cult of "the Fancy," a loose society that forged the blood sports of boxing and dog-fighting with the patronage of high-class brothels into an early kind of youth culture.[13] In this regard, Robinson himself exemplified the transformation wrought when one left the moral surety of New England. The New York papers produced daily reports of the trial of Robinson and the witnesses for and against him while Robinson's brimmed, floppy hat became the rage for young clerks that summer, creating the impression that the city had changed a whole generation of young men for the worse. Reprinted articles form Bennett's *Herald* made their way into the rural countryside throughout the Northeast in 1836 and gave credence to fears that the moral integrity of the republic was under threat.[14]

The reading classes reinforced the coupling of urban space and moral turpitude. Sermons like John Todd's warned of the "hardened pander to vice who . . . makes war upon virtue and exults in being a successful recruiting-officer of hell."[15] Best-selling books like George Lippard's *The Quaker City* (1844), based on the trial of Singleton Mercer, who murdered Mahlon Heberton after Heberton lured Mercer's sixteen-year-old sister, Sarah, to a brothel and raped her, portrayed a city that spread like a dire apparition on the middle-class conscience. In Lippard's fictionalized account of the case, a secret society in the center of Philadelphia entertained the elite of the city by kidnapping young women and forcing them into lives of vice.[16] The confluence of lurid tales in the newspapers and breathless fiction based on real events established by mid-century the image of the American city as the new Babylon.

New England Eden

As the myth of an urban Babylon arose in the second quarter of the nineteenth century, contemporary elites created a romantic foil in the New England countryside, largely out of a fictionalized past.[17] As the geographer Joseph S. Wood notes, the idealized New England village, "with a tree-shaded green, tall-steepled church, and white-clapboarded shops and dwellings," was largely a product of "Romantic New Englanders" who invented a tradition of Puritan origins for contemporary consumption. In this regard, the supposed tidiness, order, and unaffected democratic traditions of New England villages opposed the seeming chaos and danger of growing cities. According to Wood, these romantic New Englanders "manipulated a geographical image to fuse New England-as-tradition with village-as-setting . . . to create an enduring settlement ideal,"[18] even though by the 1870s over half of residents in Massachusetts in the heart of New England, themselves lived in urban areas.[19]

Like most myths, the idealized New England village began with an origin story, in this case, a founding community that exhibited a natural morality unmoored from the encrusted and pretentious rituals of the European past. This natural morality seeded a society of republican institutions and pragmatic ethics that countered the seeming chaos and ostentatiousness of growing American cities, and thereby preserved the New England village both from the aristocratic temptations of the past and the social flux of the present. In this capacity, the New England village exhibited an integrity that preserved idealized American virtue and connected its citizens to all that was original and good in the nation.

In this respect, the myth of the New England village differed from an earlier Jeffersonian rural ideal, in which agriculturalists served as a bulwark of republicanism against mercantile elites and their handmaidens in an overweening federal government.[20] Where Jeffersonian ideology proved useful to planters, yeoman farmers, and their representatives during the Federalist administration of John Adams, middle-class readers in the nineteenth century imagined the small New England village at a remove since they were not intimately tied to the economics of agriculture or the rhythms of rural life. In this way, as American cities grew increasingly diverse and raucous, the New England village served as a usable communitarian ideal, a place for the reading public to live vicariously in the midst of economic and social change.

One year before Helen Jewett's murder and the trial of her clerk-paramour Richard Robinson in New York City, Ralph Waldo Emerson mythologized Concord, Massachusetts, in a speech to memorialize the village's two-hundredth anniversary.[21] By 1835, the growth and transformation of the nearby city of Boston, coupled with the rise of the factory town of Lowell only fifteen miles to Concord's north, allowed Emerson to imagine Concord in opposition to these recent changes. Concord served as a storehouse of traditional republican mores from the Revolutionary era and before.[22]

Beginning with a description of the "river, by whose banks most of us were born" and through "every winter, [which], for ages, spread its crust of ice over the great meadows," Emerson portrayed a "little society of men" who "fish the river, plough the fields it washes, mow the grass and reap the corn . . . as did their forefathers." Just two years before, Emerson had disparagingly described Paris as a "loud modern New York of a place" lacking "history."[23] In this regard, Emerson framed history in mythological terms: a municipality's past proved itself in unchanging ways. To further this point, Emerson listed the names of Concord's founding families that still inhabited the village—"Blood, Flint, Willard, Meriam, Wood, Hosmer, Barrett, Wheeler, Jones, Brown, Buttrick, Brooks, Stow, Hoar, Heywood, Hunt, Miles"—in a fashion that Masters echoed almost one-hundred years later in *Spoon River Anthology.*[24]

Emerson's "Historical Discourse" continued through purported good early relations with the native peoples of the region: "The faithful dealing and brave good will . . . went to their hearts. . . . So that the peace was made,"[25] and as a result, the village was called Concord. This auspicious founding made for government in accordance with nature. "For the first time," according to Emerson, "[t]he nature of man and his condition in the world . . . controlled the formation of the State"[26] and made a system that was naturally just and orderly. "It was the river, or the winter, or famine, or the Pequots, that spoke through them to the Governor and Council of Massachusetts Bay."[27] This good order, based in nature, proved the "great secret of political science" and gave "every individual his fair weight in the government, without disorder from numbers." For Emerson, this represented a return rather than progress since in the "town meeting, the roots of society were reached."[28]

Tranquility ruled without interruption in Emerson's seemingly perfect civil society until the coming of the Revolutionary War, when outside forces tested the mettle of Concord's citizens: "In these peaceful fields, for the first time since a hundred years, the drum and alarm-gun were heard, and the farmers snatched down their rusty firelocks from the kitchen walls, to make good the resolute words of their town debates."[29] In the fight for independence, according to Emerson, Concord drew on its reserve of natural morality and civic order, which proved steadfast in the face of invasion. "Those poor farmers who came up, that day, to defend their native soil, acted from the simplest instincts. They did not know it was a deed of fame they were doing. These men did not babble of glory."[30] Here, Emerson, echoing Thomas Jefferson, idealized independent agriculturalists,[31] but Emerson's tribute was to the "little society of men" these farmers made, and thereby situated Jefferson's ideal citizen within a cohesive society, a rival to the collective chaos of the city for a reading public anxious about social change. Concord existed in a kind of suspended animation, maintaining native ways that stretched back one-hundred years in the face of great social flux. Describing his research into the annals of Concord, Emerson took the opportunity to shift to the present, hinting at the village's eternal qualities: "[These annals] must ever be fountains of all . . . information respecting your character. . . . They exhibit a pleasing picture of a community almost exclusively agricultural, where no man has much time for words . . ., a community of great simplicity of manners, and of a manifest love of justice."[32]

While Emerson took a celebratory tone proper for a bicentennial, his speech before the people of Concord exhibited many of the attributes of the myth of the New England village in its earliest form. Situated in the countryside, Concord was settled by simple farmers who, in their need for good order, established a society and political system that made natural morality and good sense manifest. In this myth, the flux of the American city—with its wealth, its poverty, its temptations and ostentatiousness, its chaos and crowds—represented a divergence from nature. While historians for a generation have noted that New England in the seventeenth and eighteenth centuries was a location of social, political, and legal complexity,[33] Emerson's history found that the past conformed to an idealized present.[34] Margaret Fuller, friend of Emerson, fellow New Englander, and author of *Women in the Nineteenth Century* (1845), expressed a similarly nostalgic pining for the unchanging New England village. In her travel memoir, *Summer on the Lakes in 1843* (1844), Fuller worried about a child she met in rural Illinois whose wild beauty could be "made to vanish from eyes which look too much on shops and streets, and the vulgarities of city 'parties.'" Luckily, "New Englanders of an excellent stamp" whom she called "generous, discreet, and seeking to win from life its true values" populated nearby Geneva, Illinois.[35]

Newspapers in the Northeast echoed Emerson's and Fuller's romantic notions. A letter to the *New York Express* described "New England villages" as repositories of "beauty of scenery" as well as "institutes of learning," highlighting both their pastoral charms and poised civility, places where "courtesy . . . characterize the manners of the place."[36] A short story called "The Two Neighbors" in the *Brooklyn Daily Eagle* portrayed an urban "stranger" in a similar New England idyll:

> The stranger, as he loitered by, involuntarily paused a moment to imbibe the sweet images of rural beauty and comfort . . . and it would not be strange as he passed the neat, but somewhat time-worn dwelling of farmer Howell, if he should covet still another glance at the sunny-bowed and rosy-cheeked damsel who sat at the open window of a bright summer's afternoon, busily plying her needle or perhaps braiding a straw hat for her little brother, who, meanwhile, read aloud as was the custom in this time-saving community, subject to his sister's correction, some useful and instructive book.[37]

Like Emerson's farmers, Howell resides within a singular "community," a cohesive whole. Tellingly, the story turned on the loss of Howell's farm to his son's bankruptcy in New York City and the degradation of a family tempted by the allures of fashion.[38] In this way, the New England village mixed beauty, natural morality, and social cohesion, while the city loomed degraded in the distance, a collection of individuals without the good order of a "society" or "community." According to a correspondent to the *New York Express*, "the attractive charm that hangs around a New England village has been created, and is still preserved, by a high standard of morals and untiring industry." Projecting anxiety over the ever-growing anonymity that shaped urban life by the 1840s, the correspondent claimed that in the New England village, "every man is, more or less, a check on his neighbor, and no enterprise can be projected without undergoing a rigid scrutiny, an operation which is very apt to promote a just and healthy tone of action in the neighborhood."[39]

Years before he was a well-known poet, Walt Whitman also purveyed the myth of an unchanging, naturalistic village and tinged it with nostalgia for an eternal past. While in private letters, Whitman expressed disdain for the citizens of the rural villages where, as a young man, he taught in one-room schools,[40] the poet's public writings about a visit to Montauk Point on eastern Long Island in 1849 for the *New York Sunday Dispatch* described the residents there as "a band of . . . men . . . great unshaved, gigantic-chested beings, with eyes as clear as coals, and flesh whose freedom from the gross humors of artificial life told its tale in the dark and unpimpled brown of their faces and necks." These unaffected fishermen were "thorough sons of Esau."[41] Whitman, who had spent most of his life in New York and Brooklyn, perpetuated the romantic myth of New England villages as repositories for all that was natural, unchanging, and, therefore, good for his urban audience. Eastern Long Island's rural fishermen, popularly characterized as descendants of the Puritan settlers who arrived in the seventeenth century,[42] exhibited the unaffected traits of the biblical natural man, Esau: clear-eyed, freedom-loving, unshaven, and tan. These descendants of New Englanders provided Whitman, the tourist-correspondent from the hemisphere's largest city, a story to report from a community that represented a golden age of American innocence and a place where the best of the nation abided, a look at the nation before its fall into degradation.[43]

Whitman's use of Esau to characterize the hearty rural Long Islanders he encountered on assignment from his city paper exemplified the nostalgia essential to this myth of the village. While Whitman privately felt a strong antipathy toward his rural students and their parents in the early 1840s, publicly, as a freelance reporter for the *Dispatch* (a newspaper that appealed to both working and middle-class audiences)[44] he upheld the gauzy image his readers expected from portrayals of rural Long Island, which was quickly becoming a summer retreat for New Yorkers seeking to escape the fetid miasma of the city. In this regard, Whitman displayed an ambivalence toward the city itself, much like his readers, who visited this community-of-yore vicariously, by reading his article, or literally, as tourists visiting the Long Island countryside of old "Puritan" fishing villages like Greenport, only a three-hour ride by rail from Brooklyn.[45] At the same time, Whitman's readers also conceived their own surroundings in equally opposing, and perhaps exaggerated, terms. Even as late as 1856, a year after he published his free-flowing celebrations of crowded city streets in *Leaves of Grass*, Whitman issued a warning against the "country-man trap" of the city, full of "monsters," "licentiousness," "mock auction shops," "shoulder-hitters," "thieves," "infernal rascals," and "rowdies," some "from distant San Francisco, vomited back among us to practice criminal occupations . . . who will sneak up behind you . . . and . . . knock you on the head, and rob you before you can even cry out."[46] Whitman's dire warning, published in *Life Illustrated*, was overwhelmingly aimed at a New York audience, though composed ostensibly as a guide to tourists. In the end, Whitman tipped his hand by noting that until "all the fools are dead . . . greenhorns will be deluded by New York." With this knowing wink, Whitman invited his readers to join him in the hard-nosed wisdom that the "greenhorn," an eternal Esau, could not survive the new Babylon. But Whitman's urban readers, perceiving themselves exiled from sunshine, fresh air, and comforting truths, could easily cure themselves with a weekend getaway to the New England Eden.

Paradise by Rail

By the 1850s, the Northeastern middle class had constructed a full mythology of rural New England life, replete with a history that promised that the best things remained unchanging and an ethical system that conveniently foiled the perceived complications, compromises, and dangers of the city. In this regard, the urban middle class mythologized an unadulterated village arcadia that the tourist, retiree, or commuter visited in a kind of homecoming from urban core to idealized village.[47] It is not surprising that Americans increasingly situated their cemeteries in pastoral rural locations. There, in ultimate repose, Americans returned to a mythological Eden where they found peace in the unchanging countryside and mourners meditated on eternity surrounded by unadulterated nature.[48]

With the expansion of the railroad into the hinterlands of the Northeast, the countryside became increasingly accessible to middle-class city dwellers and further allowed an idealized encounter with the village. The *New York Evening*

Post noted that "delightful" New England villages were conveniently accessible for city-dwellers by rail.[49] In an article promoting real estate near New York City in Highland Terrace, the editor Nathaniel Parker Willis proposed that soon "New Yorkers will be ready for a startling and most revolutionizing change . . . industry, necessity, or vice, could alone prefer a house in a 'block,' among disturbances and gutters, to a home unencroached upon, amid fresh air and gardens."[50] According to Ralph Waldo Emerson, by the 1850s "the morning trains . . . from every suburb, carry the business men into the city to their shops, counting-rooms, work-yards and warehouses."[51]

Andrew Jackson Downing, the horticulturalist, author, and landscape designer, made a career advising the urban middle-class on the proper way to recapture the unadulterated joys of village life. In *Rural Essays* (1853), a collection gathered and edited posthumously by George William Curtis, Downing advised his well-heeled readers against the dangers of retiring to the rural villages and "undertaking too much." According to Downing, "after ten or twenty years' hard service in the business . . . of towns," too many urban Americans carried with them the most "romantic ideas of country life," most notably "an *extravagant* notion of the purity and the simplicity of country life."[52] Downing's goal, however, was not to disabuse his readers of their fantasies of rural life so much as to return them to the proper state of mind to appreciate its charms. According to Downing, urban retirees to the country thought only of the "beauty of the scenery" and, upon moving to their new rural residences, found themselves "bored to death."[53] The fault lay, however, in themselves: "they have brought as many as possible their town habits into the country" and instead had to modulate their expectations and expenditures to be "content with simplicity."[54] Thus, for Downing, like for Whitman, city-dwellers' streetwise wisdom and fast-paced ambition made them subject to the "Sodom-apples" of cities, as if they had already bitten from a tree of urban knowledge. If they could not find within themselves the ability to "adopt the rustic habits of country life," their return to the village Eden would be impossible, even if they physically retired there.[55] However, for those "fitted to understand it . . . simply and devoutly," life in the country proved "full of pure and happy influences."[56]

Henry David Thoreau made just such a retreat. While Thoreau's *Walden* (1854) is popularly understood as the work of a reclusive philosopher in the woods, scholars like Milette Shamir understand Thoreau's retreat as an "experiment in the liberal fantasy of independence qua withdrawal into the private sphere." For Shamir, Thoreau's cabin was less a rejection of middle-class mores and more an early version of a "suburban" residence, where a "masculine definition of intimacy, based on concealment rather than revelation" provided the kind of privacy found in the male-centered study of the middle-class home.[57]

Shamir's interpretation illuminates what Thoreau sought to escape, namely, the grind of the early industrial economy. "Did you ever think," Thoreau asks his readers, "what those sleepers are that underlie the railroad? Each one is a man. . . . And every few years a new lot is laid down and run over; so that, if some have the pleasure of riding on a rail, others have the misfortune to be ridden upon."[58] According to Shamir, "Thoreau locates the desire to own a home in the primitive past" and thus "reiterates one of the most frequent conventions . . . to justify the building of the semirural cottage."[59] In this light, Thoreau echoed Downing's sentimental retiree who sought rural living as a way to reconnect to the simple, eternal, and true. Like Downing, Thoreau's idyll was dependent upon ambivalence for urban living while, at the same time, keeping one eye, warily, upon it.

Myth Made History

In the aftermath of the nation's Civil War, one whole section of the nation was left in ruins, an entire generation of young men had witnessed the grossest carnage, and civil rights themselves had been tested under the strain. Nostalgia for the New England village became part of the national mythology of its origins and a way to connect the future to an idealized past. Increasingly, historians also imbibed this idyllic mythology.

Joel Parker, professor of law at Dartmouth College,[60] gave academic polish to the mythology of the New England village in "The Origin, Organization, and Influence of the Towns of New England" (1865) by tracing the "arterial system . . . through which has circulated the life-blood which has invigorated, sustained, and strengthened [New England]; making her expand in her religious, social, educational, benevolent, and political institutions and character" to the rest of the nation.[61] New England's town system preserved "a frame of self-government, to be administered by . . . freemen[,]" which "was established from the first,"[62] and served as a model for democratic practice "through all coming time."[63]

Parker's evocation of an unchanging character of the New England village echoed the hagiography of Emerson a generation before. In this capacity, he contrasted contemporary urban unrest with the ethos of the New England village. Referring to recent riots in Philadelphia, Parker noted that the city had lost sight of its pacifist character: "Could worthy Friends . . . have bestowed upon the City of Brotherly Love the simplicity of a Quaker town . . . it would not . . . have been the most noted of all the cities . . . for the frequency and ferocity of the riots."[64] In contrast to cities like Philadelphia, New England villages "exercised upon the character of the people" a system where politics were naturally stable and efficacious: "No stumps were needed on which to utter patriotic harangues. The meeting-houses were well adapted to that purpose. It was thus that great masses of the people were influenced to an active and ardent patriotism."[65] Parker found in New England's revolutionary legacy "an industrious yeomanry," who easily converted into an armed soldiery for liberty "on the first news that the British had left the limits of Boston."[66] Accordingly, "support of the [D]eclaration was more effectual in New England than in any other of the colonies."[67] Ultimately, the honor of the Founding goes to the New England village:

> Were supplies of provisions to be had at short notice? . . . Was money required to carry on the operation of a campaign? . . . Were soldiers needed to fill ranks in the army? Was the pay which was offered inadequate . . . ? And when, by repeated drafts in this way upon their resources, the general ability was somewhat exhausted, individual inhabitants . . . became security for this additional payment, sometimes involving their whole property.

Thus, as for Emerson, the New England village proved to be the key to successful resistance to the British. And when the great conflict was over, according to Parker, the New England village abided "in the full exercise of [its] powers, requiring no change to carry the country onward to increased prosperity." As in 1776, so in 1865, New England villages, "still remain with undiminished usefulness."[68]

Twenty years later, professional historians had come to echo this mythological characterization of New England. Despite a general effort among early professionals to foster reconciliation between North and South in the generation after the Civil War, mostly through histories of Reconstruction that justified Redeemer governments and white supremacy in racialist terms,[69] the New England village remained the starting point for American democratic institutions. Edward Channing, who received his PhD in 1880 and served as an instructor and later professor at Harvard, argued in "Town and Country Government in the English Colonies of North America" (1884) that the earliest settlers of New England represented the "great middle classes," while a "large body" of settlers in the Virginia colony were poor whites "not much better than that of . . . the negro slave of his time." Channing's essay, which received the Toppan Prize from Harvard University in 1884, argued that these different origins gave rise to systems ultimately opposed. "In Virginia," Channing asserted, "the upper class took the reins of government into their hands at the start," while in New England, "the mass of the people, from the very earliest time, seized the control of affairs, fiercely resented any encroachment on what they considered their rights, and were the governing power when the Revolution burst upon them."[70] Virginia, according to Channing, was led by "Cavaliers" who oversaw a lower class who had "not as yet learned to think for themselves,"[71] whereas by the mid-seventeenth century in New England "non-freemen who had taken the oath of fidelity were admitted to a share in the carrying on of the town affairs."[72] This difference in political freedoms was born of a different cause for settlement. Virginia was "settled on account of wealth," but to New Englanders, wealth was but an accompaniment to a "pure and decent life."[73] Thus, Channing reinforced the fifty-year-old myth of the New England village as the origin of an ideal American society. In this regard, Channing's arguments echoed the contemporary "Teutonic-germ theory," where historians traced the origins of Anglo-American institutions to the tribal structures of prehistoric Germany. Though Channing himself expressed skepticism about tracing seventeenth-century New England village government to the Germanic tribes of Caesar's era,[74] he nevertheless found in New England villages the beginnings of modern republican order, the germ of the nation itself. As a senior scholar, Channing echoed these arguments in *A Short History of the United States for School Use* (1896) and his Pulitzer Prize–winning six-volume *History of the United States* (1905–1926).[75]

After a generation of formation, the romantic myth of the New England village became a stereotype. Rural New England villages, through their Puritan heritage and supposed democratic institutions, timeless mores, and natural temperance, represented a psychic refuge for middle-class readers against the social flux around them, largely represented by the perceived dangers and pretense of city life. Likewise, in the aftermath of the Civil War, the New England village held the promise that the ideals of 1776 endured.

Myth Made Fiction

Trends in popular middle-class literature also followed this pattern. Henry Ward Beecher, the charismatic minister who had spent his career preaching to ever-growing urban audiences, upon trying his hand at fiction, set his romance in the mythological New England by now familiar to readers.[76] In *Norwood; or, Village Life in New England* (1868), which was first published in Robert Bonner's *New York Ledger*, Beecher framed his love story in the nostalgic countryside:

> Since the introduction of the railways, thousands of curious travelers every summer have thronged New England, have seen its manufacturing villages, and admired its general thrift. But those who know its scenery only by the river-valleys, know little of it; and those who have seen its people . . . in cities, are little acquainted with the New England character.[77]

From there, according to Debby Applegate, the book "gave voice to Beecher's various theories" from the "spirituality of nature" and the "natural law of evolution" to his "generous vision of Reconstruction."[78] Nevertheless, though these theories proved unorthodox for a preacher of Beecher's generation and region, the myth he used to express them was familiar. Abiah Cathcart, the New England father in the novel, had "a vision of success [that] was not extravagant—a homestead and a family; and property to support and educate his children until they should be old enough to take care of themselves. That was the measure of his dream."[79] Accordingly, Abiah worked "by intelligent industry" and "never by craft," and he loved to "take his book at noon, after his frugal meal was done, and sit by his team, while the horses ground their oats." Here, Beecher asked his reader, "do you wonder . . . at such pleasure?" thereby unmasking his intended urban audience: "Then you know little of some scenes of life."[80] As Kirsten Twelbeck notes, "Norwoodites harvest the fruit of their traditional thrift in the absence of shrieking machines and discontented laborers that were a very real aspect of the age." It was as if Norwood's "tranquil dreamscapes symbolically replace[d] the killing grounds of Antietam and Gettysburg."[81] Thus, Beecher's Abiah Cathcart and the village of Norwood formed an integrated whole in the midst of disorienting change.

In *Meadow-Grass* (1896), Alice Brown capitalized on the myth of the New England village a generation after Beecher in a series of nostalgic tales of the rural countryside that echoed themes stretching back to before the Civil War. In Brown's telling, "though false ambition may have ridden us to market, or the world's voice incited us to kindred clamoring," citizens could always return to rural Tiverton, New Hampshire, in their mind's eye and experience "things as they once were, as they still are, in a certain sleepy yet altogether individual corner of country life." In Tiverton, the schoolhouse, the old watering-trough, the nearby spring "and over the gray, lichen-bearded fence, the growth of stubby pasture" remained unchanged. Though Susie Marden went out West, "she is and ever will be the little girl who made seventy pies, one Thanksgiving time, thereby earning the somewhat stinted admiration of those among us who could not cook." There was Sam Marshall, who the children were convinced would one day be a senator or even president, but who as an adult "patiently" did his haying in his field. David, who left the village and became rich, inspired the question, "Is he happy?" Another young man, who ran away from home "in quest of gold and glory," achieved happiness upon his return to Tiverton three days later "footsore and muddy," hungry, but "undaunted." According to Brown, "He never tried again . . . the wood solitudes [became] familiar to him as his own house door." The myth of the unchanging New England village reached its apotheosis in Brown's fiction as a place of eternal respite from the ambivalence of modern adult life:

> We who have walked in the country ways, walk in them always, and with no divided love, even though brick pavements have been our chosen road this many a year. We follow the market, we buy and sell, and even run across the sea, to fit us with new armor for the soul, to guard it from the hurts of years; but ever do we keep the calendar of this one spring of life.[82]

The seasons follow the unchanging rhythms of Tiverton. Children grow, some leave, and the world outside of the village changes. But Tiverton, following the patterns of the farm and their fields and the cycles of the school year, abides as a place of stability in the midst of a flux.

In *The Country of Pointed Firs* (1896) Sarah Orne Jewett likewise expressed similar nostalgia for the rural village of Dunnet Landing, Maine: "When one really knows a village like this and its surroundings, it is like becoming acquainted with a single person." The main character, a Bostonian who visits Dunnet Landing each summer to write a novel, is charmed by the escape from the ever-changing city and "returned to the unchanged shores . . . the same quaintness of the village with its elaborate conventionalities; and that mixture of remoteness, and childish certainty of being the center of civilization of which her affectionate dreams had told her."[83] In a similar vein, Margaret Deland's *Old Chester Tales* (1898) was set in a Pennsylvania village that emulated the myths of New England villages from earlier in the century. There, residents

> felt satisfaction with the conditions as well as the station into which it had pleased God to call [them]. . . . While such satisfaction is said to . . . be at variance with progress, . . . it cannot be denied that it is comfortable; as for progress, everybody knows that it is accompanied by growing-pains.

Besides, "if people choose to burn lamps and candles instead of gas" and "if they like to hear the old parson who married them—or baptized some of them, for that matter . . . the outside world may wonder, but it has no right to condemn."[84]

For two generations, amid economic and social change, the myth of the New England village offered a contrast to the American city of the Northeast. This nostalgic myth of the unchanging rural community depended upon ambivalence toward urban living on the part of the middle classes that thrived there. The village offered repose, either temporarily or in retirement, and most importantly, assured the urban middle class that the radical change and vibrancy around them, fraught as it was with unpredictability and instability, proved to be only the frothy surface of a placid and unchanging depth, where the natural values of the nation's founding survived.

CHAPTER 2

The Premodern Midwest

The hunt, the shot, the glorious chase,
    The captured elk or deer;
The camp, the big bright fire, and then
    The rich and wholesome cheer;
The sweet, sound sleep, at dead of night,
    By our camp-fire blazing high,
Unbroken by the wolf's long howl,
    And the panther springing by,
Oh, merrily passed the time despite
    Our wily Indian foe,
In the day when we were Pioneers,
    Fifty years ago.

We shunn'd not labor when 'twas due,—
    We wrought with right good will;
And for the homes we won for them,
    Our children bless us still,
We lived not hermit lives, but oft
    In social converse met;
And fires of love were kindled then,
    That burn on warmly yet.
Oh, pleasantly the stream of life
    Pursued in constant flow,
In the days when we were Pioneers,
    Fifty years ago.

—William D. Gallagher, "Fifty Years Ago"
    Joliet Signal, December 14, 1847

Forty-seven years before Frederick Jackson Turner formulated his theory of the frontier as the forge of American civilization, the poet William Gallagher captured a popular American understanding of the significance of American "pioneers" in contemporary sentimental terms. Gallagher, born in 1808 in Pennsylvania to an Irish immigrant father and the daughter of a Welsh farmer, moved, after his father's death in 1822, to southwestern Ohio.[1] While Gallagher did not live the experiences he portrayed, the poem's significance lies in its mythologizing of settlement and its wide dissemination. In the two stanzas that begin this chapter, Gallagher captured a generation of pioneering lore along the Ohio River Valley, from subsistence hunting to semi-subsistence farming, through conflict with natives to the building of homes and bearing of children, to communities "in social commerce met" by the "fires of love," which "burn warmly yet."

Gallagher's poem appears to have been published first in Cincinnati in 1846 and announced as a "New Song for the West" with a "portrait of one of the Old Pioneers of 1798," likely Israel Ludlow, one of the founders of Cincinnati, and his descendants.[2] The poem's wide distribution at a time when newspapers spoke to local audiences points to its resonance for Americans reflecting on settlement along the Ohio River Valley. By June 1846, the poem and accompanying music were being performed in New Orleans alongside popular songs like "Ah! What Delight the Soldier Knows," and the Irish Ballad, "Norah McShane."[3] That same month, the *Louisville Daily Courier* advertised print copies of the poem and sheet music for accompaniment.[4] In 1847, "Fifty Years Ago" appeared as far away from its origins as rural Springville in western New York and burgeoning Brooklyn on Long Island.[5] In December that year, it appeared in a newspaper in Joliet, Illinois, a town that had been incorporated only ten years before.[6]

While Gallagher never lived in frontier Ohio in the waning days of the late eighteenth century, his portrayal of the frontier along the Ohio River Valley marked a nascent western mythology rising in tandem with the Northeast's mythological version of the New England village. The poem's simple tropes of wildlife, campfires, Indians, home, and children proved flexible in their application and compelling in their imagery to audiences from the Gulf of Mexico to the Atlantic seaboard. In this regard, Gallagher captured an early version of many Midwesterners' nostalgic self-conception as descendants of the "wholesome" pioneers who built communities that inherited the values of their forebears. Unlike the mythological villages of the Northeast that bequeathed American values to the present, Midwestern communities stood in danger of losing their pioneering inheritance.[7]

Edgar Lee Masters portrayed his ancestors in these terms. Early in his autobiography *Across Spoon River*, Masters described his grandfather's eloquent voice in church as "always moving his pioneer listeners to tears."[8] Squire Davis Masters was born in Tennessee, relocated to central Illinois with his family in 1829, and used his inheritance to purchase property in Menard County in 1849, outside the settlement of New Salem, where Abraham Lincoln owned a dry goods store over ten years before.[9] When Edgar Lee Masters's father was born in 1845, Petersburg had a population of 714 people.[10] Lucinda Masters, his grandmother, also born in Tennessee, relocated to Alton, Illinois, and later to Jacksonville, where she met Masters's grandfather. In *Spoon River Anthology*, Masters gave voice to Lucinda's pioneering father: "We cut buffalo grass, / . . . felled forests, / . . . built school houses, built bridges, / Leveled the roads and tilled the fields." Echoing Gallagher, Masters's frontier culminated in communities that wrote the origin stories of small-town America in the twentieth century.

Frontier State

Illinois became a state from the south.[11] While historians debate the origins of the distinct culture of the Americans who emigrated during the late eighteenth century from western Virginia, along the Ohio River through Kentucky, southern Indiana, and, during the first two decades of the nineteenth century, into southern Illinois, they represented a distinct set of social and economic mores that distinguished them from emigrants that settled later in the northern part of the state. Termed variously "backcountrymen," "backwoodsmen," "frontiersman,"[12] "pioneers,"[13] or, later, "hoosiers" and "butternuts,"[14] these settlers arrived along the Ohio River Valley and beyond by chain migration, where a few settlers set up semi-subsistence farms with access to waterways and markets, most notably along the "American Bottom," bordering the Mississippi River in the southwest corner of Illinois.[15] Chain migration allowed settlers to maintain correspondence with relatives and acquaintances along the Ohio River Valley in southern Indiana and northern Kentucky,[16] thereby "fostering clusters and networks of relatives, co-religionists, or friends who perpetuated religious practices, farming techniques . . . and other familiar cultural traits."[17] Within the first ten years of the nineteenth century, the population of Illinois rose from 2,458 to 12,282.[18] Ten years later, the population had grown by 349.5 percent.[19]

Legal factors prepared frontier Illinois for settlement patterns that gestated small towns. The Land Ordinance of 1785, which established a township system for settlement of the Northwest Territories, proved to be one of the few pieces of successful national legislation to come out of the short-lived Articles of Confederation congress in the aftermath of the American Revolution. The Land Ordinance's grid of six-by-six square-mile townships aided in the orderly and cohesive system of land sales and settlement that prefaced the distinctive grid pattern of property lines and rural roads apparent across the Midwest today. While the Ordinance maintained the French system for established lots perpendicular to waterways, the majority of the Northwest Territory was structured along this grid, including territorial Illinois. Most importantly, the Ordinance required surveying *before* public sale. This system, according to one historian, "led to orderly land sales, settlement, and social harmony and helped Illinois escape the chaos, squabbling, and bitterness over sales that marred Kentucky and other states."[20]

By the end of the second decade of the nineteenth century, the Midwest's structured settlement system laid the foundation for a synergy between small-town and agricultural economies. In 1810, only Kaskaskia, the capital, and Shawneetown, the primary crossing point along the Ohio River between Kentucky and Illinois, could be considered towns. Both contained land offices, thereby providing an early connection between agricultural settlements and municipalities. Within six years, a third land office was established in Edwardsville, a village of around 150 people.[21] These land-office towns grew apace. Within three years of its founding, one visitor, Edmund Dana, described Edwardsville as containing sixty or seventy houses, "a court house, jail, public bank . . . weekly newspaper," with "excellent" land around it containing "many plantations," primarily semi-subsistence family farms of varying size.[22] By 1818, the year Illinois became a state, fourteen of the fifteen counties had a county seat, which typically contained the basic institutions of public life, "a courthouse, jail, and tavern, and possibly a general store."[23]

Central and northern Illinois, settled primarily during the two generations after statehood, exhibited the economic conditions conducive to seeding small towns surrounded by agricultural hinterlands. By the mid-1830s, inventions like the steamboat, which allowed for upriver navigation, and the completion of the Erie Canal in 1825, which connected the Hudson River and New York City to the Great Lakes, opened these regions to rapid settlement.[24] Though the more populous southern portion of the state reflected the culture of the upland Southerners who settled there,[25] in northern and central Illinois migrants from Ohio, Pennsylvania, New York, and New England, as well as immigrants from England, Germany, Scandinavia, and France, filtered into the state throughout the 1820s.[26] By then, the Algonquin peoples had struggled with Anglo-American settlement for years, especially during the War of 1812, and, during the 1820s and 1830s, when Indian removal became state and national policy. After the Winnebago War of 1827 and the Black Hawk War of 1832, when native peoples were cleared by force from northern Illinois, migration began in earnest.[27] Thereafter, a mythological Illinois frontier, which in fact was no more than about a generation old, increasingly became the backdrop upon which Illinoisans, even those whose ancestors came after statehood, memorialized their state's origins.[28] By 1835, the top two land offices in terms of sale were in the northern half of Illinois: Chicago and Springfield.[29] By 1840, Springfield was made the state's new capital, thereby recognizing the growing influence of the central portion of the state and reflecting a compromise between the two regions.[30]

While both halves of Illinois depended primarily on semi-subsistence agriculture, agriculturalists in the southern portion of Illinois used the Mississippi as the primary waterway to market, while farmers in northern Illinois increasingly looked to Chicago. According to William Cronon, despite the "five days . . . to bring an average-sized wagonload of thirty bushels of wheat to market [in Chicago,] . . . hundreds of farmers appear[ed] . . . each day" of the harvest season.[31] By the late 1840s, with the completion of the Illinois and Michigan Canal, which connected Lake Michigan to the Illinois River, Chicago contained over three hundred dry-goods and grocery stores dedicated to catering to the consuming needs of the farmers who used their meager profits to purchase supplies for the coming season.[32] By 1852, over half the city's wheat arrived from western Illinois.[33] By the late 1850s, the Illinois Central railroad connected Chicago to Centralia and Cairo in Southern Illinois; another line, the Saint Louis-Alton-Chicago, connected the Mississippi River town of Alton, through Springfield, to Chicago.[34] In this regard, according to Cronon: "branch lines demonstrated a lesson that small-town railroad promoters . . . learned repeatedly in ensuing decades: lines . . . seemed always to point toward Chicago."[35]

By the 1840s, Illinoisans were divided north and south both by the culture of their original settlers and also by their transportation networks to the rest of the world. While Andrew R. L. Cayton and Peter S. Onuf remind us that settlement in the Old Northwest "was more like an ethnic and cultural checkerboard than the proverbial melting pot,"[36] Illinois divided broadly along a north-south axis with a liminal zone in the center of the state. Southern Illinois depended upon the Mississippi River for access to markets, through the river towns of St. Louis and Alton, or via the river itself, which was navigable by flatboat to New Orleans, a route young Abraham Lincoln took in 1828 and 1831.[37] Northern Illinois proved increasingly connected to financial interests in New York through Chicago. In both regions, small towns, often county seats, served as economic hubs with skilled craftsmen, dry-goods stores, and municipal services. It is during this period that Lincoln shared ownership of a dry-goods store in New Salem along the Sangamon River. This period saw the rapid growth of towns in Illinois. Between 1835 and 1837 alone, 189 new towns were founded in the state's twenty-six counties, most of them close to woodlands, prairie, and navigable water, thereby providing ready access to fuel, fields, and markets.[38]

In his analysis of early Illinois towns, historian James E. Davis finds common traits among these incipient communities that contrasted with the New England village to the extent that when Masters settled on Main Street in Lewistown, his mother spoke nostalgically about the New England villages of her youth, though the children understood only "dimly what our mother meant about houses of the New England villages."[39] With an eye to transparent land sales and structured expansion, Illinois towns tended to be laid out according to a grid pattern similar to the Land Ordinance of 1785. In this way, Midwestern towns exhibited a settlement pattern in contrast to the New England village, which was typically organized around a common village green. Also, residential housing tended to expand to the west of the town's center, according to Davis, to "avoid wind-driven sparks" by taking advantage of the generally easterly wind patterns in the state.[40] This had the added benefit of sparing townspeople the smells emanating from butchers and tanners in the business district and contributed to residential districts with straight streets that ran perpendicular and parallel to a main street for businesses and municipal institutions.[41] Unlike the town "commons" of New England, which harkened back to shared space in English villages, the gridded pattern of Midwestern towns worked against a common space at the center. Instead, an economic thoroughfare ran through town without necessarily providing a common outdoor space. Likewise, Davis claims that residents took advantage of the gridded plats of their property and built houses with "long front lawns" for further protection from the smells and noise from the street.[42]

A contemporary booster pamphlet, *Illinois in 1837*, portrayed Illinois towns in these terms. Alton had "streets ranging above each other in exact uniformity." Beardstown grew from one cabin to two hundred "frame and brick" houses in eight years and contained "thirteen stores, eight groceries, one drug shop, two tanneries, two forwarding houses, [and] two steam flouring-mills." Belleville, the seat for St. Clair County, boasted "considerable business," and was "surrounded with a rich and extensive agricultural country, and a fine body of timber."[43] Bloomington, in central Illinois, contained "extensive business, three groceries, two taverns. . . . various mechanics and an intelligent population of about 700."[44] There were "several stores" in Lebanon and "streets [that] cross each other at right angles and are from 60 to 70 feet wide."[45] Ottawa, in northern Illinois, had between 75 and 80 families and exhibited "[l]arge additions . . . made to the town plat, by laying off additional lots on lands adjoining." Winchester, though just laid out in 1831, already had a population of 600 and "good schools, mills, and manufacturing establishments." Tellingly, only Kaskaskia and Cahokia, originally settled by the French, contained a "common field," which had to be explained to prospective settlers as "land, of several hundred acres, enclosed in common by the villagers . . . each family possessing individual interest in a portion of the field."[46]

Of the 189 towns founded between 1835 and 1837, the majority of those built more than seven miles from the nearest town survived.[47] This may explain the eclipse of Lincoln's New Salem in the 1830s by the new county seat of Petersburg only a few miles to the north, incidentally surveyed by Lincoln in 1836.[48] According to Andrew Cayton and Peter Onuf, "most settlers before the 1830s thought of community strictly in terms of family or a local network of friends," though after the 1830s, proponents of "full-blown . . . bourgeois capitalism" created a Main Street of "shopkeepers, professionals, merchants, and other people of middling rank" who promoted "self discipline" and order.[49] Towns like Petersburg, which still existed by the year of Edgar Lee Masters's birth thirty years later, exhibited this mix of pioneer origins and bourgeois stability, and thrived into the twentieth century.[50] By then, they had become touchstones of American identity.

Founding Myths

When William Gallagher's poem was published in the *Joliet Signal* in 1847, Illinois's founding mythology had come to follow a familiar narrative arc: the frontier was settled by semi-subsistence pioneers who faced a hostile native population. In the face of this hostility, pioneers improved the land and established small settlements that offered some mutual protection. However, as farms and acreage grew, isolated homesteads faced attacks. Ultimately, a climactic conflict removed what was deemed to be a native menace and, thereafter, ushered in a settled history, devoid of native peoples. Later, pioneers built small towns to serve as local economic centers for the distribution of agricultural products and acquisition of manufactured necessities.

This narrative structure was born along the Ohio River Valley. Elizabeth Perkins traces it to the years following the American Revolution where settlers in northern Kentucky and southern Indiana represented a first wave of "pioneers." By the 1840s, descendants of these settlers began to produce histories of what were popularly recalled as "Indian times."[51] According to Perkins, settlers' recollections of the first Kentucky settlements followed a simple sequence: "coming out" (arrival), "settling out" (establishment), and "improving," that provided "simple temporal boundaries ... which did not depend on ... absolute dating for its inherent meaning."[52] These three stages were interspersed with "friendly" and "unfriendly times" that marked periods of local warfare with native tribes. This remembered period of earliest settlement ended with a significant conflict and culminating battle. For Kentuckians along the Ohio River Valley during the 1790s, this final conflict took place when General Anthony Wayne defeated the Western Confederacy at the Battle of Fallen Timbers in 1794. Thereafter, the Treaty of Greenville (1795), by which the Western Confederacy ceded the Ohio River Valley to the United States, marked the end of the pioneering era.[53] Incidentally, Israel Ludlow, a likely pioneer of William Gallagher's poem, surveyed the treaty line guaranteed by the Treaty of Greenville.

The narrative arc from "coming out" to "improving" proved useful in other contexts as well. Two generations after the Treaty of Greenville, Illinoisans adapted it to their own settlement history. *Illinois in 1837* characterized Illinois as having just concluded a penultimate conflict with native peoples and presented the conflict in terms characteristic of the period:

> The country experienced almost entire freedom from their depredations after the late war with Great Britain, until 1832. In that year the savages, under their celebrated chief, Black Hawk, committed many cruel murders, and for a time excited considerable alarm in the northern parts of the state; but being effectually reduced, the remnant[s] have been since settled in the country west of the Mississippi river [*sic*], and all apprehensions of danger from the same cause in future entirely removed.[54]

According to Nick Kryczka, by the 1840s, Illinoisans transformed the so-called Black Hawk War into the culminating battle that marked the divide between the state's frontier origins and its settled future.[55] Masters himself proudly claimed that his grandfather fought in the Black Hawk War under Captain William Gillham from Morgan County.[56] Eliza Farnham, who lived outside of Peoria between 1835 and 1841 before returning east and publishing *Life in Prairie Land* (1846) about her time in Illinois, personified this mythological turn with the story of a settler who arrived "long before these lands were vacated by the Indians," and at first "depended on wild game and fruits for subsistence." Farnham's anecdote of frontier Illinois culminated in a melodramatic tale in which a mother, alone in a cabin with her children, was visited by Sauk Indians and later faced a prairie fire that threatened to engulf the homestead. The fire's "unbroken line of flame, wide as the eye could reach ... appear[ed] [like a] devouring demon sweeping the heavens" and nearly destroyed mother and children. Luckily, at the last moment, all were saved by the family's faithful dog, who, predating by a century Eric Knight's heroic canine in *Lassie Come Home*, "stood at her feet; the strong intelligence of his face fascinat[ing] her eye in spite of the danger," and led the family to the ploughed field where "the fire [had] nothing to feed on." Afterward, this pioneer woman, in Farnham's telling, "sank into the semblance of sleep, on the naked earth, among her babes, with her faithful protector crouched at her feet."[57]

Significantly for Farnham's narrative, this near-tragedy took place in a distant Illinois past. Though Illinois had been a state for only seventeen years upon Farnham's arrival, the props of the tale—Sauk Indians, a lonely cabin, a mother and children in peril, a sudden, awe-inspiring prairie fire—were the hallmarks of Perkins's "settling out" period, when lone farmsteads faced the dangers of the frontier. However, by the time Farnham arrived on the scene of her own story, frontier Illinois had given way to a settled farm-and-town landscape of the "improving" phase. While "Indian times" formed a mythological backdrop for Farnham, "our town," settled by "New-Yorkers, Bostonians, Providence people, and a few random Yankees," took a tract of "unbroken prairie" and "laid out a square mile into lots . . . and by the aid of a little capital, some notes of hand, more brains, and still more cunning, bore off the prize." Though Farnham characterized her fellow townspeople as "pretty sharp" and "thriving," as opposed to "the open-mouthed Kentuckians, Tennesseans, and Buckeyes," her description of the town's citizens neatly matches that in *Illinois in 1837*, the booster publication printed about ten years before: "the majority are . . . industrious mechanics, farmers, and tradesmen. . . . [who have] . . . expectations of becoming capitalists."[58]

By the 1840s, the myth of the New England village and the Midwestern town both featured an established small municipality as the protagonist in an origin story. But whereas the New England village served as a founding enterprise at the dawn of settlement and thereby preserved original values, the Midwestern town was the result of a mythical frontier experience, which began, in Gallagher's words, with the hunt, the shot, and the glorious chase, and culminated in "social converse met."

Lewis Atherton notes that William Holmes McGuffey's series of readers extended this myth. According to Atherton, McGuffey's readers served as the foundation, especially in the Midwest, for young Americans' conception of themselves and the rural communities they lived in. McGuffey painted a picture of a "supposedly classless society" devoid of "steamboats . . . and railroads" in which students from grades one to six "learned about horse-drawn transportation, about merchant rather than manufacturer, about artisan in place of factory laborer, of the outdoors, of birds and farm animals."[59] In one example, published in 1879, when Edgar Lee Masters was eleven years old, McGuffey exported the ideal of the well-ordered New England village to schoolchildren throughout the country. Henry Wadsworth Longfellow's "The Village Blacksmith" focuses on a single character (as in Masters's epitaphs) and situates him seamlessly into the natural order of the village,

> Under the spreading chestnut-tree
>   The village smithy stands;
> The smith, a mighty man is he,
>   With large and sinewy hands;
> And the muscles of his brawny arms
>   Are strong as iron bands.
> . . .
> Week in, week out, from morn til night,
>   You can hear his bellows blow;
> You can hear him swing his heavy sledge,
>   With measured beat and slow,
> Like a sexton ringing the village bell,
>   When the evening sun is low.
> . . .
> He goes on Sunday to the church,
>   And sits among his boys;
> He hears the parson pray and preach,
>   He hears his daughter's voice,
> Singing in the village choir,
>   And it makes his heart rejoice.
>
> It sounds to him like her mother's voice
>   Singing in Paradise!
> He needs must think of her once more,
>   How in the grave she lies;
> And with his hard, rough hands he wipes
>   A tear out of his eyes.
>
> Toiling—rejoicing,—sorrowing,
>   Onward through life he goes;
> Each morning sees some task begin,
>   Each evening sees it close;
> Something attempted, something done,
>   Has earned a night's repose.

Thanks, thanks to thee, my worthy friend,
    For the lesson thou has taught!
Thus at the flaming forge of life
    Our fortunes must be wrought;
Thus on it sounding anvil shaped
    Each burning deed and thought![60]

In this case, Longfellow's blacksmith plies an eternal trade without competition, attends church, and traverses three generations—his mother's, his own, and his children's—in a sentimental moment of hearing his daughter sing in the choir. According to Atherton, the ethics of McGuffey's readers stressed "interdependence" and "obedience to parental directions," and by "applying the eternal verities to a simple culture, uncomplicated by urban and industrial problems,"[61] enforced a "dominant middle-class code" by which "church, school, and home" furnished an education of "heart and mind."[62] This middle-class code, whether enjoyed by all residents or not, formed an ideal of a pioneering community grown to maturation for the generation of Edgar Lee Masters's parents.

In this way, the Midwestern town marked the end of a region's origin story. During the period when the New England village became the locus of American values against the moral dangers of the city, the Midwestern town became the inheritor of values of a mythological founding generation and, ultimately, a battleground for the characteristics and actualization of those values. While the New England village memorialized timeless stability in the second half of the nineteenth century, the Midwestern town became the center of conflict about the future of the country itself. Edgar Lee Masters was born into this conflict.

Civil Discord

Like Eliza Farnham, the Masters family entered Illinois history during the "improving" phase of the state. Both Squire Davis and Hardin Masters, Edgar Lee's grandfather and father, respectively, were memorialized in *The History of Menard and Mason Counties, Illinois* (1879), a volume in a series of Illinois county histories sold by O. L. Baskin & Co. Historical Publishers of Chicago during the last quarter of the nineteenth century. Each volume contained a stock history of the Northwest Territory in general and Illinois in particular with illustrations of historical and geographical interest like the "Source of the Mississippi" and "Indians Attacking a Stockade," before providing short county histories and "Biographical Sketches" particular to each volume. In its preface, the book promised to do "justice to those who . . . subscribed" by producing a "work . . . as well done as if it was patronized by every citizen in the county."[63] In other words, Baskin's county histories were vanity publications presold to subscribers for local consumption. As such, the entries on Edgar Lee Masters's grandfather, Squire Davis Masters, and his son, Hardin, give some insight into how each understood himself as first- and second-generation Midwesterners.

The History of Menard and Mason Counties, Illinois described Squire Davis Masters as a "[p]rominent . . . farmer and stock-raiser." According to his short biography, Squire Davis was "one of the self-made men" of the county, who "by industry and economy . . . has been a man of progress and enterprise." Here, then, were the tropes of the "improving" generation that entered Illinois around the time of the Black Hawk War. As markers of his contribution to the region, Squire Davis's biography highlighted his service as justice of the peace, and, in 1856, his term as a state legislator. The entry mentioned Squire Davis's Methodist faith and ended by describing him as "always . . . identifyi[ng] with the principles of Democracy," namely, the Democratic Party.[64]

Hardin Masters's biography built upon his father's narrative of progress and enterprise. While the elder Masters was described as an improver of the land through "industry and economy," Hardin's biography described him as the "son of . . . pioneers of this county." Here, then, was the son situating himself within the frontier mythology of the state. Hardin, building upon his father's pioneering legacy, completed the civilizing process, primarily through the activities of a town-dweller, through law school, admission to the bar, and "through . . . ability and popularity," by election as state's attorney in 1872 and 1876. In this way, the biographies of Squire Davis and Hardin Masters built a neat generational narrative from founding, through hard work, to community building, and finally, in the case of the son, to the upper echelons of the state's legal profession. Squire Davis's generation settled the frontier; Hardin's generation closed it.

But the biographies in *The History of Menard and Mason Counties, Illinois* also smoothed over the mid-century conflicts out of which Hardin's generation emerged to shape a post-pioneering Illinois. In the stock history of Illinois in the Baskin county series, the divisions between northern and southern Illinois read like a matter of demographics: "In the early days when Illinois was first admitted to the Union, her population were chiefly from Kentucky and Virginia. But, in the conflict of ideas concerning slavery, a strong tide of emigration came in from the East, and soon changed this composition."[65] This simplistic explanation glosses over a more complicated and long-brewing fight over the status of African Americans in Illinois that shaped the state's and the Masters' history, both during and after the Civil War. These conflicts simmered for a generation before their portrayal in Edgar Lee Masters's poetry.

Slavery and the status of free and enslaved African Americans were a source of conflict from Illinois's inception. Though the state was closed to slavery according to the Northwest Ordinance, the institution existed in Illinois until the mid-1840s, largely because of the influx of residents from slave-holding states during the first decades of settlement. While the constitution of 1818 confirmed Illinois's status as a free state, enslaved African Americans brought into the state during the nineteenth century retained their status as property. In fact, an attempt to call a constitutional convention in 1824 for the purpose of overturning Illinois's free-state status was barely rejected by the voters. Likewise, white Illinoisans often converted enslaved African Americans' legal status into long-term indentured servant contracts, thereby upholding the letter but not the spirit of the Illinois constitution.[66] In 1828, the Illinois Supreme Court recognized the right of holders of indentured servant contracts to sell the remaining years on these contracts at auction, thereby re-creating a de facto slave trade in early Illinois.[67] According to Scott Heerman, well into the nineteenth century "masters managed to create a power base that sanctioned slavery's extralegal presence in the state."[68] Accordingly, during the first three decades of the nineteenth century, "several hundred, perhaps over one thousand, [African American] servants and slaves resided in Illinois."[69]

But slavery was not a settled issue for even the earliest settlers from the Ohio River Valley. A number of biographies in *The History of Menard and Mason Counties, Illinois* highlighted their subjects' southern origins *and* their desire to leave slavery behind. T. H. Brasfield, born in Madison County, Kentucky, had "sympathies [that] were always warmly enlisted in the cause of Antislavery."[70] Squire Davis Masters's father, Thomas, left Tennessee because of "slavery prevailing."[71] Isaac Lane's father was "an Antislavery man, and left Tennessee on account of the prevalence of slavery: his son, early in life, imbibed those principals [*sic*]."[72] John Conover's parents left Kentucky, being "desirous of locating beyond the influence of slavery."[73] In fact, while *The History of Menard and Mason Counties, Illinois* made little mention of the Civil War, the debates over slavery churned just beneath its surface. No biography expressed support for the Confederacy, but the self-identification of antislavery pioneers in this vanity publication gives some hint that the issue served as a personal identifier for members of the pioneering generation. In the aftermath of the Civil War, when *The History of Menard and Mason Counties, Illinois* was published, those on the wrong side of the conflict had reasons to stay mum.

Squire Davis Masters, according to his grandson Edgar Lee, "voted against Lincoln for United States Senator [in 1858] because he thought Lincoln's policies would bring on war between the states."[74] Likewise, during the Civil War, Hardin Masters's sympathies vacillated. According to Herbert K. Russell, Hardin was "for a time ambivalent about his Civil War leanings, being first for the North and then the South." Though Hardin Masters sought to enlist on the side of the North (in 1861 he was sixteen years old), he supported the South by the end of the war and, according to his son, "I . . . was named for Gen. Robert E. Lee, for whom my father had the greatest admiration."[75] Later in life, an old charge that Hardin Masters was a "Copperhead" who had helped draft-resisters escape during the Civil War haunted Hardin when he sought legal work in Lewistown. In his autobiography, *Across Spoon River*, Masters recalled that "[a]lthough my father had tried to be a soldier for the North, a cloud followed him from Petersburg; . . . once in Lewistown he was reputed to have been a 'Copperhead.' This made trouble for him, and prevented him from getting business."[76] In this regard, the Masters family was part of a broader conflict over race, federal power, and party politics in central Illinois during the Civil War. Michael Kleen argues that it is inaccurate to divide Illinois into simply a pro-Confederate south and a pro-Union north.[77] Instead, the region of greatest conflict during the war was in the central part of the state, where the debates between Lincoln and Douglas had produced large and boisterous crowds only a few years before. Democrats and Republicans, evenly matched in Masters's central Illinois, came to regard each other's party as an existential threat.

By the election of 1860, the Democratic Party had behind it a generation of success in national and local politics. Drawing self-definition from the legacy of Andrew Jackson as the destroyer of the National Bank and advocate for the common man, middling Americans from diverse trades—craftsmen in New York, yeoman farmers in backcountry Georgia, semi-subsistence farmers in Illinois—declared themselves for "the Democracy." The Whigs, on the other hand, struggled nationally, winning the presidency only twice between 1840 and 1860. Often portrayed as the party of wealth, moral reform (including temperance, abolitionism, and so forth) and robust federal authority, especially in the economy, the Whigs often found themselves saddled with a reputation as the party of moneyed interests and moralizing busybodies, stereotypes that found their way into Masters's *Spoon River Anthology*.

In the aftermath of the collapse of the Whig Party in the mid-1850s, the explosion of violence over slavery in the Kansas Territory in 1856, and the senatorial campaign between Democrat Stephen A. Douglas and Whig-cum-Republican Abraham Lincoln, Illinois became a microcosm for political fights raging across the northern United States. The Lincoln-Douglas debates of 1858 revolved around the expansion of slavery to the west, which Douglas believed should be determined by the "popular sovereignty" of those who lived in western territories. Lincoln, on the other hand, argued for the right of the federal government to regulate the expansion of slavery into new territories. While Menard County flipped from Whigs to Democrats during the presidential elections between 1840 and 1860,[78] a look at the election of 1858 results shows how closely divided central Illinois was between the two parties and how acutely the potential for conflict existed in the state's midsection. A review of the Senatorial and House district votes in the 1858 senatorial election shows support for Douglas in the southern portion of the state and for Lincoln in the northern portion. Though representatives for Menard County supported Douglas, nearby Springfield split the vote between the two candidates. The Masters family lived in the midst of this partisan no-man's land.

Democrats in Menard County and southern Illinois tended to find their strongest support among the descendants of upland Southerners, like the Masters family, who identified with the legacy of Andrew Jackson. As Masters described Menard County in his autobiography, "[t]he county was Democratic. It had voted against Lincoln in 1860; it had voted against him again in 1864. It had opposed the war and was full of 'Copperheads,' as men were called who did not like the subjugation of the South."[79] And while many of these Illinois Democrats, like Squire Davis Masters, cited their reasons for coming to Illinois as, among other things, an antipathy toward the slave economy in the South, many also supported Douglas's doctrine of "popular sovereignty" regarding the expansion of slavery.

During the initial phases of the war, Illinois Democrats like Hardin Masters supported the Union for the sake of national integrity. Before 1863, many Americans conceived the war as an effort to preserve the Union rather than to free enslaved African Americans. In this regard, South Carolina's attack on Fort Sumter in April 1861 confirmed that the conflict was for the preservation of the republic as conceived by the founding generation. However, by late 1862, with the conflict grinding through its second year and federal troops failing to make inroads into the rebellious states, the Lincoln administration began to adjust its policy to put the full force of the US government and economy behind the Union cause. In August 1861, the federal government passed the Revenue Act, which instituted a flat tax to provide the government a ready influx of funds for a long conflict. In summer 1862, this flat tax was replaced by a progressive tax on income. In March that year, the Legal Tender Act legalized the printing of federal currency without explicit connection to a gold standard. In September of 1862, Lincoln declared the Emancipation Proclamation, which legally freed all enslaved African Americans in states still in rebellion as of January 1, 1863. In March 1863, with the Enrollment Act, the federal government instituted the first draft in US history. These acts not only strengthened the federal government's ability to prosecute the war but also transformed the rationale of the war itself, from a fight to preserve the Union to a war to secure, as Lincoln put it in November 1863, a "new birth of freedom."

But this shift in federal authority also caused alarm and growing resistance among many Midwestern Democrats, including those in Illinois, who expressed surprise or even incredulity at federal military policy during 1862 and 1863, especially the Emancipation Proclamation. Beneath a slate of endorsed Democrats, the *Joliet Signal* declared,

> We were never more surprised and mortified in our lives than when this negro emancipation proclamation first made its appearance. We firmly believe that the president has no more right or power to issue a proclamation declaring freedom to the slaves, than he has to subject the whites of the rebel States to slavery.... We hold that the President has no more right to abolish slavery than he has to abolish the institution of marriage, or any other relation or institution created and regulated by State laws.[80]

The downstate *Salem Weekly Advocate* declared that "[t]he emancipation proclamation [sic] is as unwarrantable in military law as in constitutional law."[81] The *Woodstock Sentinel*, beneath a short report of the enthusiastic reception with which New York Republicans greeted the Emancipation Proclamation, printed a short article titled "Martial Law Declared" and informed readers that "arrests for disloyalty ... shall not be interfered with by any civil process."[82] The *Mattoon Gazette* reprinted the entirety of Lincoln's letter to the Union Mass Meeting held in Springfield, Illinois, in September, 1863, one year after the Proclamation in which Lincoln addressed a hypothetical critic: "You say you will not fight to free negroes. Some of them seem willing to fight for you." On the same page, the paper quoted a speech by a Lincoln critic from Bond County in south-central Illinois:

> Lincoln is a perjured man. He took an oath to support the Constitution of the United States, but broke it by his emancipation proclamation [sic]; broke it by suspending the writ of *habeas corpus*; broke it by arbitrary arrests and imprisonment, and the banishment of innocent men, broke it by declaring martial law in Kentucky where no war existed, for the purpose of carrying elections by preventing Democrats from voting— for which purpose he caused soldiers to take possession of the polls and allow no one to vote unless he was an unconditional Union man and would support the Administration and broke it by trying to enforce a most odious "Conscription" act, in trying to drag 300,000 men in the abominable negro war against their will.[83]

In the Illinois legislative elections of November 1862, support for the Democrats in six central Illinois counties rose by 12 percent.[84] According to Jonathan

Sebastian, "the election results [of 1862] revealed a Democratic and Jacksonian view, often overlooked or at least underestimated, that persisted with a sizable percentage of the state's population."[85]

Thereafter, antiwar Democrats became known by the sobriquet "Copperhead" after the poisonous snake found in downstate Illinois and much of the mid-Atlantic and southern United States. Likewise, rumors that secret new chapters of "Knights of the Golden Circle" (KGC) were forming in Illinois further reframed antiwar Democrats as traitors to the war effort.[86] Originating in Cincinnati before the Civil War, the KGC sought to create a slave-holding empire that included the southern coastal states of the U.S. and the nations surrounding the Caribbean. However, in the context of Illinois of 1863, the KGC served as an epithet to connect antiwar Democrats to the secessionist cause. That year, letters to Richard Yates, Republican governor of Illinois, warned of pro-secession Democrats who "invest the Southern part of this state with guirillas [*sic*] the same as Missouri" and "the friends of the South [are] bold in their threats and everything indicates that civil war is almost upon us."[87] Some antiwar Democrats embraced these terms of derision and wore "breastpins made of sections of butternut, and others copper cents on their shirt bosoms, as though boasting of their disgraceful alliance with Jeff Davis."[88] Reacting to an anti-war speech by a Democrat in Moultrie County, Emeline Krats lambasted the speaker's "well known affiliations with that class of traitors, conceived in nigger slavery and brought forth in southern treason, called the Knights of the Golden Circle, now more characteristically known as Copperheads."[89] In March 1863, one correspondent from Minnesota, where a year before settlers had fought with Sioux led by Little Crow and Sleepy-Eyes, overturned the traditional narrative of "Indian times" to find a new enemy in the midst of the Midwest:

> We take back all we have said about Indians. . . . We had supposed that the fiendish malignity which could slake its savage thirst for blood in the unprovoked and indiscriminate murder of men, women and children. . . . But in reading the account of the Detroit riot,[90] given in yesterday's *Press*, where hundreds of white Copperheads were banded together like wild beasts to hunt down a parcel of poor unoffending negroes, . . . we have come to the conclusion that Indians are tolerably good Christians.[91]

In July 1863, five days after the Battle of Gettysburg and the fall of Vicksburg, a letter to the *Centralia Sentinel* warned:

> You may tell the Copperheads that their day of retribution is at hand, and whenever this army gets home, that they had better hunt their Knights of

the Golden Circle holes or leave for parts unknown. [A]lmost every man in the army has his man marked out when he gets home.[92]

According to Thomas Bahde: "With reports of approaching calamity pouring in from all over the state and all of Illinois's volunteer regiments already pledged to the federal service, all that Governor Yates could say to his petitioners was that he believed 'the organization of a Home Guard would be highly beneficial.'"[93] Accordingly, home guards, broadly known as "Union Leagues," were made up of "well-established artisans," local businessmen, attorneys, and merchants and "grew out of a desire to protect the assets that kept these men at home."[94] In this atmosphere, Copperheads like Edgar Lee Masters's father, Hardin, were increasingly perceived as a threat behind the lines.

After 1863, debate between antiwar Democrats and Unionists turned violent in central Illinois. The *Mattoon Gazette* reported on a conflict between Milton York of the 66th Illinois Sharpshooters and "a butternut roundhead by the name of Cooper, in which the latter was shot in the hip producing a serious wound." According to the *Gazette*, "Cooper is the same . . . bully who attacked the editor of the [Paris, Illinois] *Beacon*, some time since, and York . . . is a brave and daring soldier, though a mere boy." The article ended with a warning: "These roundheads ought to know better than to strike a soldier."[95] In March 1864, near the Coles County courthouse in Charleston, a group of antiwar Democrats attacked a group of soldiers from the 54th Illinois regiment and killed Major Shubal York, the father of Milton York. By the end of the short melee, five Union soldiers and two Copperheads were killed, along with twelve others who were wounded. The sheriff of Coles County, William O'Hair, assisted the attackers' escape. According to historian Michael Kleen, the "Charlestown Riot" was the result of longstanding "dissent against the Lincoln administration" generally and "Republican and Unionist actions" specifically that led central Illinois into a "trajectory of violence."[96]

By 1864, it became increasingly impossible to support the war and be against the Republican Party without raising the charge of being a "Copperhead," "Roundhead," "Butternut," or secret member of the "Knights of the Golden Circle." After Lincoln's reelection in 1864, the peace position came to be equated with treason and, after the war, these antagonisms continued to resonate in central Illinois.[97] Edgar Lee Masters grew up with the legacy of these conflicts, which, for him, differentiated the small towns where he grew up. There was Petersburg,

peopled by Virginians, Marylanders, Tennesseans, and Kentuckians. . . . [F]or breeding [and] civilization, [it had] all [the] good human qualities I have ever known. . . .

and, Lewistown, nearly forty miles to the northwest,

> inhabited by a people of tough and muscular minds, where political lines were bitterly drawn by the G[rand] A[rmy] [of the] R[epublic]. . . . It was this atmosphere of Northern light and cold winds that clarified my mind . . . to the beauty of Petersburg.[98]

Masters drew from both in imagining Spoon River, a Midwestern town fraught with nostalgic images and ambivalent undertones that were partially the result of the smoldering legacy of the Civil War in Illinois.

A War by Other Means

Edgar Lee Masters was born in 1868 under the shadow of the war. In the presidential election that year, Ulysses S. Grant, victor of the campaigns in the West and destroyer of the Army of Northern Virginia in the East, was elected on a Republican ticket that promised to remake the South through a long and thorough Reconstruction. The Masters family lived until 1869 in Garnett, Kansas, where Edgar Lee's father had unsuccessfully attempted to practice law, before returning to Petersburg, where Masters lived until 1880. In his later years, Masters's memories of childhood in Petersburg formed a nostalgic backdrop to his adolescence in Lewistown and his young adulthood in Chicago. His periodic visits to his grandfather's farm during the 1890s bolstered these sentimental memories and provided him with family lore that stretched back to the pioneering generation of the 1840s. According to Masters, "I stored many memories at this time of my life."[99]

In middle age, Masters sympathetically recalled Petersburg as a burgeoning town in a fashion that echoed the boosterism of *Illinois in 1837*: "the town had two railroads, several coal mines, a woolen mill, some factories, a small brewery and a winery." Likewise, echoing the idyllic confluence of nature and community found in William McGuffey's readers, Masters recalled "luxuriant forestry," "heavy greeneries" and the Sangamon River, "picturesque, yellow and muddy as its waters are when closely seen."[100] In this regard, Petersburg represented the ideal of a Midwestern town, "sixteen blocks long and half that many wide, a town of 3000 in a valley framed by hills."[101]

But for Masters, the legacy of the Civil War, when Copperheads and Union Leaguers battled over the wartime policies of the Lincoln administration, also resonated. This legacy manifested itself acutely after the Masters family relocated to Lewistown. While his eleven years there proved to be "as long as twenty years in a later period in life," and though it was in Lewistown that he began to love literature—"Shelley took me aloft on wings of flame"[102]—and discovered his passion for writing, Lewistown also proved to be challenging for his father, saddled as he was with the epithet "Copperhead" and the reputation as a Southern sympathizer. According to Masters, it was about this time that he

> read the Bible through and through; and by the time I was fourteen or so, I was skeptical of it as a revelation. The attitude of some of the leading citizens toward my father helped to solidify my opposition to churches and to the religion they preached. They were the banker, the merchant, and their retainers, all men of small natures and inveterate prejudices and village ignorance of everything really good and beautiful. These men made it as hard as possible for my father in politics and in his profession.... [H]is captivating personality did not win over these bitter Calvinists.... What they did took bread from my mouth.[103]

With these memories, Masters synthesized the latent social conflicts left over from the Civil War with the rising social divisions apparent in the war's aftermath and forged them into the personal grievances that shaped his later portrayal of small-town Illinois. The victors of the conflict—the bankers, the industrialists, and the "Calvinists"—proved to be the inherited enemies of Hardin's ilk, and, ultimately in Masters's view, the despoilers of the Midwestern communities built by his grandfather's generation.

The legacy of the Civil War in central Illinois manifested itself as economic conflicts in the second half of the nineteenth century. Increasingly during these years, the railroad, local banks, grain elevators, and the city of Chicago came to represent the legacy of Lincoln for many rural Illinois Democrats like Hardin Masters, who were inclined to antiwar sympathies during the early 1860s.[104] In his later years, Edgar Lee Masters described Lincoln as giving rise to "other slaveries more powerful in America ... as a result of the War" and he reminded his readers that it was from the Illinois Central Railroad that "Lincoln received [a] handsome fee."[105] By then, railroads in Illinois dominated the agricultural transportation network for primarily two reasons. First, between 1861 and the fall of Vicksburg in 1863, the traditional river route to New Orleans was closed to central and southern Illinoisans, who increasingly depended upon access to markets in Chicago to sell their crops. Second, during the war, rails carried troops and supplies through the state, first to supply General Grant as he battled his way south and, later, to facilitate the mopping-up operations as the eastern theater became the location of the war's culminating battles. In this environment, railroad corporations thrived. The Illinois Central, for example, saw the value of its dividends rise 4 percent in 1862, 6 percent in 1863, 8 percent in 1864, and finally, 10 percent by 1865.[106] By the middle of the 1860s, according to William Cronon, the railroad had emerged as "the chief link connecting Chicago with the towns and rural lands around it, so [that] the city came finally to seem like an artificial spider suspended at the center of a great steel web."[107]

In reaction to the power that grain elevators, railroads, and the Chicago stock exchange seemingly had over prices, Midwestern farmers in the 1870s organized into Granger parties, based in local Grange halls that were initially founded to provide a meeting place for farmers who faced social isolation in the west. By 1877, in the Supreme Court case *Munn vs. Illinois*, farmers' advocates successfully argued that state governments had the right to regulate the prices that grain elevators charged to store farmers' wheat, thereby providing redress for the falling prices caused by the overproduction of crops. By the 1880s, these local Granges had formed into state-level "Alliance" parties that won control of state legislatures, stood poised to shape national legislation, and paved the way for the unified People's (or "Populist") Party of the 1890s.

Beneath this seemingly progressive platform of government regulation lay an older argument about the fight of the people against elite interests.[108] Manifesting itself throughout the nineteenth century as a populist ethos that appealed to Thomas Jefferson's legacy, activists as diverse as Jacksonian Democrats during the late 1820s, antimonopoly artisans during the 1830s, free-soil advocates during the 1840s and 1850s, and Midwestern farmers during the 1870s all appealed to Jefferson's legacy. While Lawrence Goodwyn claims that "the old Jacksonian resonances of Whig-Democratic conflict, containing as they did still older rhythms of the Jeffersonian-Federalist struggle, were all but obliterated by the massive realignment of party constituencies" after the Civil War, populist activists nevertheless broadly embraced three positions that they loosely traced back to Jefferson.[109] First, the natural citizenry of a republic was the egalitarian average, yeoman farmers and urban skilled artisans, overwhelmingly white men, whose work gained them financial independence and, therefore, republican liberty.[110] This bred an egalitarian ideology grounded in the idea of political liberty as the hallmark of equality rather than enforced economic parity. Second, financial elites, driven by the pursuit of profit rather than ideals of political liberty, were the greatest threat to the majority of citizens. Elites, through wealth and influence, insinuated themselves into government in pursuit of ill-gained profit, likely through the oppression of the laboring classes. The Democratic Party, therefore, typically opposed legislation like high tariffs on foreign goods as examples of government power wielded for the benefit of a minority of economic elites. Third, drawing upon Jefferson's theological liberalism, these populists often opposed the moralism of the Second Great Awakening and the reform movements that grew from it, initially the abolition of slavery and, later, the prohibition of alcohol. These were supported by political rivals like the Whigs and the Republicans and, later, prohibitionists in the nineteenth and early twentieth centuries. Accordingly, the goals of moral reformers were framed as the work of meddlesome busybodies, a strain of New England Protestants, industrialists, and financiers who sought to undermine the financial and social liberty of the common people. Throughout the nineteenth century, political egalitarianism (for white males), antielitism (against industrialists and bankers), and antimoralism (against, for example, advocates of temperance) shaped the ideology of these populists who appealed to Jefferson's legacy.

After the Civil War, as the value of staple crops fell when production outstripped demand, Midwestern farmers blamed economic elites that they perceived as nefariously benefiting from their economic plight. Grain elevator operators and railroads, who monopolized access to markets in American cities, had seemingly inserted themselves into the natural relationship between the farmer and the consumer and parasitically siphoned off the farmer's legitimate profit through their monopoly of the transportation network. And while crop prices fell, the value of farmers' debt remained static, thereby benefiting those who held a farm's mortgage, typically a bank. This formed a three-headed oppressor that undermined farmers' economic independence: the local grain elevator, which set the purchasing price of the farmer's crop; the railroad, which sometimes controlled the local grain elevator or depressed prices through control over access to markets; and the bank, which held a farmer's mortgage and threatened to take his land in the event of bankruptcy. While Grangers formed farmers' cooperatives and banks during the 1870s, later farmer activists increasingly interpreted the problem as caused by a system under the control of moneyed interests in faraway cities like Chicago and New York who threatened the economic viability of regular Americans.[111]

During the 1870s, the short-lived Greenback Party, made up primarily of farmers whose crops benefited from the inflationary effect of federal currency, explicitly connected their goals to Thomas Jefferson's legacy. They argued in their 1876 platform that "it is the duty of the government to provide . . . a circulating medium, and insist, in the language of Thomas Jefferson, that 'bank paper must be suppressed and the circulation restored to the nation, to whom it belongs.'"[112] Likewise, Populists like James H. "Cyclone" Davis used Jefferson as a "yardstick for viable political remedies," especially the "radical and agrarian side of the tradition":[113]

> Let us waft a message to Mr. Jefferson and tell him that there is another *hereditary high-handed aristocracy* in our land, with far more stupendous

accumulation of property, held in single lines of "corporate names" or titles, whose castles, palaces, mansions and estates, the kings and princes of Britain's realm cannot rival. Tell him, too, that the remorseless princes of our land hold parchment titles to more land in our Union than the original thirteen States, for which he and his generation suffered, bled. [W]ith an unrelenting spirit of tyranny, they have reduced our great industrial masses to tatterdemalion slaves. . . .[114]

In this regard, both Greenbacks' advocacy for the continued circulation of federal currency and, later, the Populist Party's appeal for the free coinage of silver were symbolic of a larger fight against debt-holding interests, banks— which constituted a danger to the economic liberty of the common people— and distant financial elites, who controlled transportation networks and stock exchanges and whose influence on crop prices left farmers at the mercy of their debtors.[115]

When Edgar Lee Masters divided Spoon River between the moralizing financial elite and the noble, but often tragic mass, he echoed this long-standing American rhetorical appeal to the legacy of Thomas Jefferson. While the Greenbacks of the 1870s and the Populists of the 1890s rivaled the Democratic Party at the state level, many Democrats like Masters sympathized with their hostility toward Republican Party dominance and the acceleration of the industrial economy after the war. According to Masters, Jefferson's influence was not "bourgeois" since there was no "remnant of monarchy in any of his practices or principles."[116] Recalling his days as a boy in Lewistown some fifty years later, Masters viewed his father's professional and personal struggles in these ideological terms. Hardin Masters's law career stalled because of his Jefferson-like antipathy for the overreaching power of financial elites exemplified by Lincoln's war. In this regard, Masters traced the family's financial struggles in the late 1870s to his father's Virginian descent and repudiation of the Union cause.[117]

To young Masters, the ideological division between his father and Lewis-town also manifested itself in his home. His mother, Emma, had "imbibed a sort of theological doctrine—probably from her father, a Massachusetts Methodist minister—which was that the will had to be broken." Accordingly, "their marriage was the conjunction of two kinds of Methodism: New England's and that of the Middle West . . . distinguished by 'gospel love,' not by gospel hate"; Emma Masters "to the last . . . hated the Middle West and its people."[118] Edgar Lee Masters took his father's side in his divided home and remembered Hardin as "athletic," "strong," and of "quick mind. . . . My father loved a horse, and loved racing, and he loved sports of all kinds. . . . His good looks, his gay spirits, his physical strength and prowess . . . made him a man to be hailed wherever he went in that country."[119] According to Masters, his father rebelled against his mother's "nervous dyspepsia" and attempts to "break [his] will" by visiting saloons and philandering.[120]

Edgar Lee Masters, therefore, understood the differences between his mother and father as an extension of broader American debates: Lewistown "Calvinists" and his mother's "New England" Methodism against Hardin's sympathy for Jefferson's legacy, perceived in the Masters's house as an easygoing egalitarianism, an inclination to free thinking, and antipathy toward economic and moral elites. Even after his father forced Masters to leave Knox College after only one year, discouraged his desire to pursue a career as a writer, and pushed him into the law, Masters felt an affinity for Hardin Masters and the values he represented: a kind of lost America, a country that in the last generation had gone astray from its founding principles and had been, instead, overtaken by capitalists and prudes, the descendants of Union Leaguers and Lincoln men, dousers of the "fires of love" kindled by the pioneering generation, and perpetrators of the war that squelched the "social converse" of his father's youth.

From Mythology to Realism

While Masters was growing up in central Illinois and discovering a passion for literature and at the same time cultivating a disdain for Lewistown, a number of regional authors sought to distinguish Midwestern literature from the more genteel eastern variety. Their realism was shaped by the Midwest of the late nineteenth century.

A Midwestern literary tradition had been building since the 1870s and 1880s, as authors like Edward Eggleston and Mark Twain—taking inspiration from the humorous tales of the Old Southwest by authors like Johnson Jones Hooper—imparted a literary style broadly termed "realism" onto their work, with colloquial dialogue and ironic twists of fate.[121] Eggleston introduced his book *The Hoosier School-Master* (1871) with the promise that "our life . . . was not less interesting, not less romantic, and certainly not less filled with humorous and grotesque material [than the lives of rural New England]."[122] According to Ima Honaker Herron, Eggleston's realism "dealt unromantically with social conditions," and helped establish this trend in Midwestern literature.[123] Later Midwestern realists like Joseph Kirkland, an Illinoisan and Civil War veteran, drew from European precedents like Émile Zola, Gustave Flaubert, and Thomas Hardy, seeking to "reproduce, on American soil . . . unflinching realism," as he claimed in the preface of his novel *Zury: The Meanest Man in Spring County,*

A Novel of Western Life (1887).[124] *Zury* is a story of a pioneer child who achieves wealth and stability not through "social commerce met," but by hard bargains and financial acumen. While his pursuit of profit sours him on humanity, he is eventually redeemed by a schoolteacher from Boston, Anne. Kirkland's vernacular dialogue and unblemished look at the effect of pioneer living on early Midwesterners contrasted with the glossier accounts of pioneer mythology from earlier in the century, such as Eliza Farnham's.

Ronald Grosh, quoting Jay Martin, notes that the historical context of the late-nineteenth-century Midwest proved conducive to realism: "the Civil War . . . and the domination of business and politics by the frontier spirit contributed to the 'gradual decline of romantic idealism, [and] the rapid growth of materialism in public and private life.'"[125] David Marion Holman likewise claims this realistic style was "appropriate for the region . . . because the history of the Midwest and its inhabitants is inextricably entangled with populist idealism," thereby making "the discrepancy between the ideal and the actual, between theory and practice . . . the heart of Midwestern social realism."[126]

E. W. Howe wrote realistic tales of rural communities of a much grimmer variety. Fifteen years Masters's senior, Howe began his career in fiction with *The Story of a Country Town* (1883), which portrayed the town of Twin Mounds through the eyes of a narrator who grew up in a place where "in the dusty tramp of civilization westward . . . our section was not a favorite. . . . [N]o one in the great outside world talked about it, and no one wrote about it."[127] According to Ronald Weber, Howe's Twin Mounds was ruled by "petty business affairs, heated biblical disputes, zeal for public office"[128] and it offered an unadulterated look at rural life in the Midwest that presaged Masters's own. According to Henry Nash Smith, Howe's Twin Mounds was a place of "grim, savage religion, of silent endurance, of families held together through no tenderness, of communities whose only amusement is malicious gossip."[129]

As agrarian reform politics grew from its Midwestern base to national influence in the 1880s, a parallel transformation of the realistic tales of the Midwest grew into critiques of social and economic dislocation that fused clear-eyed portrayals of life in the region with sympathy for the farmer and antipathy toward a seemingly new and particularly rapacious kind of capitalism. Wisconsinite Hamlin Garland's series of stories of farm life in the "Middle Border" states, *Main-Travelled Roads* (1891), offers the best example of this kind of reform realism.[130] Garland began the short story, "The Creamery Man," with a description of the progress from frontier to farmland that presaged Frederick Jackson Turner's thesis of three years later.[131] The "tin-peddler had gone out of the West" and "passed into the limbo of things no longer necessary" as the "creamery man [took] his place."[132] The creamery man of the story, Claude, a handsome and friendly collector of cream on the rural farms of the county, courts "Yankee" Lucindy, whose father owns a farm of middling status. At the same time, "Dutch" Nina, a German girl from a prosperous farming family also on Claude's route, mistakes Claude's kindness for courtship. While Lucindy hopes to marry a refined member of the middle class, Claude dreams of marrying Lucindy, and Nina wants to marry Claude, who will treat her like a "Yankee wife," since she knows that "Yankee girls did not work in the fields."

Claude unwittingly fosters Nina's fantasy by convincing her to spend less time working in the field, which causes her German mother and father much grief and also causes Nina's hands to grow soft, her color to fade, and her figure to fill out, for which Claude, over a number of months, compliments her. When Lucindy visits Minneapolis, she returns better dressed and actively cool to Claude's advances since she now aspires to the urbane manners of the city rather than the country ways of the creamery man. Meanwhile, Nina's mother grows suspicious of Claude's intentions and attacks him during one of his weekly visits "like a she grizzly bear, uttering a torrent of German expletives, clutching at his hair and throat."[133] Nina, however, defends her wished-for beau and throws her mother to the ground in a scene reminiscent of the slapstick fights between the Duke and King in the *Adventures of Huckleberry Finn*. While Nina's mother is prostrate on the ground, Claude douses her with water:

> The mother sat up soon, wet, scared, bewildered, gasping,
> "Mein Gott! Mein Gott! Ich bin ertrinken!"
> "What does she say—she's been drinkin'? Well, that looks reasonable."
> "No, no—she thinks she is trounded."
> "Oh, drowned!" Claude roared again. "Not much she ain't. She's only just getting cooled off."[134]

Once Claude discovers that the newly bourgeois Lucindy is lost to him, however, he returns to Nina's farm and asks her to go for a ride,

> "Get your hat," he said, "and we'll take a ride."
> "With you?"
> "With me. Get your best hat. We may turn up at the minister's and get married—if a Sunday marriage is legal."
> As she hurried up the walk he said to himself,
> "I'll bet it gives Lucindy a shock!"
> And the thought pleased him mightily.[135]

In its humor, Garland's tale meditates on change in the region: as the tin-peddler gives way to the creamery man, so, too, Lucindy acquires sophistication at the cost of disaffection from her community, Claude gains a wife and farm while losing his rambling life as the creamery man, and Nina becomes a "Yankee" wife at the expense of her German heritage. Garland's story, then, is tinged with nostalgia: change also means loss. Thus, attributes of each character "passed into the limbo of things no longer necessary." Garland's rural community moves on an anxious continuum from frontier to civilization, unlike the mythological New England village, which remained steadfast in the midst of flux. In this fashion, Garland evoked feelings of nostalgia and ambivalence about the Midwest in general and its small towns in particular.

Garland's *Many-Travelled Roads* also fused realism, populist sentiment, and a plea for economic justice that reflected political and literary trends in the Midwest. In "Under the Lion's Paw," the farmer Timothy Haskins is exploited by the land speculator Jim Butler, who put "[e]very cent he could save . . . into land at forced sale" and thereby lived off the misfortunes of hard-working farmers. When Haskins desires, but cannot afford, a farm owned by Jim Butler, he agrees to purchase seed and materials on consignment from the town supplier, to work the land of the farm, and eventually to purchase it for $2500. Thereafter, "Haskins worked like a fiend, and his wife, like the heroic woman that she was, bore also uncomplainingly the most terrible burdens."[136] Over three years, the Haskins family improved the farm, but Butler doubles the price of the rent, or offers to sell it at $5500. Farmer Haskins is aghast:

> "*What!*" almost shrieked the astounded Haskins. "What's that? Five thousand? Why that's double what you offered it for three years ago."
>
> "Of course, and it's worth it. It was all run down then; now it's in good shape. You've laid out fifteen hundred dollars in improvements, according to your own story."
>
> "But *you* had nothin' t' do about that. It's my work an' my money."
>
> "You bet it was, but it's my land."
>
> "But what's to pay me for all my—"
>
> "Ain't you had the use of 'em?" replied Butler, smiling calmly into his face.
>
> Haskins was like a man struck on the head with a sandbag; he couldn't think; he stammered as he tried to say: "But—I never'd git the use—You'd rob me! More'n that: you agree—you promised that I could buy or rent at the end of three years at—"
>
> "That's all right. But I didn't say I'd let you carry off the improvements, nor that I'd go on renting the farm at two-fifty. The land is doubled in value, it don't matter how; it don't enter into the questions; an' now you can pay

me five hundred dollars a year rent, or take it on your own terms at fifty-five hundred, or—get out."[137]

In this case, Garland injects economic panic into a genre traditionally populated by vernacular tales of the Midwest; hard work ultimately proves to be Haskins's undoing. In this way, Garland translated contemporaneous arguments of agrarian activists against grasping elites into compelling fiction that framed Midwestern rural life in deeply ambivalent terms. According to Robert Bray, Garland "was able to see the agrarian dilemma partly in terms of social class conflict, partly as the inexorable march of finance capitalism."[138] Ultimately, Garland himself became an activist in the Populist movement.[139]

These Midwestern realists reflected Edgar Lee Masters's own conception of his upbringing in central Illinois. While Masters remembered fondly his grandfather's farm, the countryside surrounding it, and the people of Petersburg from his youth, these memories were darkened by Lewistown, which came to represent for Masters the postwar United States, a nation of capitalists and prudes who undermined not only his father's livelihood and his idyllic Petersburg, but also the ideals that he believed had built the region and founded the nation. In this regard, Masters's contrasting of Petersburg with Lewistown echoed the myth of the New England village, with the new city looming in the distance. However, Masters's two countervailing communities were in the same region, roughly the same size, and part of the same history that made Illinois a state of fields and little towns. In this way, Masters fused his memories of both places when he conceived Spoon River. But first, he had to go to Chicago.

CHAPTER 3

Frontiers

Closed and Opened

The process to which democracy was ever and ever will be a remorseless foe is the accumulation of all power in the hands of a few men.

—Edgar Lee Masters, *The New Star Chamber* (1904)

In 1892, Edgar Lee Masters, now twenty-four years old, unsure about his new career as a lawyer, and frustrated by his failure to make a living in Lewistown, stepped off the small-gauge train in Havana on the Illinois River and awaited the midnight train to Chicago.[1] For the last four years, he had stewed on the fact that the career he had prepared for was not the work he wanted to do. According to a diary entry from one year earlier, he was "financially stranded, with an ill cultivated talent, no audience, no prospects, fighting the habit of years to give half of my mind to law when, alas, either law or poetry demands the whole attention."[2] On the train to Chicago, Masters wondered "what Chicago would look like, how it would begin" and was surprised at how it was "difficult to tell when we left the prairie" and where began "the new subdivisions springing up all around." The city was, he recalled, "in anticipation of the World's Fair."[3]

Chicago in 1892 was on the cusp of self-redefinition after over two generations of growth, destruction, and breakneck rebirth. Before the famous fire of 1871, Chicago had grown from mid-sized frontier town to burgeoning Midwestern city and during the Civil War benefited from its relative distance from the fighting by supplying Union armies with ready-made clothing, soap, candles, wheat, beef, and pork. By the 1860s, the horse-drawn streetcar lines cut their way north and west from Lake Michigan into the prairie.[4] The population of the city nearly quadrupled between 1850 and 1860[5] and, by 1865, Chicago had six hundred saloons and grocers to support its growing population,[6] 64 percent of which were immigrants—mostly in industry—and 34 percent in unskilled trades.[7]

The Chicago Fire of 1871 temporarily stymied the city's breakneck growth. While the legend of the fire quickly mixed fact and fiction in the story of the city's rebirth, the fire nonetheless, in Frederick Law Olmsted's estimation, inspired "very sensible men . . . [to] the conviction that it was the burning of the world."[8] The destruction offered a mythic break with Chicago's recent past, allowing boosters "to look no further back than October 8, 1871, for [the] city's origins" and freeing Chicagoans from the era's sense of aimless industrial growth.[9] Unlike the cities of the Northeast, Chicago seemed to have no history, and therefore no burdensome Eden from which it had fallen.[10] Though the fire could not burn away the divisions between classes and ethnicities and between middle-class mores and perceptions of moral degradation that industrial cities in the East had experienced two generations before, the rebuilding effort offered Chicago boosters a "model for initiative and innovation."[11] While the old cities of the East had a past, Chicago was the future.

But optimism after the fire ran up against ongoing social unrest. By the early 1870s, Chicago labor was roughly divided between activists shaped by the ideology of the "Internationals," who sympathized with the broader international socialist movement and were primarily of German and Eastern European origin, and Anglo-American workers who adhered to the artisan activism from earlier in the century that sought redress through political democracy.[12] The Great Railroad Strike of 1877 brought Chicago labor activism to national attention. In the aftermath of the depression of 1873, overproduction caused falling wages and unemployment nationwide. By July 1877, a new vagrant law allowed the Chicago police to harass the unemployed and labor organizers indiscriminately in an attempt to suppress protest in the streets.[13] In mid-July, a railroad strike that began at the B&O Railroad hub in Maryland spread through the Northeast. On July 24, the strike spread to Chicago, St. Louis, and Kansas City, and to sympathetic trades outside of the railroad industry.[14] On July 25, there were open battles between the Chicago Police Department, the Illinois National Guard, and strikers, leading the *Chicago Tribune*, the voice of capital in the city, to proclaim a "Red War."[15] Similar instances of violence continued at roughly decade-long intervals throughout the rest of the century: at the Haymarket Square Riot in 1886 and the Pullman Strike in 1894.[16]

In the midst of this foment, Chicago prepared for the World's Fair of 1893, known as the "Columbian Exposition" in honor of the four-hundredth anniversary of Columbus's arrival in the Western Hemisphere. When the House of Representatives chose Chicago over New York for the right to host the Fair, the *Tribune* crowed, "Chicago Wins!" and "Congressmen Agree Upon Chicago's Unequaled Merits as a Site." A cartoon on the front page of the February 25, 1890, issue of the *Tribune* showed Uncle Sam greeting Chicago-as-Columbia with the words "Uncle Sam Awards the World's Fair Prize to the Fairest of All His Daughters." Surrounding the overjoyed "Chicago" was a fainting St. Louis, an aged New York, and a weeping Washington.[17] The World's Fair and the White City that housed it represented for Chicagoans evidence that their city had joined the ranks of world-class metropolises.[18] The fair covered 600 acres of Chicago's lake shore and included architectural designs that required 36,407 cartloads of materials, including 20,000 tons of iron, and 70,000,000 feet of lumber to build the structures that housed the exhibits.[19] Whereas St. Louis, New Orleans, New York, and Philadelphia owed their origins to Europe, Chicago was American-born. The Fair would showcase the city as the true heir to Columbus's "discovery."

When Edgar Lee Masters arrived in 1892, Chicago was "alive with people from all the surrounding states who had come to the city to make money during the World's Fair."[20] Though he worked unhappily for a short time as a bill collector for the Edison Company, a job he called "intolerable," in May 1893, Masters went into partnership with another young lawyer, Kickham Scanlan, and opened a practice in the Ashland Building the same day as the Columbian Exposition opened in Hyde Park on Chicago's near South Side.[21] On Dedication Day, nearly one million people witnessed the parade and, at the dedication ceremony in the Manufactures [*sic*] Building, which housed an exhibit space of forty-four acres, the director general of the exposition, Colonel George R. Davis, claimed, "This rich heritage is ours, not by our own might, not even by our own discovery, but ours by the gift of the Infinite."[22] The day after the opening ceremony, the *Tribune* described the fair as "Ready for a World" and waxed, "the Mind Cannot Grasp What Is Seen in the Eye's Sweep."[23] Masters simply called it "the most beautiful thing that has ever existed on this earth."[24]

It is unlikely that Masters saw Frederick Jackson Turner give his famous address on the significance of the frontier on American history at the World's Fair that summer; both the *Chicago Tribune* and the *New York Times* ignored Turner's address. But Turner's talk gave academic polish to the local temperament that summer in the White City and to two generations of pioneering mythology behind it. According to Turner, the Midwest was the culmination of a process of Americanization that began in the forests of the Atlantic coastal backcountry after the American Revolution. Nation-building took place on the frontier, where Europeans, distant from continental influence, necessarily lost their European habits.[25] According to Turner,

> It begins with the Indian and the hunter; it goes on to tell of the disintegration of savagery by the entrance of the trader, the pathfinder of civilization; we read the annals of the pastoral stage in ranch life; the exploitation of the soil by the raising of unrotated crops of corn and wheat in sparsely settled farming communities; the intensive culture of the denser farm settlement; and finally the manufacturing organization with city and factory system.[26]

For Turner, this process drove "growth of nationalism and the evolution of American political institutions." By implication,

> The Middle region was less English than the other sections. It had a wide mixture of nationalities, a varied society, the mixed town and county system of local government, a varied economic life, many religious sects. In short, it was a region mediating between New England and the South, the East and the West.[27]

This admixture had its own "national tendencies" where "[o]n the tide of the Father of Waters, North and South met and mingled into a nation." Turner, a native Midwesterner and a professor at the University of Wisconsin, framed the region as the culmination of this nationalizing process, making the Midwest the first harvest of the American frontier. By implication, Turner's vision of the frontier necessarily perceived Chicago as its first fruit, separating the older cities of the East from this process. Turner's "Middle regions" had the "most important effect . . . in the promotion of democracy here and in Europe."[28] Chicago, then, could thereby claim, along with the Midwest, to be truly American, in the heart of the continent, connected to the East, but destined to surpass it both in power and in democratic promise. According to Henry Nash Smith, this ideal was born of the pioneering myth of a frontier that "fostered economic equality . . . [and] made for an increase of democracy." Accordingly, the frontier promised "a rebirth, a regeneration, a rejuvenation of man and society."[29] The *Tribune* summed up Turner's sentiments by calling the Chicago Fair an "Epoch in Human Progress."[30]

At the same time Chicagoans celebrated their ascension over the older cities like New York, rural Midwesterners sought redress from the economic hegemony of the Northeast. In 1892, the same year Masters arrived in Chicago, state-level agrarian activists met in Omaha, Nebraska, and nominated former Civil War general, James B. Weaver, as the People's (or Populist) Party candidate. According to the Populist platform:

> The people are demoralized. The newspapers are largely subsidized or muzzled, public opinion is silenced, business prostrated, our homes covered with mortgages, labor impoverished, and the land concentrated in the hands of capitalists.[31]

At the Omaha Convention, the Populists generated a platform (and published it symbolically on July 4th) that embraced economic justice by government regulation of the railroads and communication, more democracy through the direct election of senators, a graduated income tax, the free coinage of silver and, in a plea for support from workers in the cities, a regulated work week. Weaver's campaign gained more support than any previous third party, electing eleven representatives to the House that year and winning several governorships. In this regard, the Populists appeared to augur sweeping change in US domestic policy coming from the Midwest.[32] Frederick Jackson Turner himself situated this farmer's political revolt against railroads and banks, those perceived perpetrators of high debt and low prices, as a poignant example of the frontier shaping national policy.

But within two years of his arrival, the glow was coming off Chicago for Masters. While his law practice continued to find cases, it was "not so prosperous as it had been during the World's Fair."[33] His sputtering love life often forced him to patronize a local saloon "to inquire about girls; and occasionally in this way I found one in a room somewhere near." While he expressed a "fear of women of this stamp" he "did not know what else to do."[34] Masters also returned to Lewistown occasionally after the Fair, at one point to avoid the unrest caused by the Pullman Strike of 1894, and visited his grandfather's farm outside of Petersburg. There, Masters expressed nostalgia for the seemingly unchanging ways of country life that had appealed to urban dwellers in the Northeast for the last two generations, "My grandfather . . . and my grandmother . . . were the same as they had ever been":

> My grandmother still milked her cows, she still churned, and cared for the house, she still sat at the head of the bountiful table and laughed and told stories. And we rested under the old maple trees, . . . and [my grandfather] told about the time that Lincoln had stood under the very shadows of these trees and tried a case before him as a justice of the peace.[35]

In this way, Masters's grandparents symbolized for him the ideal of Midwestern pioneers: connected to the land, steady in their habits, strong in their form, and under threat from changes wrought by the American economy in the late nineteenth century.

A Cross of Gold

In the intervening years between the presidential elections of 1892 and 1896, Populism's impact on national politics and the two political parties grew apace. William Jennings Bryan's nomination at the 1896 Democratic convention in Chicago proved a watershed moment for the party, when Democrats shifted from postwar defensiveness to an activist platform that took its cue from the Populist Party of four years earlier. Bryan, himself an Illinoisan who settled in Nebraska, led the break with the policies of Democratic President Grover Cleveland with his famous "Cross of Gold" speech, which placed the debate over gold versus silver coinage at the heart of the campaign.[36] When Hardin Masters (now a state's attorney and downstate Democratic politico) arrived in Chicago in July to serve as a delegate to the Democratic National Convention at the Coliseum, he brought a ticket for his son.

Forty years later, Masters quoted the penultimate moment of Bryan's speech to the convention in his autobiography, "You shall not press down upon the brow of labor this crown of thorns, you shall not crucify mankind upon a cross of gold." To Masters, this moment represented a reawakening of a Jeffersonian ideal he equated with his father, and, by extension, the Democratic Party as it existed before the Civil War:

> And as the vast crowd rose in ecstasy and cheered, and as the delegates marched about yelling and rejoicing for the good part of an hour I sat there . . . resolving that I would throw myself into this new cause which concerned itself with humanity. . . . A new life had come to me as well as to the Democracy.[37]

That night, Masters and his father assured each other that Bryan "would sweep the country" and make it possible for regular Americans to take the country back from "banks and syndicates" who had controlled the country and "robbed the people" since 1861. These elites made it impossible, according to Masters, for young people to succeed in America without selling themselves to "financial oligarchs." Bryan was Jackson and Jefferson reborn. He would smash Eastern elites and save the country from economic exploitation.[38]

But when Masters went to campaign for Bryan in central Illinois, he found the citizens of Petersburg less enthusiastic. After he gave a halting speech in favor of

Bryan, during which "something in my mental constitution . . . would not loose my tongue," his cousin, Nell, who was married to a local farmer, "teased me, and called attention to some of my mispronunciations." At the Masters's farm later that day, his grandfather told him that he planned to vote for the Prohibitionist ticket that year. His uncle likewise rejected Bryan's arguments for the free coinage of silver and called Bryan an "anarchist" for his support of Illinois Governor John Peter Altgeld, who had pardoned three of the protesters accused of attacking police officers at the Haymarket Square riot in 1886. According to Uncle Will, the governor of Illinois "was no better than a murderer." Even a hired hand that worked for Masters's grandfather dismissed Bryan on the argument that the free coinage of silver would cheapen the few dollars he made. Masters returned to Chicago "considerably dispirited."[39] That November, though Bryan won much of the South and West, the Republican nominee, William McKinley, won the electoral college with support from the more populous Northeast and much of the Midwest. As some small consolation to Masters, Menard County, home to Petersburg and his grandfather's farm, went for Bryan.

After the election of 1896, Masters turned to professional and domestic concerns. He courted Helen Jenkins, the daughter of a Chicago railroad executive, "impressed by her piety, which I took as the equivalent of goodness, [and] by her chastity which was fuel to my passion."[40] After a falling out with his partner, Kickham Scanlan, during arbitration on behalf of the streetcar union, Masters met his next law partner, Clarence Darrow, who also had an office in the Ashland Building. Darrow had recently added to his firm former governor Altgeld, who had lost his bid for reelection in the Republican sweep of 1896.

Darrow is remembered today as the defense attorney in the notorious Loeb and Leopold murder trial (1924) and in the case *The State of Tennessee v. John Thomas Scopes* (1925), in which he faced William Jennings Bryan. However, when he met Masters, Darrow was known as a lawyer who defended radicals and labor interests. Darrow began his career as a small-town lawyer born, as he said, "in the Western Reserve of Ohio,"[41] and soon relocated with his family to Chicago where he represented the Chicago and North Western Railway Company.[42] During the Pullman Strike of 1894, however, Darrow changed his legal loyalties and defended Eugene Debs, president of the American Railway Union. That same year, he mounted an unsuccessful insanity defense of the assassin of Chicago Mayor Carter Harrison.[43] Since the early 1890s, Darrow had worked actively for the Populists in Illinois and was instrumental in the creation of the "Popucrats," Illinois Democrats who took the platform of the Populists as their own. Darrow's work on behalf of Populist issues within the Illinois Democratic Party helped pave the way for Bryan's nomination in 1896 by both the Democrats and the Populists.[44]

In his autobiography, Masters was cagey about his professional relationship with Clarence Darrow. Darrow does not appear in the index and is referred to in the text as a "criminal lawyer" who "was not in good odor in Chicago," though he "posed as an altruist and as a friend of the oppressed." However,

> the man had charm, he had plausibility, and he lavished praise upon me. ... He offered me what I thought was a fair percentage of the partnership earnings. ... There was a chance now to be at ease on the score of money, and to have some opportunity for poetry.[45]

This antipathy for Darrow came only with the hindsight of their strained end. During the 1890s, Masters's work in Darrow's law office allowed his populist sympathies and legal work to come together. Relatively soon after this period Masters claimed, "I am deeply interested in sociological matters" and "in championing the cause of the under-dog," though he eschewed socialism, saying, "I prefer to remain a Democrat."[46] While Masters was never happy as a lawyer, his political passions found some outlet in the law offices of Clarence Darrow.

The law also proved profitable for Masters, especially when he became a partner in the firm after Altgeld died. By the early 1900s, the law offices of Darrow, Masters, and Wilson cleared between $25,000 and $35,000 annually for the partners, which, according to Masters's biographer, Herbert Russell, equaled about $250,000 in modern terms.[47] In 1904, Masters perhaps reached the pinnacle of his career as a lawyer when, along with Darrow, he argued the case *U.S. Ex Rel. Turner v. Williams* before the United States Supreme Court. In the case, Darrow and Masters unsuccessfully sought to prevent the deportation of the British anarchist and labor organizer John Turner, who had been detained and slated for deportation under the Anarchist Exclusion Act of 1903. Turner had been arrested carrying pamphlets with titles such as "The Legal Murder of 1887" (a reference to the execution of four activists arrested during the Haymarket Affair) and "The Essentials of Anarchism." Masters and Darrow argued that the Act was unconstitutional and claimed to the high court that no power "is delegated by the Constitution to the general government ... over the beliefs of citizens, denizens, sojourners, or aliens, or over the freedom of speech or of the press."[48]

By 1900, Masters's writing began to intersect with his political sympathies for the downtrodden. In 1908, he founded the Jefferson Club and oversaw the Democratic Party's Jackson Day banquet that year, which culminated in an address by William Jennings Bryan. The banquet program ended with a poem (perhaps written by Masters) that reflected the Jefferson Club's faith in the Populist cause and echoed Masters's penchant for classical. "Praise him who keeps the faith unfurld, / Who undismayed beneath sky / Hath wrought Atlantean deeds."[49] Surrounded by Chicago au proclaimed their literary independence from the East, Masters compose writings that sought to combine his interest in literature a justice. Though he moved mostly on the outskirts of Chicago's literati, he found himself surrounded by the kind of literary culture he had dreamed of joining as a young man in Lewistown. After Bryan's defeat in the election of 1908, Masters quit the Jefferson Club and "went back to . . . my poetical studies with a sense of vast relief."[50]

Little Room and Press Club

While Chicago was preparing for the World's Fair and the People's Party prepared to challenge the Northeastern economic elite on a national scale, a group of Midwestern authors and critics began to form a cohesive literary society based in the city. Masters went to Chicago with hopes of becoming a writer, and though he carried a portfolio of the poetry he had written in Lewistown, his search for legal work overtook much of his time during his first years in the city.[51] Nonetheless, Masters arrived in Chicago just as the city was becoming a hub for regional literature.

By 1896, Hamlin Garland had relocated to Chicago and become an active member of the "Little Room," an informal club of artists, social reformers, and philanthropists who gathered around the matinee productions of the Chicago Symphony Orchestra and included members such as fellow author, Henry Fuller; the future editor of *Poetry*, Harriet Monroe; the literary critic, Henry Morton Payne; teacher and dramatist, Anna Morgan; sculptor, Lorado Taft; and painters, Charles Francis Browne, Joe Leyendecker, Ralph Clarkson, and Ralph Fletcher Seymour. Even the architect Louis Sullivan attended meetings.[52] The gatherings of the Little Room served as "a bridge between the Chicago artist and his local society," where Chicago philanthropists such as Mrs. William Armour, Mr. and Mrs. Eugene Field, General and Mrs. A. C. McClurg, and Mr. and Mrs. Potter Palmer patronized local artists.[53]

But Masters's perception of the artists and patrons of the Little Room was generally sour. He called them "dilettanti [who] practiced a haughty exclusiveness,"[54] and his aversion to their salon-style meetings reflected his personal anxieties. In this way, Masters situated himself outside of Chicago literary society in terms that echoed the anxieties of populism itself. Masters brought to Chicago his father's antipathy toward moralistic posturing, especially when it expressed an exclusivity that hinted at class and regional origins along Illinois's north-south axis. Specifically, his father's struggle with the town elite of Lewistown, many of whom were veterans of the Grand Army of the Republic, coupled with his own rejection of his mother's New England upbringing, allowed Masters a convenient means by which to characterize threatening rivals in terms that echoed a contemporaneous critique of the industrial and "northeastern" legacy of the Civil War. For Masters, the denizens of the Little Room, though Mid-westerners like himself, were "snobbish."[55]

Instead, Masters attended the "Press Club," so named since most of the members were journalists, where "politics, whiskey, horseplay, lubricity, sentiment and independence" shaped the gatherings.[56] Opie Read, a Tennessee native by way of Arkansas, served as president of the club off and on for over twenty years. Though Read worked as a Chicago reporter, most of his well-known works were about the rural countryside. His book, *The Jucklins* (1896), which told the story of a schoolteacher in rural North Carolina, sold, at least according to Read, one million copies.[57] Masters first met Read when he attended the Press Club with law partner and fellow poet, Ernest McGaffey. According to Masters, the Press Club was a refuge of epicurean cheer for a small-town boy adrift:

> I would sit beside someone like Opie Read, and thus have my pride salved for its wounds of the day. For with my economic problems thus measurably settled, I started . . . to enjoy the roaring city. . . . Whenever there was a bear dinner at the Press Club, or a haunch of venison served, I was invited . . . and with a guest card given me at once I sometimes dropped in to see Opie Read surrounded by a group of admirers as he told stories of Arkansas and Kentucky.[58]

At a Press Club meeting during the summer of the World's Fair, President Grover Cleveland, who had given a speech at the White City, arrived unexpectedly, perhaps to hobnob with the reporters who gathered there, or to investigate the Club's libertine reputation. Nearly ten years before, Cleveland had been embroiled in a sex scandal during which he admitted to having fathered an illegitimate child. As Opie Read recalled in his book *I Remember*, the Press Club was unfazed by the president's visit:

> One night a ponderous man gazed somewhat in awe upon them. Upon him had fallen a hard day and now he seemed to put aside his cares as though . . . his cloak suddenly become too hot for him. The girls withdrew and . . . [journalist] John McGovern remarked to the fat man:
> "Mr. President, I trust that you may pardon the almost unwonted freedom of our institution and not go away offended."

And Mr. President Cleveland . . . shook himself with a laugh. "My dear sir, I have often been told that I'd make a good sheriff, and that the best of sheriffs, you know, may look back upon a time when they were rounders [a person who habitually visits saloons]. Don't let my presence put restraint upon your festivities."

[McGovern continued] "Mr President . . . we greatly admire you, not more for your statesmanship than for your moral bravery. When confronted with scandal not many men would command that the truth be told. . . . Mr. President, an old-time philosopher delivered himself of this bit of wisdom when asked as to what time a man should marry: 'A young man not yet and an old man not at all.' Do you agree with him?"

"That course, sir, would render mankind what we term illegitimate. Affinity and love are the best judges of marriage."

McGovern turned to me. "What do you think of it?"

"I think that if I were a woman I would never be the wife of a scribbler, no matter how much I might love him."

"You are right," McGovern agreed. "A woman is false to herself when she weds a writer, an actor or a preacher."

"How about a president?" Cleveland laughed.[59]

In this light, the goings on of the Press Club were similar to the "sporting" culture of New York City nearly fifty years before, where young clerks from the countryside built a rakish culture around blood sports and brothels. However, since most of the reportage of this earlier libertine culture was immersed in the language of moral peril and shaped by the religious sensibilities of the 1840s, the self-reflections of those who indulged in this subculture are mostly lost to us.[60] On the other hand, many of the authors, who, like Masters, arrived in Chicago in the 1890s, recorded their memories of the "Gay Nineties" in Chicago over thirty years later with confident retrospection.[61] For example, as a middle-aged man, Opie Read recalled a preacher catching him with a "disreputable wench" during his youthful days in Tennessee:

Report reached my mother and she wrote to me a letter blotted with her tears. Home I went again and kneeling with her in prayer resolved to mend or at least to patch my evil ways. Ah, but hard is it to make a saint out of a bounding animal, though I did try, for to our town there came an evangelist and opened up a general supply store of forgiveness and morality. It was but natural that I should scoff at it all, but a girl who had dazzled me with her smile and entranced me with her talk induced me to go up to the mourners' bench. She sat beside me . . . stroked my hair, put her cheek against my own, but the beast was still within me for I wallowed in the hope that I might kiss her.[62]

Likewise, Masters recalled Lewistown in similarly moralistic terms,

> New England and Calvinism waged a death struggle on the matter of Prohibition and the church with the Virginians and free livers. . . . The politics of the town, with the ever recurrent matter of the saloon, grew intolerable.[63]

Both Read and Masters, publishing with twenty-five years' hindsight, recalled their youthful frustrations with a worldly wise, cosmopolitan tone, as if each had escaped a repressive environment that squelched something essentially theirs: in Read's case, his youthful sexuality, in Masters's a desire for "free" living.

Unlike the clerks of 1840s New York, Masters and Read reached middle age in a period of shifting discourse regarding human sexuality, primarily toward a Freudian conception of repression, which gave them the language and even the ethical imperative to outgrow the nineteenth-century moralisms of their hometowns. While Freud had been formulating his theory of repression since the late 1890s, his visit to the United States in 1909 inaugurated the dissemination of his ideas to such an extent that by the time Read and Masters reflected on their youthful libertinism, Freudian psychology "had become a conspicuous— indeed, unavoidable—part of the American cultural landscape."[64] Indeed, "by the 1930s, even . . . moviegoers could learn about . . . 'psychoanalysis'"; Freudian psychology had become the "fad of 'modernity.'"[65]

In this context, Masters, and others of his generation and libertine inclination reframed the antics of the Press Club of the 1890s into a social critique of their upbringing. By the mid-twentieth century, critics had come to accept this retroactive reframing at face value. For example, Bernard Duffey, in his book *The Chicago Renaissance in American Letters: A Critical History* (1956), claimed that members of the Press Club had their predecessors in the frontier Midwest:

> [Members of the Press Club] represented the life of the rural county seat . . . [and the] . . . familiar though disruptable feature of western life since frontier days. . . . [T]he deliberate drive against respectability [of the Press Club] . . . was little more than a magnification of one kind of life to be found in varying guises across the back country . . ., a host of rural philosophers, village free thinkers, disenchanted paragraphers, corner saloons, and makeshift brothels, Huck Finn's Pap, or Puddinhead Wilson, was as indigenous to Midwestern life as was Aunt Polly.[66]

But Duffey's interpretation has the story backward. The "rural philosophers" and "village free thinkers," with their "drive against respectability" from "frontier days," proved to be figures constructed in hindsight. Twentieth-century writers like Masters adopted an ideology by which they read themselves back into the towns of their youth as village free thinkers and rural philosophers—community exiles—able to explain their memories with a new language that portrayed the moral strictures of their upbringing as narrow-minded hypocrisy, as old-fashioned, as "unrealistic."

Spasmodic, Obscure, and Fragmentary

As a poet, Masters wrote on the cusp of a set of twentieth-century ideas and literary trends that historians and critics loosely term "modernist." While the sharp outlines of modernism are contested, historian Dorothy Ross offers a practical definition:

> [Modernism] follows from the subjective direction taken by romanticism . . ., but look[s] for meaning and value in a cosmos devoid of God and an amoral inner and outer nature demystified by Darwinian biology. Turning inward, [modernists] found resources that could be refashioned and set to the Apollonian or Dionysian ends of order or release. . . . In their effort to construct meaning, modernists . . . transformed alienation, the sickness of modern man, into an heroic stance of the intellectual and artist.[67]

Freud's theory of human psychology, likewise, ostensibly disconnected as it was from Christocentric ethics or abstract philosophy, proved to be "central," according to Ross, for modernists who had an "uneasy relationship with American society."[68]

Virginia Woolf famously placed the beginning of modernism "on or about December 1910." When quoted outside of its context, the statement appears both glib and surprising. How can a literary movement be dated to a particular month? However, according to Woolf, a change took place between the death of Victoria in 1901 and the ascension of George V in 1910:

> The change was not sudden and definite. . . . But a change there was, nevertheless; and, since one must be arbitrary, let us date it about the year 1910. . . . All human relations . . . shifted—those between masters and servants, husbands and wives, parents and children. And when human relations change there is at the same time a change in religion, conduct, politics, and literature. Let us agree to place one of these changes about the year 1910.[69]

Woolf's quote is often used to signify the shift in Anglo-American literary culture to the modern since it pinpoints what was a slow-moving, amorphous, but nonetheless fundamental change in sensibilities in the early twentieth century. Incidentally, the first issue of the *Journal of Educational Psychology,* where psychologists E. C. Sanford and W. H. Burnham reported on Freud's visit to the United States in 1909, was published in 1910.[70]

However, in its context, Woolf's date served a much more targeted purpose as a response to a charge by the contemporary British novelist, Arnold Bennett, who argued in "Is the Novel Decaying?" that a younger generation of authors, of which Woolf was a member, had forgotten the purpose of the novel itself: to create characters who "vitally survive in the mind." According to Bennett, authors like Woolf had grown beholden to "cleverness" and Woolf's third novel, *Jacob's Room* (1922), proved this overly clever turn.[71]

While Woolf agreed with Bennett about the state of the novel, she blamed, instead, Edwardian authors of Bennett's generation who, upon recognizing the "iniquities of the Victorian social system" changed from "novelists into reformers," which made them "better men, but worse artists."[72] For Woolf, social consciousness had turned authors of realistic fiction into scolds and pedants, blind to the essence of an individual's "character." Whereas art captured contradictions, nuances, and essential tragedies in characters, portraying them in the round, authors of Bennett's generation had, in their quest to expose social disparities and injustice, lost sight of the artist's charge to illuminate the world in all its ambivalent meaning. For Woolf, Edwardian authors overlooked "the spasmodic, the obscure, the fragmentary, the failure" in human lives for the sake of a kind of aesthetic social engineering.[73] Younger authors like Woolf found some inspiration in the works of Henry James, for whom the "persistent themes of the divided self, moral ambiguity and unreliable narrative," exemplified the essence of character.[74] According to Woolf, modern authors

> have no fixed scheme of the universe, no standard of courage or morality to which they . . . conform. The man himself is the supreme object of their curiosity. . . . [T]he man himself, the pith and essence of his character, shows itself to the observant eye in the tone of a voice, the turn of a head, some little phrase or anecdote picked up in passing. . . . Thus . . . whole chapters of the Victorian volume are synthesized and summed up.[75]

In this light, Woolf's declaration of 1910 as the moment of change was not so arbitrary: it implied that authors of the first ten years of the twentieth century missed a cultural shift and abandoned good art for moral posturing. Populist novelists like Hamlin Garland reflected this missed opportunity. While Garland was lauded for his portrayal of rural life in the Midwestern hinterland, and by the early twentieth century, had achieved a national audience, his short stories and novels represented a hybrid of vernacular tales and reform ideology whose goal was to elicit sympathy and reform. This reformist inclination found voice in other contemporary works in the United States, including Frank Norris's *The Octopus: A Story of California* (1901) and Upton Sinclair's *The Jungle* (1906).

Masters himself was subject to this kind of writing. In 1900, he claimed, "I was making money at law, but I was not getting rich. . . . And all the while material for creative work was accumulating so fast within me that I was on the point of bursting. What was to be done with it?"[76] In the play *Maximilian* (1902), Masters wrote a critique of America's intervention in the Philippines after the Spanish-American War through a portrayal of the collapse of Emperor Maximilian's reign in nineteenth-century Mexico.[77] In *The New Star Chamber* (1904), Masters collected his essays on the state of US democracy in the aftermath of Bryan's two failed campaigns and argued, "out of the process of producing and distributing wealth have arisen those laws which struck at human liberty."[78] Later, Masters continued to try his hand at drama. In *Althea* (1907), *The Trifler* (1907), *The Leaves of the Tree* (1909), *Eileen* (1910), and *The Locket* (1910), he turned his increasingly unhappy domestic life and series of misbegotten affairs into broad meditations on relations between men and women.[79]

But it was Masters's poetry that most suffered from Edwardian moral posturing. For example, *The Blood of the Prophets* (1905) situated contemporary social injustice in classically themed jeremiads. In "Ballade of Dead Republics," the populist bugbear of money-power played the role of republic-destroyer:

> Tell me ye King-craft of to-day
>   Where is Athens, who made men free;
> Then sank into stupor by the way,
>   Subdued by the Spartan tyranny?
> And Rome that staggered to death, perdie,
>   Stabbed by the sword of Hannibal,
> And bled by patrician infamy—
>   The Dragon of Greed destroyed them all![80]

And in "On a Picture of John D. Rockefeller," Masters compared the leaders of modern capitalism to parasitic despoilers:

> In thou, Columbia, dost from this, thy son—
> The condor beak and python eyes—recoil,
> Bethink thee of the years that Freedom's soil
> Was husbanded by devil-feet which run
> To scatter lies and wrongs; until thereon
> Huge growths do thrive, once meadow, by the toil
> Of Pioneers; where now resort for spoil
> The mouths and beaks that hunt for carrion.[81]

Where once grew fertile fields worked by the hands of pioneers, now only carrion existed, fit for the hungry mouths of capitalists.

Much to Masters's frustration, this populist poetry in a ponderous style attracted few readers. This might not have been entirely his fault. According to John Timberman Newcomb, Masters's poems appeared during a nadir in the popular reception of new verse. According to Newcomb, "[t]he status of poetry in the United States hit bottom between 1900 and 1905" when the "fireside poets" of the nineteenth century—poets like Longfellow and Whittier—monopolized the cannon of American verse, and new poets and critics "assumed that the art was in precipitous decline." Newcomb notes that before 1905, "no serial publications devoted themselves primarily to verse by living Americans" and "[n]o ongoing national prizes remunerated poets."[82] Masters himself was forced to publish *A Book of Verses* (1898) with the "dubious" Chicago firm Way and Williams, "which kept [Masters's] manuscript for two years, [and] agreed to publish [it] only after he threatened to sue." The press ultimately went bankrupt the day Masters's book came out.[83] This was not an unusual situation for aspiring poets in the early twentieth century, and Masters was often forced to self-publish his work before *Spoon River Anthology*.

While Masters's programmatic reform literature exemplified the pedantic and moralistic tone that Woolf complained of in her critique of Edwardian fiction, and he faced an arid publishing environment for poetry generally, he also started to move in circles that prodded his style toward something more avant-garde and outlets that would encourage this transformation. During these years, Masters met William Marion Reedy, the gregarious and corpulent editor of *Reedy's Mirror*, which, by the second decade of the twentieth century, published in the vanguard of contemporary literature in the Midwest. Reedy, a fellow Midwesterner six years Masters's senior, met the lawyer and furtive author through Ernest McGaffey,[84] who had also introduced Masters to the Press Club years before. Reedy was part of the revival of verse in periodicals represented by other small, self-consciously literary and avant-garde journals like Harriet Monroe's *Poetry: A Magazine of Verse*, which, according to John Timberman Newcomb, created "a space for contemporary American verse where there none had been."[85] While Reedy had edited the magazine since 1896 and covered topics as diverse as Henry George's single-tax theory and Democratic politics, during the early twentieth century the journal began to provide space to new poets, including Vachel Lindsay, Sara Teasdale, Carl Sandburg, and Ezra Pound.

According to Masters, "*Reedy's Mirror* was famous in St. Louis and Chicago. ... In the next thirteen years, Reedy was more and more a national figure."[86] While even as late as 1915, Reedy was still publishing editorials on Henry George and weekly columns on the stock market, the *Mirror* also published authors and on topics that reflected burgeoning interest in the aesthetically austere, ethically amoral, and psychologically complex. In a fashion that presaged Woolf, the *Mirror* rebelled against the fatuous state of Edwardian literature. In *The Law of Love: Being Fantasies of Science and Sentiment Inked into English to Cheer Up the Gloomsters* (1905), Reedy laid out his ideal melding of spirit and matter that gave some hint as to how poetry could capture this unseen union:

> Life is but force. Matter holds together by force. Matter, therefore, has life. ... We have exalted the soul too much. .... It is nothing without the body. The body gives the soul its form and effect; its character.[87]

Like Woolf, Reedy despaired of finding a literature that reflected "an awareness of human imperfection and aspiration"[88] and critiqued popular authors like Upton Sinclair, who, to Reedy, proved to be more propagandist than artist.[89]

Reedy was at first unimpressed by Masters's writing.[90] The *Mirror* reviewed *Maximilian* with only faint praise and said of his drama *Eileen*, "Mr. Masters knows how to do things of this sort, but whether they are worth doing is another question."[91] While Masters continued to send poetry to the *Mirror* for publication, Reedy preferred to publish Masters's thoughts on contemporary legal and political matters, including an anonymously written screed against Woodrow Wilson that lambasted the Democratic nominee in 1912 for his "condemnation of Jefferson, and his preference for Hamilton." Nevertheless, Masters himself had grown dispirited with politics by that time and, after the campaign of 1912, "resolved to have no more to do with politics and to stick by poetry."[92] Reedy, on the other hand, recommended Masters "lay off on formal and classical poetry,"[93] though he sent him a copy of J. W. Mackail's *Select Epigrams from the Greek Anthology* (1906), perhaps to inspire him to economize his lugubrious verse. In his introduction, Mackail described ancient epigrams as "little more than stories told shortly in elegiac verse."[94] In this way, Reedy steadily inspired the transformation of Masters's poetry from pretentious, pedantic, and reform-minded verse with classical overtones to the tight character studies of *Spoon River Anthology.*

Masters also met another Midwestern author who inspired a change in his poetry during this period.[95] Masters read Theodore Dreiser's *Sister Carrie* (1900) when it was first published and claimed it gave him "a sense of refreshing realism, and honesty that meant something."[96] Dreiser consulted Masters for a book on Charles Tyson Yerkes, the Chicago financier who by the 1890s monopolized control over much of the city's streetcar system. Dreiser's "skeptical daring" in the book *The Financier* (1912) impressed Masters for its "treatment of evil, and sin, and ... unmasking of the passing show."[97] In later years, however, Masters claimed that Dreiser "didn't know much about literature" and that "his ... stories betray the fact that money and lust figure in his psyche."[98] This criticism of Dreiser revealed a certain pattern in Masters's reflection on authors generally celebrated: received opinion was likely wrong and perhaps nefarious. In this way, Masters practiced a form of self-imposed literary exile that preempted popular rejection.

By the end of the first decade of the twentieth century, Masters still wrote in the moribund style that reflected the populist temperament of authors like Hamlin Garland and his emotional investment in the Bryan campaigns of 1896, 1900, and 1908. Likewise, the Democratic Party itself, after 1912, shifted from the Populist agrarian ideology of William Jennings Bryan to the more urbane Progressivism of Woodrow Wilson, with attendant support for an activist government based on a model of robust federal power. By 1913, therefore, Masters found himself increasingly left behind by contemporary literary and political trends.

Later that same year, Carl Sandburg, then a young and relatively unknown poet and reporter for the *Chicago Day Book*, a short-lived daily penny newspaper aimed at Chicago's working class,[99] visited Masters while covering a case involving the Waitresses' Union and the Hotel and Restaurant Keepers' Association.[100] In addition to discussing the case, Masters and Sandburg talked about poetry, especially Sandburg's own, which Masters claimed "cannot be called poetical, nor ... important," but also contained a "refreshing realism ... off on an entirely new trail."[101] These new trends in poetry made Masters anxious and defensive:

> Harriet Monroe had started her *Poetry: a Magazine of Verse* ... and Reedy had written me [about it]. ... So far as I knew about it I thought the magazine an efflorescence of that group in Chicago which had founded the Little Room. ... I had cast my fortunes with the Press Club crowd. ... A few years before this [William Vaughn] Moody [a poet of Masters's generation] had stirred admiration with his formal odes, and one had to wonder what was going on and in what direction Chicago letters would run, if they ran at all.[102]

A younger generation of poets, publishing in Monroe's *Poetry* magazine, as well as *Reedy's Mirror*, now received the attention formerly reserved for the "formal odes" of Masters's cohort of authors, those that arrived in Chicago in the 1890s.

In the March 1913 issue of *Poetry*, Monroe published a short article by Ezra Pound, a poet nearly twenty years younger than Masters, who served as a cheerleader for new trends in verse. Pound, a college friend of the poet William Carlos Williams and the poet H. D. (Hilda Doolittle), had decamped to Europe in 1908 and, within a few years, rejected the "moral generalizing" of contemporary poets in favor of poetry that captured the "specific tone of a personality . . . or the emotions of a single moment."[103] From London, Pound and H. D. proclaimed a type of poetry they called *Imagism* that sought to divorce verse from the overwrought style of contemporary poets and, instead, capture the "image," which presented "an intellectual and emotional complex in an instant of time."[104] In *Poetry*, Pound famously laid out the "don'ts" of Imagism: "use no superfluous word, no adjective, which does not reveal something. Don't use such an expression as . . . dulls the image. . . . [T]he natural object is always the *adequate* symbol. Go in fear of abstractions." Likewise, a "rhyme must have in it some slight element of surprise if it is to give pleasure."[105] In the same issue, Frank Stewart Flint, in the article "Imagisme," offered three dictums of Imagism:

1. Direct treatment of the "thing," whether subjective or objective.
2. To use absolutely no word that did not contribute to the presentation.
3. As regarding rhythm: to compose in sequence of the musical phrase, not in sequence of a metronome.[106]

Masters, aware of changes in contemporary verse and the significance of Monroe's new magazine as a repository of these changes, must have felt some anxiety about these proclamations in *Poetry*. One of the few poems William Marion Reedy published by Masters during this period, "For a Dance" (1914), exhibited many of Pound's "don'ts",

There is in a dance
    The joy of children on a May day lawn.
The fragment of old dreams and dead romance.
    Come to us from the dancers who are gone.

What strains of ancient blood
    Move quicker to the music's passionate beat?
I see the gulls fly over a shadowy flood
    And Munster fields of barley and of wheat.

And I see sunny France;
    And the vine's tendrils quivering to the light.
And faces, faces, yearning for the dance
    With wistful eyes that look on our delight.[107]

Here, Masters sought the "musical phrase," and a set of rhymes that could "surprise," but strained against the formal style that Reedy discouraged. Even in his autobiography, written twenty-five years later, Masters wondered "what was going on." His marriage gave him some degree of stability, though little joy, and his law practice provided him with a substantial living, though it had not yet made him rich. Furthermore, his unfulfilled and increasingly untenable status as a poet frustrated him. In early 1914, Masters submitted "The Altar" to Reedy, which began "My heart is an altar whereon / Many sacrificial fires have been kindled / In praise of spring and Aphrodite" and asked the reader to "murmur a little Doric prayer / Over the ashes which lie scattered around the altar." Reedy responded, "damn it man you're not Doric, you're American."[108]

In May 1914, Masters's mother visited his family in Chicago and was, uncharacteristically, "wonderfully humorous." During the visit, they discussed memories of Lewistown and Petersburg and "reinvested . . . in those incarnations that had long since surrendered their sheaths to the changes of those years."[109] Soon after, Masters began to write short poems that united an earlier idea for a novel that captured the "microcosm of the Spoon River country"[110] with his desire to write poetry that gained the attention of William Marion Reedy and the generation of younger authors around him. Masters had a number of precedents for a collection of tales from rural America, including Hamlin Garland and E. W. Howe's writings and Clarence Darrow's *Farmington* (1903), which had been reviewed positively in the *Tribune*.[111] However, the most immediate inspiration was most likely William Marion Reedy's ongoing demand that Masters write something "American." In reaction, Masters wrote the first poems of *Spoon River Anthology* partially in jest (he later called them "rampant yokelisms") and, in a letter to Reedy, asked, "is this American?"[112] Nearly twenty years later, he remembered the genesis in these terms:

> [T]here was implicit in Reedy's criticisms the idea that I should do something distinctly American, that my experience and background should not go unexpressed, and should not be smothered under verses of mere skill, which did not free what was really within me. . . . [H]e implied in all that he said that I should use life for poetry. I was trying to do that; I was doing it, but not the way I did it in the Anthology. . . . [W]hen I sent him the first pieces of the Anthology . . . back came a letter immediately saying that this was the stuff. I was astonished . . . and his extravagant praise seemed like irony. I . . . scrawled at the top "Spoon River Anthology" and laughed at what seemed to me the most preposterous title known to the realm of books.[113]

In hindsight, Masters's astonishment is not surprising. As his biographer Herbert Russell notes, Masters proved notoriously unable to discern quality from trash in his own writing, and none of his later works achieved the renown of *Spoon River Anthology*, even though he soon quit the law and dedicated himself to writing for the next thirty years. Nevertheless, with the first installment of *Spoon River Anthology* in *Reedy's Mirror*, Masters suddenly found himself on the forefront of the Midwestern, and perhaps even the international, literary zeitgeist. Latent in these poems, however, was his preceding decade of life in Chicago, his Populist politics, his Press Club libertinism, and behind these, the nostalgia and ambivalence he felt for his youth in the little towns of Petersburg and Lewistown.

Garlands and Graves

The poems by "Webster Ford," a pseudonym Masters had used before, that appeared in *Reedy's Mirror* under the title "Spoon River Anthology" were organized in a fashion similar to the epigrams in Mackail's *Greek Anthology*, separated by a Roman numeral and titled with the speaker's name. The first seven made clear that the speaking characters, Hod Putt, Ollie McGee, The Unknown, Cassius, Serepta the Scold, Amanda, and Chase Henry, spoke from the grave. Some of the names changed when the "garlands," as Masters called them, were collected into the book *Spoon River Anthology*. For example, "Serepta the Scold" became "Serepta Mason" in its final version. However, these titles, given from either ignorance ("The Unknown") or reputation ("the Scold") called these characters by the names society gave them. These individuals spoke from within the "microcosm" that shaped their reputation. And though the reader was a stranger, the dead felt obligated to acknowledge their public reputations before revealing their private realities. In these short epitaphs, the citizens of Spoon River struggled to be known.

The first epitaph, "Hod Putt," has been noted by many critics as echoing the colloquialism "hard put," or one who has suffered a difficult life, often financially. In this case, Masters's populist sensibilities were readily apparent, though framed in the austere style of the Greek epigrams and the economical language admired by Imagist poets:

> HERE I lie close to the grave
> Of Old Bill Piersol,
> Who grew rich trading with the Indians, and who
> Afterwards took the bankrupt law
> And emerged from it richer than ever.
> Myself grown tired of toil and poverty
> And beholding how Old Bill and others grew in wealth,
> Robbed a traveler one night near Proctor's Grove,
> Killing him unwittingly while doing so,

For the which I was tried and hanged.
That was my way of going into bankruptcy.
Now we who took the bankrupt law in our respective ways
Sleep peacefully side by side.

Here, Masters exhibited his populist sympathy for people subject to the vicissitudes of the capitalist economy. Both Hod Putt and Bill Piersol were of the pioneering generation of settlers in the Midwest. However, though Piersol went bankrupt, he, inexplicably for Hod, grew richer than ever afterward. Hod Putt followed the opposite direction down the economic ladder, fell into poverty, committed a crime, and was hanged, achieving his own kind of bankruptcy. While it ends on an egalitarian note, the poem portrays the economic iniquities addressed by Populist reformers in the late nineteenth century and Midwestern authors like Hamlin Garland, who infused their work with rural anxieties. In Masters's epitaph, the reader's sympathies follow the unlucky Hod Putt, but despite this populist undertone, Masters's economy of style and ambivalent resolution left the reader with an amoral result: both ne'er-do-well thief and successful bourgeoisie sleep peacefully. This amoral affect catered to modernist suspicion of Edwardian reform-minded literature and was interpreted by Masters's contemporaries, at least those engaged by *Spoon River Anthology*, as the element that made these epitaphs "realistic."

In another of these first poems, Chase Henry, the town drunkard, has the last laugh at the townsfolk who scorned him:

In life I was the town drunkard;
When I died the priest denied me burial
In holy ground.
The which redounded to my good fortune.
For the Protestants bought this lot,
And buried my body here,
Close to the grave of the banker Nicholas,
And of his wife Priscilla.
Take note, ye prudent and pious souls,
Of the cross-currents in life
Which bring honor to the dead, who lived in shame.

Here, the modernist charge that reform-minded literature was unrealistic aligned with Masters's antipathy for "Calvinist" Lewistown. Chase Henry was refused burial by one denomination and, inexplicably, given a plot by another. This fortunate happenstance put him close to the ostentatious grave of those who likely disparaged him in life. Neither the Catholics, who refused Chase burial, nor the Presbyterians, who gave him a desirable plot, are judged; both are subject to the same "fortune" and, as pious souls, reminded to "take note" of life's "cross-currents," as if their prudence made them not only prudes, but also fools. In the end, the fickleness of fate brought honor, inexplicably, to Chase Henry. His authoritative final pronouncement provides little meaning beyond a vague sense of the amorality of the cosmos in the face of earthly human morals.

Masters's other poems from this first garland exhibited a similar ambivalence toward this rural community and its above-ground values. The Unknown cages an injured hawk and now searched Hades for its soul. No reason is given for his lost identity. Cassius mocks the absurdity of his gravestone that called him "gentle" when he had spent his life fighting "slanderous tongues," only to "submit to an epitaph . . . by a fool!" Serepta the Scold was known for her moralistic grandstanding, but blames the "unseen forces that govern the processes of life" for her shrewish ways. The village believed Amanda died in childbirth, much to her husband's grief, but in fact, "he slew me to gratify his hatred." In all these cases, it was impossible to know the "truth" of these radically subjective epitaphs, but in reading them, it became apparent that the townspeople still lived in the shadowy twilight of the irony, hypocrisy, and tragedy that plagued them in life.

In this way, Masters's epitaphs exhibited situations of great human moral import without any clear moral framework. Since Masters's dead speak authoritatively about the ultimate destination of the living, their spasmodic, obscure, fragmentary and failed lives left the reader with a deeply ambivalent sense of any underlying cosmic order. In Spoon River's epitaphs, Masters took the ideological inclinations he built over a lifetime and presented them within an amoral system: downtrodden populists sink into peaceful sleep beside successful businessmen; drunkards are luckily buried; the pious cannot overcome fortune; scolds sometimes wish they were not; a complimentary gravestone is slander, but Masters infused his last poem, the eighth of this first garland, with nostalgia. Titled "The Hill," this longest of the eight poems is spoken by no particular person, but in a voice familiar with the little town of Spoon River. Ending each stanza with "All, all are sleeping, sleeping, sleeping on the hill," the poem asked where were "Elmer, Herman, Bert, Tom and Charley / The weak of will, the strong of arm, the clown, the boozer, the fighter? / . . . The tender heart, the simple soul, the loud, the proud . . . / Where are Uncle Isaac and Aunt Emily / And old Towny Kincaid and Sevigne Houghton / And Major Walker who had talked / With venerable men of the revolution? / . . . Lo! The babbles of the fish-frys of long ago, / Of the horse-races of long ago at Clary's Grove / Of what Abe Lincoln said / One time at Springfield." In this final poem of the first series, Masters left no doubt that he was talking about a single small town in rural Illinois and, with first names and nicknames and titles of relatives long gone, with memories of social gatherings and historical events and locations fraught with memory, he cast a spell of familiarity. The speaker of "The Hill" talks like one townie to another, and with the recollections shared, nostalgically repopulates Spoon River.

In his next installment of poems, Masters capitalized on the morally ambiguous themes of his first garland. They included an unhappily married lawyer who died in his office and was buried with his beloved dog, the village poetess who was murdered one night by the "Yahoos of the street," and "Knolt Hoheimer," who died at the Civil War battle of Missionary Ridge and asked what the words "Pro Patria" meant on his gravestone, anticipating the more biting irony of Wilfred Owen's famous poem of World War I, "Dulce Et Decorum Est." But Masters still maintained his anonymity, perhaps because of some reticence to affix his name to such unusual verse. That same spring, he published an article in the *Mirror* under his own name (or at least his initials) on "Futurist Poets," where he crankily charged the poets Donald Evans and Allen Norton with inauthenticity and hoped that their laments proved to be the pretense of youth, since "poets who are really tired and disillusioned keep still."[114]

Another garland appeared in the June 26 issue of the *Mirror* with ten new poems, including one by the lovelorn schoolteacher Emily Sparks and the banker Nicholas, whose grave lay close to the drunkard, Chase Henry. Readers who had followed "Spoon River Anthology" learned that Nicholas lost all his money when the bank collapsed and then suffered the inequity of hearing the organ he bought for the church play while Deacon Rhodes, who broke the bank, worshipped after his acquittal for fraud. In the July 3 issue of *Reedy's Mirror*, Harry B. Kennon, in an article called "Spoon River Cemetery," "visited" the fictional Illinois town, and described it as a "shunned . . . acre, baking under the August sun." There, he saw "obscene tinfoil" shining through the wreath of a soldiers' monument for "Knolt Hoheimer." Kennon went on to describe the Spoon River, "a creek now" by a "desolate, lonely, uninviting city of the dead that calls peremptorily to the unlovely, dead-alive town in the distance." There, a "poet" took thoughts and "weave[d] them into garlands" with a weed called "Life Everlasting."[115] It is difficult not to imagine Masters and Reedy giggling a little over this visit to fictional Spoon River.

Masters published garlands through the summer of 1914. By autumn, letters of inquiry began to arrive in the *Mirror*'s offices addressed to "Webster Ford," which Reedy forwarded to Masters at the summerhouse he was renting on

Lake Michigan. In October, *Poetry* magazine recognized Masters's new verse as deserving "more than casual recognition," since "tradition" had "served to lead [Webster Ford] . . . to a little cemetery in a small town—it might be any small town—in the United States, where death reveals life in a series of brief tragic epitaphs." *Poetry* reprinted three of the poems, including "Doc Hill," who cared for the sick of Spoon River at "all hours of the night" because "my wife hated me, my son went to the dogs. / And I turned to the people and poured out my love to them." *Poetry* also reprinted "The Hill," thereby capturing both the ambivalence and nostalgia that characterized Spoon River from its inception.[116] In 1915, Harriet Monroe claimed that Masters found inspiration for *Spoon River Anthology* in Sandburg's free verse when it appeared in *Poetry* magazine: "*Poetry* had furnished the spark which kindled a poet's soul to living flame, and burned out of it the dry refuse of formalism."[117] In retrospect, Masters claimed with characteristic tartness, "Harriet Monroe and her associate editors could not help but feel regretful to learn that my *Spoon River Anthology* was being published in a St. Louis periodical. . . . But while I knew Harriet Monroe . . . she knew nothing about me until *Spoon River* loomed."[118] That same month, Harry Kennon, who had "visited" Spoon River back in July, claimed that the "work of [Webster Ford] makes a reading man glad—and glad again—of letters."[119] Finally, in November, William Marion Reedy published an editorial titled "The Writer of Spoon River" in which he claimed that "inquiry as to the identity of the author has been widespread and persistent. Literary folk in this country and in Europe have almost shown anger that the author of such a work . . . should be kept concealed under a pseudonym." After revealing Masters's identity and listing his previous publications, Reedy claimed,

> Mr. Masters makes great literature of his comprehensively various epitaphy by the virtue of the impersonality of the work in which he makes so many other personalities live. . . . Each person's story is not only *a* life, it is *life*. . . . Theirs is a terrible truthfulness. Seldom . . . does he portray a life or a character that you do not say, "I knew that man in *my* town."[120]

According to Reedy, Masters had taken the genre of Midwestern life and infused it with "tragedy or comedy, . . . pity or terror or absurdity in just a few lines. . . . Spoon River is New York or Chicago or St. Louis and these dead folk are saying to each of us, 'You, too!'"[121]

By December 1914, William Marion Reedy, Harriet Monroe, and the readers of *Reedy's Mirror* recognized in Masters's microcosm the truth of the whole. The "impersonality" of the work made many personalities rich in vitality, but unmoored from any cosmic structure. No apparent narrator gave meaning to their utterances; instead, the dead spoke in profoundly subjective tones, as if each passing encounter offered a chance to explain someone's eternal meditations. Taken together, Masters's garlands left the reader with one universal truth: everything is spasmodic, obscure, and fragmentary.

On December 31, 1914, Masters signed a book contract with the Macmillan Company for a bound version of *Spoon River Anthology.*

CHAPTER 4

Rampant Yokelisms

Do you remember, O Delphic Apollo,
The sunset hour by the river, when Mickey M'Grew
Cried, "There's a ghost," and I, "It's Delphic Apollo";
And the son of the banker derided us, saying, "It's light
By the flags at the water's edge, you half-witted fools."

—Edgar Lee Masters, "Webster Ford," *Spoon River
Anthology* (1915)

By the time Macmillan published *Spoon River Anthology* in April 1915, Masters's poems had already made a stir in the literary community around *Reedy's Mirror*. William Marion Reedy had revealed Masters as "Webster Ford" and, when a poem appeared as the last epitaph in the book version of *Spoon River Anthology* under the same name, savvy readers understood the reference.

All three characters in the poem, Webster Ford, Mickey M'Grew, and Ralph Rhodes personify representative types in *Spoon River Anthology*. All are situated in a moment when their reaction to an inexplicable apparition reveals the town's underlying social fault lines. When, almost twenty years later, Masters claimed that the book was ordered with "the fools, the drunkards, and the failures c[oming] first, the people of one-birth minds got the second place, and the heroes and the enlightened spirits came last" he elided the extent to which his populist sympathies, along with his distaste for financial and moral elites, resonated.[1] In the character of Webster Ford, Masters solidified the role of the exile as the moral center of Spoon River.

Mickey M'Grew mouths the simple superstitions of the pioneering generation. By this point, the reader already knows that Mickey dreamed of going to college but ended up giving all his saved money to his down-on-his-luck father. The reader also knows that Mickey will meet his end by plunging to his death while cleaning the town's water tower. Jennie M'Grew, Mickey's wife, also saw an apparition "on a sunny afternoon" and understood it as death, "something black, / Like a blot with an iris rim—/ That is the sign to eyes of second sight." For both of the M'Grews, unseen forces shape the world. Sometimes death unexpectedly greets you on a sunny day.

The banker's son counters the M'Grews' superstition. Ralph Rhodes, who ruined his father's bank "with loans / To dabble in wheat" and who ultimately moved to New York, grew "sicken[ed] of wine and women," and committed suicide by walking into traffic, opposes Mickey and Webster, and sees only the logical in the apparition: it's a trick of the light. Since the poem "Webster Ford" appears well after "Ralph Rhodes" in the book version of *Spoon River Anthology*, the reader is aware that the confident materialism shown by Ralph at the river ultimately saps his will to live. In an earlier poem, Ralph's father, Thomas Rhodes, rails against "liberals" and "navigators into realms intellectual" who ultimately learn that their "boasted wisdom" cannot "keep the soul from splitting into cellular atoms." Old Man Rhodes considers this just deserts since "we, seekers of earth's treasures / Getters and hoarders of gold" face hard reality "self-contained, compact, harmonized, / Even to the end." Ralph Rhodes's interpretation of the apparition on Spoon River and his bitter end prove to be the legacy of his father's cynicism.

In this regard, Mickey and Ralph are products of their fathers' generation. The M'Grews are examples of the populist characters of *Spoon River Anthology*, who, after the pioneering generation, fall into a downward economic cycle controlled by financial and legal forces—the bank, the courts, or by faraway entities in Chicago or New York—beyond their control. Populists in *Spoon River Anthology* are either crushed or unbowed by happenstance, which arrives in ways that the pioneering ethics of independence and fortitude can no longer successfully navigate, but merely forbear.

On the other hand, Ralph Rhodes, son of the town banker, is confident of his ability to see the world as it really is, rather than as the "half-witted fools" Mickey and Webster. However, in following his father's materialism, Ralph ruins his father's bank and saps his will to live. When the wine and women no longer satisfy him, he cannot face his "theft." Residents like Rhodes represent the elite strata of Spoon River, who live the hypocrisy of moralistic posturing and rank materialism. This elite hypocrisy elicits little sympathy in Masters's treatment; the Rhodes of Spoon River slide easily into scandal and financial ruin. In this regard, Masters's antipathy toward his father's remembered oppression at the hands of the elite of Lewistown manifested itself in his creation of a hypocritical and grasping elite in Spoon River. Ralph Rhodes and Mickey M'Grew are one page apart in *Spoon River Anthology*, almost at the center of the book itself.

This is not to say that every character in *Spoon River Anthology* easily fits into the populist-elite drama.[2] Lucinda Matlock and Fiddler Jones both lie peacefully on the Hill. And there are many individuals in the graveyard who come from middle-class homes or are unburdened by circumstances beyond their control. Nevertheless, *Spoon River Anthology* displays a latent ethical framework that exhibits sympathy for the downtrodden and animosity toward the elite, which reflects Masters's populist sensibility and echoes his more reform-minded writings from earlier in the century. In a similar fashion, Masters embedded moral arbiters throughout Spoon River's cemetery, of which Webster Ford is the exemplar. Coming at the end of the book, he has the final word.

Webster Ford exists outside of the populist-elite drama. He has no relatives in Spoon River's graveyard and his interpretation of the apparition is profoundly different from his friends': Webster sees Apollo, who cursed the mythical Cassandra with foresight that no one believed.[3] And though he hides his vision of Apollo "for fear / Of the son of the banker," and carries the vision until it "perished with [Mickey] like a rocket which falls / And quenches its light in the earth . . .," Apollo returns to Webster "in an hour / When I seemed to be turned to a tree with a trunk and branches."[4] For Webster, it is "vain . . . to fly the call of Apollo." Instead, Webster Ford advised the reader to "[f]ling yourself in the fire, die with a song of spring, / If die you must in the spring," for it is a better choice than to die "rooted fast in the earth." Here, then, is the exile's appeal. Webster, in-but-out of Spoon River, understands the town in a way that separates him from it. Rooted in place, he's doubly exiled: psychologically, from Spoon River, and physically, from the rest of the world. While he sympathizes with Mickey's tragic mysticism and is cowed by Ralph's cold materialism, he is distinctly disconnected from both. In the apparition on Spoon River, Webster senses a set of forces at work exemplified by a complex and amoral cosmos, neither purely Mickey's nor Ralph's, a presence in the form of Apollo that gives him knowledge of a life unfettered by religiosity or materialism, a knowledge that echoes Walt Whitman's worship of the world for the mystical qualities manifest in its infinite complexity. But unlike Whitman, Ford cannot express this to others in a way they understand. Cassandra-like, Webster's audience understands only in hindsight. In his appeal to passersby, Webster echoes Whitman from "Calamus" ("leaves of me . . . fit alone for urns of memory . . . for hearts heroic, fearless singers and livers.")[5] and ends his lament with an entreaty to the patron of his unrequited foresight: "Delphic Apollo!"

Exiles in *Spoon River Anthology* express Masters's long-held nostalgia for and ambivalence toward his mythological town, which proved to be a projection of Petersburg and Lewistown in the last quarter of the nineteenth century. Masters conflated both in the fictional community of Spoon River, and thereby mixed his romanticized populism, through which he recalled the "southern" town of Petersburg, with the equally fantastical bourgeois materialism and hypocritical moralism of "northern" Lewistown. Within each were memories of early Illinois: its settlement patterns along a north-south axis, its gridded little towns, its pioneering mythology, its political conflicts during the Civil War that translated into economic conflict thereafter, Copperheads and Union Leaguers, farmers and lawyers and bankers, his "Virginian" father and "Yankee" mother—all fit broadly into categories of honest-tragic populists like Mickey, moralistic-materialist elites like Ralph, and a few town exiles like Webster, who reflect on their home with a mix of fondness and foreboding.

Populists: Affliction and Fortitude

Populist characters in *Spoon River Anthology* do not explicitly refer to the political movement that ran candidates in the national election of 1892 or the party that nominated William Jennings Bryan along with the Democrats in 1896. However, the personal struggles of the individuals termed "populist" here echoed the Jeffersonian pose of nineteenth-century populists, namely, that nefarious forces bankrupted the nation's pioneering-farming legacy. Accordingly, Aaron Hatfield represents the ideal of the pioneering generation at its founding moment:

> Better than granite, Spoon River,
> Is the memory-picture you keep of me
> Standing before the pioneer men and women
> There at Concord Church on Communion day.
> Speaking in broken voice of the peasant youth
> Of Galilee who went to the city
> And was killed by bankers and lawyers;
> My voice mingling with the June wind
> That blew over wheat fields from Atterbury;

While the white stones in the burying ground
Around the Church shimmered in the summer sun.
And there, though my own memories
Were too great to bear, were you, O Pioneers,
With bowed heads breathing forth your sorrow
For the sons killed in battle and the daughters
And little children who vanished in life's morning,
Or at the intolerable hour of noon.
But in those moments of tragic silence,
When the wine and bread were passed,
Came the reconciliation for us—
Us the ploughmen and the hewers of wood,
Us the peasants, brothers of the peasant of Galilee—
To us came the Comforter
And the consolation of tongues of flame!

Here, Aaron, named for the brother of Moses and the high priest of the Israelites, personifies a generation that stretches back not only to the first settlers of Spoon River, but also to their brethren in ancient Galilee, unchanged in the nearly two thousand years since the days of Jesus. This generation's fortitude and simple faith, through war and tragedy, against "bankers and lawyers," drew from God's anointed peasantry. Nearly twenty years after the publication of *Spoon River Anthology*, Masters claimed that Aaron Hatfield was a characterization of his paternal grandfather, Squire Davis Masters, who settled a farm outside of Petersburg and whom Masters visited throughout his childhood and during his early days in Chicago.[6] While Masters nostalgically memorialized his grandfather as a deeply religious peasant, John Hallwas reminds us that "Masters' grandfather was not a plowman, or a hewer of wood ... but a gentleman farmer who rarely did any physical work at all."[7] Nevertheless, Aaron Hatfield represents a founding generation in *Spoon River Anthology* whose descendants succumb to the town's fall from grace; his progeny are the victims of this fall.

Barry Holden and Nancy Knapp are examples of this victimized second generation. Nancy explains her descent into madness through a series of events seemingly out of her control:

Well, don't you see this was the way of it:
We bought the farm with what he inherited,
And his brothers and sisters accused him of poisoning
His father's mind against the rest of them.
And we never had peace with our treasure.
The murrain took the cattle, and the crops failed.

And lightning struck the granary.
So we mortgaged the farm to keep going.
And he grew silent and was worried all the time.

The explanation of these events is both apparent and mysterious to Nancy. She
is able to recount the circumstances of her decline in the order in which they
occurred, and though she offers to explain the "way of it," she cannot support
her explanation with any sense of underlying forces. Her husband received an
inheritance, her brothers- and sisters-in-law turned against him, disease killed
the cows, crops failed, lightning struck, and the mortgage became necessary.
Events descend sequentially into disaster outside of Nancy's ken, held together
only by two ominous "thens":

Then some of the neighbors refused to speak to us,
And took sides with his brothers and sisters.
And I had no place to turn, as one may say to himself,
At an earlier time in life: "No matter,
So and so is my friend, or I can shake this off
With a little trip to Decatur."
Then the dreadfullest smells infested the rooms
So I set fire to the beds and the old witch-house
Went up in a roar of flame,
As I danced in the yard with waving arms,
While he wept like a freezing steer.

While Nancy is aware that her home becomes "the old witch-house" and the
dreadful smells that filled the rooms are as real as disease and lightening, madness
happens to Nancy without any self-recognition. Instead, her interpretive move
characterizes her grieving husband as a helpless steer, thereby forever saddling
his memory with the degradation of the farm itself.

Nancy's brother Barry achieves some clearer understanding of the causes of
his plight, but this does little to preserve him from a similar act of desperation:

The very fall my sister Nancy Knapp
Set fire to the house
They were trying Dr. Duval
For the murder of Zora Clemens,
And I sat there in court two weeks
Listening to every witness.
It is clear he had got her in a family way;
And to let the child be born
Would not do.

While neither Duval nor Clemens appear in *Spoon River Anthology*, it is clear from Barry's description that a respected member of the town's elite, Dr. Duval, impregnated Zora Clemens and, because his reputation would be ruined with the birth of a child out of wedlock, he killed Zora. In this case, Masters hints at the fatuous hypocrisy of the town's elite, but only through our inference. Barry makes no such judgment, but accepts, instead, the social stricture that this birth "would not do." However, this unwanted pregnancy inspires Barry to weigh his own plight against Dr. Duval's:

> Well, how about me with eight children,
> And one coming, and the farm
> Mortgaged to Thomas Rhodes?

Here, Barry identifies himself as a populist character in Spoon River. Children and mortgages happen to Barry, seemingly out of his control. His plight is sympathetic, but Masters does not direct us toward empathy. We know Barry much as Webster Ford knows Mickey M'Grew and Thomas Rhodes. Like Webster Ford, we are soothsayers whose understanding of others' plight cannot save them:

> And when I got home that night,
> (After listening to the story of the buggy ride,
> And the finding of Zora in the ditch,)
> The first thing I saw, right there by the steps,
> Where the boys had hacked for angle worms,
> Was the hatchet!
> And just as I entered there was my wife,
> Standing before me, big with child.
> She started the talk of the mortgaged farm,
> And I killed her.

As in the case of his sister Nancy, Barry is buffeted by events that break him. Though he is able to compare his plight to Dr. Duval, Duval commits murder to uphold his reputation. Barry, on the other hand, faces economic ruin and acts out of frenzied desperation, destroying himself and his family. While Dr. Duval is a hypocrite and a criminal, Nancy and Barry are victims of circumstances that drive them both to madness.

Not all populists are so afflicted in *Spoon River Anthology*. Jefferson Howard exemplifies a spirit of independence and pride that allows him to forbear unfortunate circumstance,

> My valiant fight! For I call it valiant,
> With my father's beliefs from old Virginia:
> Hating slavery, but no less war.

I, full of spirit, audacity, courage
Thrown into life here in Spoon River,
With its dominant forces drawn from New England,
Republicans, Calvinists, merchants, bankers,
Hating me, yet fearing my arm.
With wife and children heavy to carry—
Yet fruits of my very zest of life.
Stealing odd pleasures that cost me prestige,
And reaping evils I had not sown;
Foe of the church with its charnel dankness,
Friend of the human touch of the tavern;
Tangled with fates all alien to me,
Deserted by hands I called my own.
Then just as I felt my giant strength
Short of breath, behold my children
Had wound their lives in stranger gardens—
And I stood alone, as I start alone!
My valiant life! I died on my feet,
Facing the silence—facing the prospect
That no one would know of the fight I made.

A number of critics have noted that Jefferson Howard is modeled on Masters's father,[8] Hardin; Masters himself offered many easy clues, especially the reference to a Virginian descendant struggling against the town's power-elite of "Republicans" and "Calvinists." However, many critics overlook the extent to which this character, though identified as a lawyer in other poems in *Spoon River Anthology*, also suffers from forces outside of his control in a fashion similar to Nancy Knapp and Barry Holden. While Hardin Masters moved to Lewistown to seek greater economic opportunity, Jefferson Howard is "thrown into life" in Spoon River, "tangled" in a fate alien to him. His adversarial stance toward the town's elite, then, is a product of his father's beliefs from "old Virginia," which take the decidedly un-Virginian stance of "hating slavery, but no less war." Jefferson's struggles, therefore, are born of the "zest of life," which he engages "valiantly," which, though forgotten by his children, nonetheless allows him to live proudly unbowed by the elite forces of Spoon River. Whereas Nancy Knapp and Barry Holden are driven toward destruction and death, Jefferson is driven toward life, which manifests itself in the "human touch of the tavern" and in "spirit, audacity, and courage." In this regard, Jefferson is admirable for his joie de vivre and forbearance in the face of adversity. His memory of his pioneering roots connects him to the sympathetic characters in Spoon River.

There are a number of similarly proud populists in *Spoon River Anthology*, many of whom react to adversity with a forbearance that mark them as inheritors of the pioneering generation. Mrs. George Reece, for example, sees her husband, the bank cashier, jailed for the crimes committed by banker Thomas Rhodes and his son, Ralph, but still raises her children and "sen[ds] them forth into the world all clean and strong" on the advice of Alexander Pope: "Act well your part, there all the honor lies." Mrs. Purkapile's husband runs away for a year and returns with the tall tale that he'd been kidnapped by pirates on Lake Michigan, but she, "out of respect for my own character . . . refused to be drawn into divorce / By . . . a husband who had merely grown tired / Of his marital vow and duty." Ida Frickey, "a penniless girl" arrives poor in Spoon River and dies the heir of the McNeely fortune. Jack McGuire shot the town marshal but was only given fourteen years in prison after his lawyer struck a deal with the judge. In the end, McGuire "served [his] time / And learned to read and write." Daisy Fraser's debauched reputation cannot undermine her moral clarity:

Did you ever hear of Editor Whedon
Giving to the public treasury any of the money he received
For supporting candidates for office?
Or for writing up the canning factory
To get people to invest?
Or for suppressing the facts about the bank,
When it was rotten and ready to break?
Did you ever hear of the Circuit Judge
Helping anyone except the "Q" railroad,
Or the bankers? Or did Rev. Peet or Rev. Sibley
Give any part of their salary, earned by keeping still,
Or speaking out as the leaders wished them to do,
To the building of the water works?
But I—Daisy Fraser who always passed
Along the streets through rows of nods and smiles,
And coughs and words such as "there she goes,"
Never was taken before Justice Arnett
Without contributing ten dollars and costs
To the school fund of Spoon River!

The populist characters of *Spoon River Anthology*, whether broken or indefatigable, are subject to circumstance. In this regard, the reader is invited to sympathize with these characters, but not necessarily to identify with them. These are the noble or tragic downtrodden of the town, much as the idealized farmer of Populist ideology from the late nineteenth century. These romanticized common folk represent a memorial to Masters's childhood memories of his grandfather's generation in Petersburg and their descendants. However, Spoon River was populated by the remembered citizens of Lewistown as well, who in Masters's mind represented elite forces that drove the town from its pioneering Eden toward the modern sins of moral hypocrisy and economic exploitation.

Elite: Moralism and Greed

For Masters, moralism and greed on the part of the American elite reflected a broader falling away of American mores in the aftermath of the Civil War. The American republic, according to Masters, was conceived by "a few free spirits ... [who] set it to follow a career of justice to the common man upon a fresh soil," but "[a]rmed with the theology of a rural Methodist, Lincoln crushed the principles of free government," making it possible for the "exploiter to grow fat, for his best accomplice is the religious imposter, the church." Ultimately,

> [a]ges may be required ... to ... see the work of Lincoln, whose only literacy was out of the Bible, and who developed an oratory from it, inspired by its artifice of emotional reiteration, and equipped with its sacred curses and its dreadful prophecies. With this manner of molding a people[,] events of a materialistic basis have cooperated to hypnotize ... America.[9]

The town of Spoon River is haunted by Masters's jeremiad against the postbellum sins of religiosity and materialism, which Masters drew from his bitter memories of Lewistown and characterized as "Republican," "Yankee," and "Calvinist."

A. D. Blood, the prohibitionist and erstwhile mayor of Spoon River, and Thomas Rhodes, the president of the bank, personify the twin-headed transgressions of the town's elite. Rhodes, whose mortgages broke the farmers of Spoon River and whose illegalities eventually destroyed the bank, represents the cynical core of the town's elite:

> Very well, you liberals,
> And navigators into realms intellectual,
> You sailors through heights imaginative,
> Blown about by erratic currents, tumbling into air pockets,
> You Margaret Fuller Slacks, Petits,
> And Tennessee Claflin Shopes—
> You found with all your boasted wisdom

How hard at the last it is
To keep the soul from splitting into cellular atoms.
While we, seekers of the earth's treasures,
Getters and hoarders of gold,
Are self-contained, compact, harmonized,
Even to the end.

Rhodes's sneering list of "liberals" and "navigators" names some of the more prominent exiles in Spoon River. Margaret Fuller Slack, named after the nineteenth-century transcendentalist, dreamed of being an author, married instead, gave birth to eight children, and died of lockjaw from a needle. Petit the poet wrote in "little iambics" and only realized after death that nature speaks with the roar of Homer and Whitman. Tennessee Claflin Shope "asserted the sovereignty of my own soul," echoing Ralph Waldo Emerson, and ended his epitaph with "Peace to all worlds!" For Rhodes, these exiles represent the greatest threat to his materialistic worldview, which is blind to anything but "cellular atoms" and the "earth's treasures" that form the foundation of his relationship with the cosmos.

While Rhodes lambasts the poets and the mystics in Spoon River from the grave, A. D. Blood, the town moralist, attacks earthier individuals,

If you in the village think that my work was a good one,
Who closed the saloons and stopped all playing at cards,
And haled old Daisy Fraser before Justice Arnett,
In many a crusade to purge the people of sin;
Why do you let the milliner's daughter Dora,
And the worthless son of Benjamin Painter,
Nightly make my grave their unholy pillow?

Daisy Fraser, quoted above, was the town harlot who noted that it was she who contributed most to the town's school fund through her court fees compared to the elites who controlled the bank and the newspaper. Dora Williams, daughter of the milliner, after her affair with Reuben Painter, married well twice, was widowed twice, and with her fortune, moved to Paris where she wed a Count, only to be poisoned by him and buried in Rome. In these cases, Daisy and Dora both represent fallen women for A. D. Blood, who is capable only of anger at the town's ignorance of his moral rectitude. Steeped in self-righteousness, Blood cannot understand the ironic justice of Benjamin and Dora's coupling on his grave and, behind it, an amoral universe that mocks his pinched morality. When poor Oscar Hummel appeared drunk on Blood's doorstep late one evening, the moralist beat him to death.

Religious hypocrisy and materialistic greed run like an undercurrent through Spoon River. They curdle the best intentions and reveal the character of the secretly profligate. Mrs. Benjamin Painter hounded her husband out of the house because she loathed the "smell of whiskey and onions . . . / And the rhythm of Wordsworth's 'Ode.'" George Trimble gave up his pursuit of economic justice for prohibition and church membership, though he lies now in the graveyard "unwept of all." Williard Fluke, when his wife took ill, visited a prostitute called "Cleopatra" (perhaps Daisy Fraser) but was troubled by bad dreams and, when Christ told him to confess his sins, dropped dead before the image of his blind child sitting in the front pew. Henry Bennett, wise and "grave of mind," rails against his wife's inheritance and her marriage to "that mount of brawn," Willard Shafer. Deacon Taylor belonged to the "party of prohibition" but died of cirrhosis of the liver. The debonair Lucius Atherton, with curled mustache, tight trousers, and a diamond stud, ended his days "a gray, untidy, toothless, discarded, rural Don Juan." When Homer Clapp discovered that Lucius seduced his beloved Aner Clute, he set his mind to work as the head accountant of the canning factory, only to lose everything and realize that "only death would treat [me] as an equal of other men." Sexsmith the Dentist claims a "moral truth is a hollow tooth which must be propped with gold" and proves his argument by celebrating the eviction of Daisy Fraser by the canning works.

Each of these characters manifests varying degrees of the extremes of A. D. Blood and Thomas Rhodes, and through their misguided illusions of power, religiosity or wealth, are framed in nefarious terms. Unlike the populist characters of the town, readers are invited to judge these individuals by their shortcomings. However, rather than originating solely from the downtrodden populists of Spoon River, who are either victimized or unbowed, the judgment the reader aims at these elites is formed by the underlying ethics of the town's exiles, some of whom escape Spoon River, but many of whom represent an ethical structure that infuses the book with the ambivalence and nostalgia Masters felt for his own upbringing.

Exiles: Prisoners and Escapees

Exiles, like Webster Ford, live disconnected from Spoon River through knowledge of the limitations of the town itself. They know the amoral cosmic forces that shape people's lives, and they understand the hypocrisy and fruitlessness of the local moral structures and materialistic concerns that make a rival claim to this knowledge. In this regard, Masters's exiles are, in Whitman's terms, "both in and out of the game and watching and wondering at it,"[10] but unlike Whitman's Bard in *Leaves of Grass*, Masters's exiles are often incapable of making themselves, in Webster Ford's terms, "fearless singers and livers."[11] Herbert Marshall, for example, begins a lament of his broken engagement with an attempt to lay mutual blame:

> All of your sorrow, Louise, and hatred of me
> Sprang from your delusion that it was wantonness
> Of spirit and contempt of your soul's rights
> Which made me turn to Annabelle and forsake you.
> You really grew to hate me for love of me,
> Because I was your soul's happiness,
> Formed and tempered
> To solve your life for you, and would not.
> But you were my misery. If you had been
> My happiness would I not have clung to you?

At first, Herbert comes to the convenient argument that Louise wanted more than he could provide, namely to "solve your life for you." But then, Herbert takes this justification and reads into it cosmic ramifications:

> This is life's sorrow:
> That one can be happy only where two are;
> And that our hearts are drawn to stars
> Which want us not.

Masters finds in this family drama the tragedy of modern life: humans aspire to transcendence in a cosmos that is indifferent to those aspirations. While Herbert's explanation of his infidelity is convenient to the point of being laughable, it has an underlying ethos that embraces life despite an indifferent universe. He also recognizes the irony of this embrace.

George Gray expresses similar wisdom:

> I have studied many times
> The marble which was chiseled for me—
> A boat with a furled sail at rest in a harbor.
> In truth it pictures not my destination
> But my life.
> For love was offered me and I shrank from its disillusionment;
> Sorrow knocked at my door, but I was afraid;
> Ambition called to me, but I dreaded the chances.
> Yet all the while I hungered for meaning in my life.

And now I know that we must lift the sail
And catch the winds of destiny
Wherever they drive the boat.
To put meaning in one's life may end in madness,
But life without meaning is the torture
Of restlessness and vague desire—
It is a boat longing for the sea and yet afraid.

George lives an internal exile in fear of chances and sorrow, but now, in death, he realizes life is something into which one must "put . . . meaning." It is this sentiment that marks George's modernist temperament, which shapes the ethos of the town's exiles. Most residents of Spoon River sleepwalk with illusions of an ordered cosmos where traditional bromides about the farm, church, and bank are mouthed daily, but belied by both human action and inexplicable circumstance. For the town's exiles, both those who escape and those who do not, life is to be lived in spite of the amoral qualities of the cosmos. In life, Thomas Ross Jr. catches hints of these amoral qualities:

This I saw with my own eyes:
A cliff-swallow
Made her nest in a hole of the high clay-bank
There near Miller's Ford.
But no sooner were the young hatched
Then a snake crawled up to the nest
To devour the brood.
Then the mother swallow with swift flutterings
And shrill cries
Fought at the snake,
Blinding him with the beat of her wings,
Until he, wriggling and rearing his head,
Fell backward down the bank
Into Spoon River and was drowned.
Scarcely an hour passed
Until a shrike
Impaled the mother swallow on a thorn.

But the broader meaning of these hints, the necessity to embrace life in spite of its underlying absurdity, comes to Thomas only after death, when he connects the cliff-swallow's life to his own:

As for myself I overcame my lower nature
Only to be destroyed by my brother's ambition.

Whereas the populists of Spoon River like Mickey M'Grew or Daisy Fraser elicit sympathy and benevolent support from the reader, and town leaders like Thomas Rhodes and A. D. Blood offer cartoonish examples of nefarious elites, Spoon River's exiles offer blunt wisdom that invites the reader to meditate on a cold universe.

Other exiles realize this truth in life and thereby live quietly with the knowledge of it. Professor Newcomer learned that the "urge of nature made a man / Evolve from his brain a spiritual life . . . in a futile waste of power." Theodore the Poet spent his youth waiting on the "shore of the turbid Spoon" watching for crawfish to appear from their muddy burrows and later "watched for men and women / Hiding in burrows of fate amid great cities, / Looking for the souls of them to come out." Richard Bone, who carved the town's gravestones, "chiseled whatever they paid me to chisel / And made myself party to false chronicles" as the historian "who writes / Without knowing the truth, or because he is influenced to hide it." Griffy the Cooper teaches that you "are only looking around the interior of your tub" when you "think your eye sweeps about a wide horizon"; you are, instead, encumbered by the "taboos and rules and appearances" that "are the staves of your tub." Schroeder the Fisherman drops crumbs in the water "just to see the minnows bump each other" and throws corn to his pigs to watch "them push and squeal and bite" and concludes, "if there's anything in man—/ Spirit, or conscience, or breath of God / That makes him different from fishes or hogs, I'd like to see it work!" Shack Dye, the African American blacksmith who "shook as I saw some horse-shoes crawling / Across the floor, as if alive" realizes that the practical joker, Walter Simmons, used a magnet to move the horseshoes and ultimately charges that "everyone of you, you white men . . . didn't know any more than the horse-shoes did / What moved you about Spoon River."

A few of these exiles manage a symbolic escape from Spoon River. In this regard, Russian Sonia and Dorcas Gustine provide two examples of exiles who live at peace with their status. Both exhibit the pluck of unbowed populists like Jefferson Howard, but situate their success in ironic wisdom as much as life-embracing verve. Russian Sonia, an emigrant to Spoon River, mocks the town's moral standards in happy repose,

> I, born in Weimar
> Of a mother who was French
> And German father, a most learned professor,
> Orphaned at fourteen years,
> Became a dancer, known as Russian Sonia,
> All up and down the boulevards of Paris,

Mistress betimes of sundry dukes and counts,
And later of poor artists and of poets.
And forty years, *passée*, I sought New York
And met old Patrick Hummer on the boat,
Red-faced and hale, though turned his sixtieth year,
Returning after having sold a ship-load
Of cattle in the German city, Hamburg.
He brought me to Spoon River and we lived here
For twenty years—they thought we were married!
This oak tree near me is the favorite haunt
Of blue jays chattering, chattering all the day.
And why not? for my very dust is laughing
For thinking of the humorous thing called life.

While Masters did not give Sonia's husband, Patrick Hummer, an epitaph in *Spoon River Anthology*, it is easy to imagine that he stood as both an economic leader of the town, and also, quite possibly, a subject of some gossip for his exotic wife. However, Sonia, daughter of a German academic, orphan, exotic dancer, and libertine, settles down to a "marriage" in Spoon River and celebrates the ruse and the life she lives within it. In this regard, she exemplifies the vigor of Jefferson Howard while, at the same time, exhibiting an understanding of the absurd cosmic order that gave her the life she loved.

Dorcas Gustine also embraces her status as an internal exile in Spoon River, and thereby achieves a kind of escape. She introduces herself and her status as a truth teller,

I was not beloved of the villagers,
But all because I spoke my mind,
And met those who transgressed against me
With plain remonstrance, hiding nor nurturing
Nor secret griefs nor grudges.

And then reframes the legend of the Spartan boy who hid a wolf under his cloak and, without complaint, let the animal devour him rather than reveal his secret. She rejects the bravery of the Spartan, and claims, instead,

It is braver, I think, to snatch the wolf forth
And fight him openly, even in the street,
Amid dust and howls of pain.
The tongue may be an unruly member—
But silence poisons the soul.
Berate me who will—I am content.

Clear-eyed and honest about the seeming amorality of life in Spoon River, these exiles clue the reader to the "terrible truthfulness" of life that William Marion Reedy celebrated in his November 1914 review of Masters's poems. In this fashion, Spoon River's exiles affirm modernist notions of life as it really was, without affected theological structure, yet still hopeful for human transcendence. While Masters portrayed his populist characters nostalgically, wrapped in the mythology of the pioneering period, or sympathetically, as innocent creatures shipwrecked by modern circumstance, and the town's elite as materialistic prudes, the truth-tellers of the village are moderns.

Alice Corbin Henderson, associate editor of *Poetry* magazine, echoed the ethos of Masters's exiles in her June 1915 review of *Spoon River Anthology*,

> Mr. Masters makes life seem precious. Humorous, squalid and noble at the same time, an affair of broken wings, splendid hopes, draggled aspirations, and smothered beauty, life is yet too amazingly vital to be discarded even by those who have themselves taken the final step to discard it![12]

In this regard, Henderson echoed Reedy's celebration of the book's truth-telling. For Henderson and Reedy, portraying life in terms of "a cosmos devoid of God and an amoral inner and outer nature,"[13] proved the realism of Masters's work. When Henderson—herself a native Midwesterner—visited "a little Illinois town on the old canal" in preparation for her review, she mouthed the ethos of Masters's exiles: "The square stone houses," she noted, "built of lime-stone quarried from the hills, and the old frame houses of the pioneer colonial pattern, seemed to hold in hiding the secret lives of the people of whom Mr. Masters had written." In this regard, Henderson used Masters's Spoon River to project her own ambivalent nostalgia for rural Illinois onto the town's landscape. Masters's sensibility seemed suddenly to reveal a small town's underlying grim vitality: "Deserted by the tide of progress ... there was an air of memory and regret about the place; a provincial richness and a sense of desolation."[14]

Within five years, Masters was credited with beginning a literary "revolt from the village" among authors who similarly sought to reveal the "draggled aspirations" of Americans in the prototypical Midwestern town.

CHAPTER 5

Reception

> The year 1914 was miraculous, not only in
> Chicago but over America. But right through
> history one can see that these joyous
> periods come into being only to be quickly
> wiped out. . . .
>
> —Edgar Lee Masters, *Across Spoon River*

Edgar Lee Masters thought *Spoon River Anthology* appeared at the end of an era. In one sense, he was correct. Middle-class reform activism in the early twentieth century, often termed "Progressive," eclipsed the Populist politics that captivated Masters in the final years of the nineteenth century. While Progressives like Jane Addams, Robert LaFollette, and Walter Rauschenbusch arose in tandem with the Populist movement, their focus on the plight of the urban poor, political corruption, and the degradation of industrial workers soon overshadowed the Populists, who largely disappeared as a political force after 1896. Populist influence in the Democratic Party likewise faded. Beginning with the Wilson administration, the Democratic Party shifted from the ideology of agrarian activism and monetary inflationism that gave William Jennings Bryan his political energy to a platform that pursued an increasingly regulated industrial economy through robust federal power. In 1913, the Wilson administration shepherded through the enactment of the Federal Reserve System to regulate monetary policy, an expansion of bankers' power anathema to Populists like Bryan.[1] By 1915, as the Wilson administration moved closer to war, William Jennings Bryan, then Wilson's Secretary of State, resigned in protest. Masters had been averse to Wilson since the 1912 campaign and, in hindsight, claimed Wilson had "ruined America for years to come" and his supporters "showed with terrible results what they were in their essential beings, and what they meant to America as Americans."[2]

But in another sense, Masters published *Spoon River Anthology* at the beginning of a literary era that shaped sensibilities throughout the twentieth century. While he had spent his young adulthood in Chicago in the 1890s and aped some of the popular reform literature of the first decade of the twentieth century, by 1915, Masters began to move among proto-modernist authors like Dreiser and Sandburg and wondered at the advent of Chicago's bohemian culture: "The town had studios where there were painters and sculptors, it had the precursors of flappers, and here and there men and women were living together in freedom, just as they did in Paris."[3] While Masters claimed that Harriet Monroe and the staff at *Poetry* ignored his work before *Spoon River Anthology*, by 1915 he was welcomed into the magazine's circle where "we had many happy gatherings . . . and where I saw the frequent visiting poets from New York and elsewhere who had come hastening west to see what it was that had struck Chicago."[4] There, Masters mingled with leading lights of a new literary sensibility, including Siegfried Sassoon, Wallace Stevens, and Willard Wattles, though he must have felt his age among these younger poets.[5] For John Timberman Newcomb, Masters, along with poets like Amy Lowell, Robert Frost, Carl Sandburg, and Vachel Lindsay, "drew upon regional and urban vernaculars, colloquial diction and syntax, and realist modes of verbal representations to create a poetry of everyday experience that was widely accessible to non-specialists, yet still sufficiently complex and nuanced to attract the admiration of literary connoisseurs."[6] Yet Masters was also a liminal poet, caught between the Edwardian themes of an older generation of writers and the poetic structure and style of a younger one. If we accept Masters's claim that he was taken aback by the popularity of his "rampant yokelisms," the overwhelmingly positive reaction to *Spoon River Anthology*, both among connoisseurs and the general public, was something of a lark. This might explain why Masters was never able to pull off a second act: since he did not conceive of himself as part of a revolution in poetry, when the opportunity to publish a second collection came quickly in 1916, he fell back on a less compelling, but more familiar style from his early years in Chicago.

Critical Reception

During the heady days of *Spoon River Anthology*'s first appearance, Masters met the poet and critic Amy Lowell, who descended on Chicago like "an Italian diva."[7] By 1915, Lowell had established herself as an arbiter of what was being called the "New Movement." Descended from a prominent New England family, Lowell's early poetry followed many of the conventions of the era. However, in 1913 she discovered the work of H. D. and visited Ezra Pound in London, arriving with a letter of introduction from Harriet Monroe. In 1914, Lowell's poem "In a Garden" was published in *Des Imagistes*, the first of many anthologies of modernist verse during these years, alongside the works of H. D., Ezra Pound, and William Carlos Williams:

> And I wished for night and you.
> I wanted to see you in the swimming-pool,
> White and shining in the silver-flecked water.
> While the moon rode over the garden,
> High in the arch of night,
> And the scent of lilacs was heavy with stillness.[8]

By 1914, Lowell's book of verse, *Sword Blades and Poppy Seed*, established her as one of "America's primer poetic innovators"[9] and her anthologies defined the "New Movement" for general consumption. In *Some Imagist Poets: An Anthology* (1915), she included a variation on modernist dicta that defined the new verse for readers:

1. To use the language of common speech, but to employ always the exact word, not the nearly exact, nor the merely decorative word.
2. To create new rhythms—as the expression of new moods—and not to copy old rhythms, which merely echo old moods....
3. To allow absolute freedom in the choice of subject....
4. To present an image (hence the name: "Imagist")....
5. To produce poetry that is hard and clear, never blurred nor indefinite.
6. Finally, most of us believe that concentration is of the very essence of poetry.

According to Adrienne Munich and Melissa Bradshaw, Lowell's "views on literary history" in these anthologies "definitively shaped conceptions of the literary scene" during the second decade of the twentieth century.[10]

Lowell recognized in *Spoon River Anthology* a collection of verse that drew upon the New Movement style to portray a rural Midwestern reality. In her *Tendencies in Modern American Poetry* (1917), she anointed Masters as one of the new poets of the American avant-garde. Accordingly, "no author to-day shows more clearly the breaking down of an old tradition"[11] while exploring a place where tradition seemingly reigned supreme. Echoing William Marion Reedy's positive reviews from the fall of 1914, Masters embodied a "new movement" in poetry, which, with "Realism, Direct Speech, Simplicity," represented "the most revolutionary [poetry] that America has yet produced" in its lucid detail of small, poignant Midwestern lives.[12] Lowell argued that Masters's legitimacy as a "new" poet drew upon the pioneer myths of the previous century, perhaps supplied by Masters himself. His ancestors, "a sturdy stock and a pioneering one," had moved "ever Westward, to newer, cruder, freer lands" and produced, over time and in Turnerian terms, "a new beauty, a differing religious concept" in preparation of a final stage, an "era of accomplishment" that "shakes the world again, [as] mankind takes another step on its eternal path."[13] Lowell also recognized elements of the stock characters of Spoon River, the hypocritical elite, the tragic populist, and the observant and knowing exile,

> I believe that . . . [t]he ugliness, the bitterness, the materialism, with which he believed himself surrounded, have been burnt into his soul, so that now he gives them out perforce. There are hints of beauty in his poems, but they are almost smothered under other things. Here is strength, vigour [sic], vividness; here, too, is coarseness, brutality, cynicism.[14]

While Lowell reviewed Masters's long and unsuccessful career as an author before *Spoon River Anthology* and claimed that even his new verse lacked "beauty of form and syllable," he nevertheless held "infinite sympathy for the cramped, monotonous lives of ugly little towns" and saw "through a bitter mist; misery can cramp souls as well as bodies." For Lowell, Masters portrayed the people of Spoon River "with extraordinary precision and clarity."[15]

Like many of Masters's early highbrow reviewers, Lowell vacillated between portraying Spoon River as emblematic of Midwestern towns in particular, and reading Masters's book as a meditation on humanity in general. On the one hand,

> These are strange tales. So brutal that one wonders, if life in our little Western cities is as bad as this, why everyone does not commit suicide. . . . We can see the cemetery, the Court House, the various churches, the shops, the railroad station, almost with our physical eyes.[16]

On the other,

> [Masters] raises local politics to the realm of a world force. . . . Indeed, "Spoon River" might be called an epic of everyday life [since] humanity varies very little throughout the ages.[17]

In this way, Lowell sensed within Masters's rendition of Midwestern towns the lucidity of the internal exile, keenly aware of the ways in which "our institutions and our social fabric frequently jar upon our sensibilities, that thought in America is in advance of custom, and that personality being at variance with the official life results in a painful chafing."[18] Here, Lowell channeled Webster Ford and the other exiled characters of Spoon River, who extracted universal truth from local tragedies and reprised William Marion Reedy's claim that the poems explored humanity's plight through a focused look at the intimately local—a perspective achieved through familiarity and skepticism, an exile's perspective on, but not of, Main Street. Lowell described a poet whose image of the rural Midwest was both neutral and invested, sympathetic and repulsed, local and universal. In this way, she solidified the parameters by which contemporary artists and critics understood Masters.

Lowell's generally positive reception of *Spoon River Anthology* echoed highbrow critics who saw in Masters a poet who valued precision and austerity. In *The Egoist*, Ezra Pound described Masters, whom he identified by the pseudonym Webster Ford, as "calling up the reality of the Middle West" while at the same time "dealing with life directly, without circumlocution, without resonant, meaningless phrases" since "[g]ood poetry is always the same; the changes are superficial."[19] The critic Van Wyck Brooks likewise saw the universal in Masters's desperate community:

> The immense and legitimate vogue of this book is due to its unerring diagnosis of what we all recognize, when we are confronted with it, as the inner life of the typical American community[,] when the criterion of humane values is brought to bear upon it in place of the criterion of material values with which we have traditionally pulled the wool over our eyes. . . . Poets, painters, philosophers, men of science and religion, are all to be found, stunted, starved, thwarted, embittered, prevented from taking even the first step in self-development, in this amazing microcosm of our society.[20]

And while Brooks found none of the nobility in Masters's pioneering generation or his tragic populists, he found a universal truth that in the United States "a race . . . has never cultivated life for its own sake."[21]

More traditional literary venues lauded Masters's work while also noting the novelty of his verse. Lawrence Gilman, in the venerable *The North American Review*, celebrated *Spoon River Anthology*'s free verse and, in terms that Masters himself would have applauded, claimed that "the aesthetic Calvinists" would demand silence from Masters, in spite of his "extraordinary" work. In Spoon River, according to Gilman,

> are tragedies, sordid or touching, horrible or grim; pitiful romances, scandals, little histories of violence and tenderness, of patient waiting and rebellious enduring; grotesque comedies, preposterous melodramas; a humanity that is universal.[22]

Gilman, like many literary critics at the time, sought to characterize Masters's collection of poems in modern terms, calling it the "cinematographing of narrative verse," and offered that it presented "a kind of moving-picture in the form of fictional verse." While Gilman claimed that "it is not easy to declare with confidence" that *Spoon River Anthology* was poetry, the book nevertheless "seizes you, engrosses you, haunts you" and was "a miracle of veracious characterization." In November 1915, *The North American Review* printed a letter that responded to Gilman's suspicion that *Spoon River Anthology* was not really poetry by claiming that Masters's verse proved to be a "sharp flexible style, like a clean blade, [that] cuts away all frippery," adding a metaphor of modern progress to Gilman's "cinematographing."[23] William Stanley Braithwaite's *Anthology of Magazine Verse for 1915* called *Spoon River Anthology* "the most widely discussed volume of verse published this year," which "by sketching the human characters . . . brings the universal, infinite varieties of human nature into the fabric of a single community."[24]

But not all critics were positive. Floyd Dell in *The New Republic*, though he admired the book, wondered if "*some* aspects of our American scene" benefited from a more lighthearted "comedic view of life" as opposed to Masters's dark ironies.[25] In the *Bulletin of the American Library Association*, Jessie Rittenhouse admired *Spoon River Anthology*'s "many high notes," but criticized Masters for seeing "life entirely through its negative phases":

> I think it comes to a very doubtful thing as to whether it is well to dig in graves to the extent that Edgar Lee Masters does, because if you are digging in graves you are pretty sure to find something ghoulish.[26]

Whether celebratory or critical, the literary reception of *Spoon River Anthology* revolved around the portrayal of Spoon River as representative of the rural Midwest while, at the same time, serving as a microcosmic portrayal of the universally human. In this regard, the book was understood not as a collection of separate poems, but instead, as a whole; Spoon River's dead were individuals, but also as human types, who, in their particularities, represented recognizably universal traits. The dead of Spoon River had led lives whose meaning resonated symbolically as they contended with the amorality of the cosmos, which seemingly decided their fates oblivious to human ethical systems or conceptions of the divine. Spoon River, therefore, offered a stage onto which the dilemmas of modern American life—the inequities of modern capitalism, the hypocrisies of American moralism, and the ironies of thwarted human aspirations—displayed themselves through average Americans. Implicitly, the literati who read *Spoon River Anthology* in the first years after its publication sympathized with the perceptive exiles in Spoon River who lucidly understood the limits of their fellow citizens' radical subjectivity. Whereas nearly one hundred years before, the New England village had offered a receptacle for what was good and unchanging in the face of ambivalence about urban growth, in the first decades of the twentieth century, Spoon River seemed to offer an unadulterated look at the cosmic truth of a place so typical it could be anyplace. While most of the citizens of Spoon River fetishized their individual lives, the reader, alongside the town's exiles, patronized their claims and concerns and read into them broader meaning.

Popular Reception

Popular audiences interpreted the book differently. Even before the Macmillan edition of *Spoon River Anthology* appeared on April 15, 1915, word of Masters's work reached New York. In an April 4, 1915, feature on the poet, the *New York Times* reported that the English critic, John Cowper Powys, had declared Masters "the natural child of Walt Whitman."[27] Powys, who published his first novel that year, had spent the previous ten years in the United States lecturing for the American Society for the Extension of University Teaching, an organization based in Philadelphia which, since 1890, had supported lecturers and correspondence courses to introduce Americans to higher education. Powys's position as a lecturer for the American Society, whose mission was to "bring the ideals and methods of university training ... to every American ...," positioned him as a natural ambassador from higher culture to the popular press.[28] Powys's comparison of Masters to Walt Whitman became a steady refrain for the remainder of 1915 and further marked Masters's collection of poems about a fictional Midwestern town as something particularly American, which, like Whitman's poetry, nevertheless aspired to universal claims.

By way of introduction, the *Times* article duplicated Masters's full entry from *Who's Who in America* and recognized the extent to which *Spoon River Anthology* was a departure for Masters, whose *Who's Who* entry conveyed "but little of the personality of the man whose 'Spoon River Anthology' . . . has been attracting attention in the Middle West." Contrary to his previous work, Masters claimed that *Spoon River Anthology* had already garnered popular attention. During 1914 "the letters began to pour in":

> They came from New York publishers, the Dean of Cornell University . . . literary people in England and all over the United States; I am getting them yet, every day or so, all of which encouraged me to go through to a finish.

Tellingly, this introduction of Masters to a popular audience displayed a keen interest in assuring readers that the poet's politics proved innocuous: "Mr. Masters is not a socialist . . . although he has been charged with socialistic tendencies." Masters affirmed this claim: "There is an undefined something in the socialistic doctrine which is lacking and which prevents my becoming a member." Instead, "I prefer to remain a Democrat" who is "keenly interested in championing the cause of the under-dog [*sic*], particularly in the field of labor."[29]

Some significant themes that resonated throughout the popular press in 1915 appeared in this *New York Times* profile. Whereas critics like Amy Lowell and William Marion Reedy emphasized the degraded state of many of Masters's characters, and thereby found in them a realism lacking in most contemporary literature, the *Times* softened Masters's critiques and emphasized his unpretentious personality. The poet lacked any affect, and instead displayed, "the earmarks of the lawyer and businessman, and none of the traits or mannerisms of those who aspire to be called poets." Masters was "modest" and "unassuming," "wrapped up in his home and family," and a man who wrote poetry "as a diversion at such times as he can tear himself away from a busy and successful law practice." In this regard, the novelty of an unpretentious lawyer-cum-poet lent credence to his reports from rural America: "I always had in mind that I would write a novel about a small community, . . . including every interest and every piece of machinery you find in the big world or metropolis, because you do not find human nature in a small community alone—you find it everywhere."[30]

Conveyed without obvious ideology, Masters's universal themes insulated him from charges of hiding within Spoon River a radical political program during a period when socialism increasingly carried with it the taint of an urban, foreign ideology. Such was the view of the popular press, even though prominent socialists like Eugene Debs and William "Big Bill" Haywood were native-born and of rural origins. Instead, Masters was a "Democrat" who championed "the under-dog," situating him in a more benign tradition of social critics. In this *New York Times* portrayal, Masters proved to be no pretentious aesthete with a harebrained and dangerous social agenda. Instead, he was born in a small town, made his way to a solid career in the big city, and retained his sympathy for the "under-dog."

Reviews of *Spoon River Anthology* in the popular press echoed these themes throughout the summer and fall of 1915. The *Evening Public Ledger* of Philadelphia called it a "record of real life, American in many ways, too ironical, too bitter perhaps, but so intensely expressed that you can't help living through the experience set down." And though reading the book depicted experiences that were "not of the highest," Masters at least "leaves you to avoid everything he has written about and make your own life better."[31] Another review understood *Spoon River Anthology* as a kind of journalism, and, with some minor errors of fact, claimed it proved that high literary publications elided true human experience: "These poems were published from week to week in Reedy's Mirror, an Illinois newspaper. . . . The Spoon River Anthology is another instance of the remarkable quality of our journalism. Better things may be found in the newspapers than in the professedly literary publications."[32] These early reviews mark a rising dilemma for readers in the popular press: What was *Spoon River Anthology*? Was it a collection of moral directives that taught through negative examples? Was the book realistic reportage of life in the rural Midwest? Was it psychology or philosophy? Or anthropology? While literary critics like William Marion Reedy found in *Spoon River Anthology*'s ironic and tragic tales an unalloyed look at the vicissitudes of an amoral cosmos, popular reviewers sought a message and an underlying moral system and generally found a sympathetic portrayal of the lives of common people. Here was a harmless populism that offered no overarching political program or aimed itself at any particular class. According to Narayana Chandran, "Masters cautiously underplay[ed] the alarming implications of . . . social transformation . . . lest the Spoon River dead sound like his Populist mouthpieces."[33] Instead, *Spoon River Anthology*'s dark undercurrents bubbled to the surface as individual anecdotes, typical of any American community and edifying in their moral import.

Throughout the summer of 1915, reviewers of *Spoon River Anthology* in the popular press increasingly interpreted the book as an apolitical critique of American society through individual shortcomings. While the book was critical of elements of American life, its criticism was aimed at human foibles explored individually. Masters threatened no obvious class or social system. In this way, *Spoon River Anthology*'s lambasting of hypocrisy and greed accomplished what Masters's early reform-minded literature could not: popularity without heavy-handed polemic, social critique without explicit policy. Reviewers in the popular press, therefore, often embraced the book's sympathy for the underdog from the perspective of Main Street's exile, who saw morbid ironies under the town's placid surface, but remained tacitly sympathetic toward the core goodness of everyday Americans. In this way, reviewers in the popular press sympathized with the exiled characters in *Spoon River Anthology* in a way subtly different from that of highbrow literary critics. Whereas the literati read into Masters a hard truth that echoed Virginia Woolf's claim that great literature exposed "the spasmodic, the obscure, the fragmentary, the failure" in everyday life,[34] popular readers found in Masters's exiles quiet advocates for the downtrodden who were separated from the masses by their perspective on moral degradation, but nevertheless tacitly on the populist's side in the face of elite greed and moralistic hypocrisy. Masters effectively wrapped contemporary sympathy for the common man, a position familiar to readers after twenty years of Populist rhetoric, within twentieth-century modernist verse, and thereby found receptive reviewers in the popular press who read the work as presenting universal, all-American themes in an easily accessible but unorthodox style. In this light, the reader was party to residents' plight without being morally culpable for their lot. Masters invited readers to visit Spoon River as one of its exiles, both in and out of the game, from which one could act simultaneously as both moral arbiter and voyeur.

In June 1915, the *New-York Tribune* described Masters as "a young, practicing attorney of Chicago, Illinois." The paper asked Masters this question: "What Can Poetry do for Our Republic?" Masters rose to the opportunity to opine on themes that had shaped him since the 1890s. He called on "boys and girls" to "resist contaminations of all falsities . . . in all matters of worldliness." Based on his authority as having "lived shoulder to shoulder with men not in the commonly accepted atmosphere of the professional poet," he condemned "hedonistic materialism" that treated "the less efficient . . . with injustice" by which "the whole state is corrupted and its destiny lowered." Poetry, on the other hand, "can unify and strengthen . . . enlightened souls so that they shall be a governing force, supplanting those materialists who would continue to make of men a commercial commodity." Here, then, was the cartoonish Thomas Rhodes, the town banker, who claimed "we seekers of earth's treasures, / Getters and hoarders of gold, / Are self-contained, compact, harmonized, / Even to the end." In this regard, Masters smoothed the political contours of his older reform literature and fit them neatly to the characters of *Spoon River Anthology*. A pinched, materialistic purview was the nation's problem; economic injustice and structural inequity were not. Reform required overcoming spiritual apathy. Whitman, claimed Masters, (seconding John Cowper Powys's characterization of him as the new American bard), was the poet "who made the commencement in the direction of a new authenticity," while "The New England school" of poets like Longfellow and Emerson, fireside poets of the previous century, could not "match [Whitman] in vitality or in vision." In this critique of nineteenth-century New England poets and his equation of himself with Whitman, Masters relocated the New York bard in the West, and perhaps implicitly criticized Robert Frost's *North of Boston*, which also appeared in 1914 to critical acclaim. The true poets of the republic appealed, like Whitman, to "large audiences" lying "hidden and torpid against sonnets which simulate the emotions. . . ." Real American poets, instead, understood that "[p]oetry is a popular art when it concerns itself with life, and the best art demands that that concern shall be fresh and intimate."[35]

The columnist Jay House, in a review in the *Topeka Daily Capital*, captured the populist undertones of Masters's verse with a jarring metaphor: "*Spoon River Anthology* . . . bares with a phraseological scalpel the sordidness, the narrowness, the shame, the misery and woe that lurk beneath the calm exterior of the rural community."[36] House, in this regard, proved to be a particularly receptive consumer of Masters's latent populism. Born a Midwesterner of Masters's generation in 1870, House had created a public persona of a folksy truth-teller in the (relatively) big city of Topeka, who nevertheless understood the realities of Midwestern small-town life.[37] House's columns and quips ranged in topics from politics to cuisine and were presented in a commonsensical and often humorous style that overlay an undercurrent of detached irony. For example, according to House,

> There is a good deal of talk about the automobile, but a mule 17 hands high and weighing in the neighborhood of 1600 pounds attracts more attention than a $6000 car.[38]

And on the topic of rural cultural refinement:

> A country boy is always greatly surprised to learn that town people do not consider bologna sausage a delicacy.[39]

But on the topic of moral hypocrisy, House was more pointed:

> If it were not for the patronage of the respectable "white gemman" up town[,] booze peddling in the bottoms would die a natural death. . . . If the emoluments of street walking came only from the lower stratas [*sic*] of society[,] street walking soon would become a lost art.[40]

Embedded within these jokey quips and commonsense claims lay a social critique sympathetic to Masters's underlying populism in *Spoon River Anthology*.

House expressed a bemused affinity for average citizens in rural America, who were impressed by big mules and befuddled by refined cuisine. While ultimately patronizing, House typically positioned his readers to celebrate, humorously, the unaffected ways of the average. On the other hand, House aimed his ire at hypocritical elites, "white gemman up town," who mouthed moral platitudes while consuming alcohol and patronizing prostitutes. For literary critics, Masters had written poetry that was new in its form, themes, and especially in its cold amorality. On the other hand, popular reviewers like House better gleaned the populist undertones in Masters's Spoon River, where a few internal exiles (not so unlike House writing from Topeka) sympathized with the underdog and understood the turpitude of those who claimed moral and social superiority.

While House's admiration for *Spoon River Anthology* reflected support from a former hotbed of populist sentiment like Topeka, popular reviews across the country also celebrated Masters's moral posturing. In the summer of 1915, the *New York Times* extended its admiration of Masters and waxed anthropologically about the significance of the rural Midwestern town to understanding human nature in moral terms: "the village community presents a microcosm of life and an opportunity to study character impossible to the more hidden and complex life of the city." In this regard, the small town offered a control group without dependent variables. "The weakling or the criminal in a village community has no defenses, no subterfuges: every spring of his action is open to him who can analyze it." Masters's power as a poet, therefore, was grounded in his experience as an interpreter of humanity generally: "looking back to his youth in the environs of Spoon River—[Masters] has reconstructed the life of the neighborhood, so as to give us a complete group of portraits." And in matters of ethics, "he never blurs his values, one sees in an instant what made or unmade a character."[41] By the fall of 1915, this became a common refrain by popular reviewers across the country, who read in Masters's verse a moral *comedia*, whose stock characters spoke to individual human foibles. For a reviewer in the *Guthrie Daily Leader* (Oklahoma), the book proved to be a "gasping sense of reality as though present at a private rehearsal on Judgement Day."[42] In an end-of-year review of literature, the *New York Times* called the book "an epic" whose power lay not "in any sense a matter of form, but of psychology" since the book, through the exploration of a "great body of types" showed "the sinister, the satiric, the pathetic, the beautiful, phases of humanity."[43]

However, some popular reviewers echoed highbrow debates about the book's claims to be poetry. In the *St. Louis Post-Dispatch*, published in the same city as *Reedy's Mirror*, a reviewer asked whether Masters's work constituted "literature or not" and noted that a reviewer in the *Kansas City Star* questioned the book's "humanness," for "they know it is literature [but] they do not know how to classify it." Likewise, the *Post-Dispatch* noted that the *Boston Transcript* wondered whether *Spoon River Anthology* could be "considered poetry alone" and that the *Chicago Herald* claimed, despite the contention of John Cowper Powys, that *Spoon River Anthology* was not "poetry in the old-time accepted sense of the word." Ultimately, Masters's book was "too big for the scope of petty measurements."[44] The *Press and Sun-Bulletin* of Binghamton, New York, also declared that *Spoon River Anthology* decidedly "isn't poetry," though it nonetheless had "the great virtue of wide popular appeal to those who are weary of artificialities and believe in seeking inspiration from the soil" since "the author . . . has not shirked . . . the highest duty of any writer, to paint life as he sees it."[45]

And yet as readily as popular reviewers argued about Masters's form while generally celebrating his treatment of his subjects, there also arose a steady stream of parodies of his style. Herbert Russell notes that these parodies "affirm the ancient adage that imitation is the sincerest of flattery" and that "[i]n 1915 and 1916 in particular, *Spoon River Anthology* was the most imitated book in America."[46] These parodies exhibited the extent to which the poems in *Spoon River Anthology* offered a poetic form by which universal foibles could be explored through individual plight—in these cases, for humorous ends. For example, from the *New-York Tribune* in July 1915, the cult of inventiveness came in for mockery through the absurd machinations of George Gazookus,

> I spent most of my struggling years
> Attempting to invent a sleigh
> To run in summer time
> And people called me crazy,
> Though shops upon the Avenue
> Display and sell their summer stuff
> In January;
> Yet are they deemed astute business men
> Who run these wild emporia
> As I lie here, out Brooklyn way you know,
> Below the sub-soil,
> I think I could have put my years to finer uses.
> I should have labored to invent
> A cemetery dictograph
> For after reading "Spoon River Anthology,"
> It occurs to me that Edgar Lee Masters
> Would have bought a bale of them.[47]

For Gazookus, suffering was caused by bad luck, and his solution, realized too late, was for a better invention, a cemetery dictograph to record the dead's gripes with industrial efficiency. The reader, however, while sympathizing with Gazookus's plight, recognizes the folly of his postmortem revelation and its kinship to the bad ideas he had while alive. In this regard, these parodies capitalized on Masters's marshaling of the exile's perspective by understanding the speaker's lament better than the speaker himself. Gazookus was both sympathetic and pathetic in terms similar to Masters's own degraded populists. Likewise, on September 1915, a subway rider unburdened his gall for a subway guard:

> Much has been said in criticism of you, friend Subway Guard,
> And it is only right that you be given your just dues
> When the occasion warrants it.
> I hereby record my esteem for you; esteem which is prompted
> By your earnest endeavors to avert mishaps and accidents
> By bellowing in accents loud and insonorous
> "Watch Your Step."
> But it peeves me exceedingly
> When you continually admonish me in ungentle tones to
> "Use Both Doors"
> When I often experience considerable difficulty
> In using
> One.[48]

Here, then, the regimented chaos of city travel is reduced to an inconvenient demand to a disgruntled commuter. While the reader readily empathizes with the speaker, the small tyrannies that make for mass transit are experienced at an ironic remove, and thereby portrayed as both important and petty. In a similar vein, a fictional commuter railed against a fellow traveler:

> Some day—ah, sweet and poignant my revenge—
> I'll get him! Throttle him and thrust
> Him on the ground.
> Between his writhing lips I'll jam
> A funnel,
> And within its gaping mouth hot oil
> I'll pour, mixed with red hot
> Cinders.
> And the while, the fumes of Sulphur and
> Asafetida[49] I'll blow
> Into his upturned face.

Who is the guy?
He is the simplike nut who's too
Lazy to pull down the window ahead of mine
In the D., L. & W. R. R. tunnel,
And who contents himself, in spite of all
Commuteristic conventions,
By merely drawing down his shade.
Blast him![50]

In this case, Homeric rage at a small inconsideration on the train allows readers to laugh at impolite fellow-riders and, at the same time, recognize the trivial frustrations of modern life when compared to Homer's heroic Achilles. In the series "Fox Meadow Tennis Club Anthology" P. W. meditates on the poor etiquette of a liberal-minded club mate,

When first you joined the club,
How pleased the members were to play with you, Clyde Duble!
You had a modest, deprecating way whenever you won,
And smiled good-naturedly without excuse when defeat met you.
But now they slink away when you come near the court.
And men turn animated listening faces to their friends as you approach.
But who could blame them?
Oh, Clyde! To think that you could sink so low
As publicly to state you *like* mixed doubles.[51]

In this parody of Masters's style, the politics of competition and gender are both poignant and small-minded.

These parodies, while reflecting what Russell calls flattery, also exhibited the flexibility of Masters's social-commentary-through-individual-travails. Likely the readers of these variations on Masters's style found them funny both by their application of *Spoon River Anthology*'s grandiose treatment of common lives and for their easy application to mundane struggles: the pathetic pursuit of profit, the autocracy of guards at the subway station, the oafishness of fellow commuters, and the inconvenient accommodations of a tennis club member. In each case, the humorist assumed the reader's familiarity with the subjects parodied, while at the same time, positioned the reader to observe human folly ironically. In the same way, Masters situated his readers in a familiar-but-distant stance and thereby wrote poems both poignant and cold; these parodies elicited laughter by assuming the meaningful in the mundane and the ethically universal in the particular, all through the removed position of an observer intimate with the drama portrayed.

Reaction

According to Herbert Russell, Masters met his newfound literary success with ambivalence: "From the start of his fame he showed an impatient and antisocial side and often tried to avoid people."[52] Masters's old antipathy toward the American literati came to the fore, apparent from his early Chicago days when he joined the Press Club over the more literary Little Room, whose members he called the "dilettanti." For Masters, "[f]ame became an irritant" since it did not "pay very well, introduced him to people he did not like, and ate up time at an alarming rate."[53] Even over a decade after *Spoon River Anthology*'s successful first printing, Masters recalled in the *American Mercury* that he "stood embattled" because "the publishing houses were all in the East, and didn't want books of verse, and would scarcely take one from a Westerner." Despite his success, Masters continued to sympathize with the outsider status of his exiled characters. Perhaps a bit defensively, Masters used this rhetorical position to justify "the freedom I took, and the rebellion I asserted against the technical groves and academicians."[54]

Nevertheless, the popularity of *Spoon River Anthology* during 1915–1916 encouraged Masters and his publisher to produce a second book of verse posthaste. Macmillan published *Songs and Satires* in spring 1916, and under Masters's byline identified him as the "author of *Spoon River Anthology*." However, in *Songs and Satires* Masters reprised much of his earlier style (in fact, many of the poems were reprinted from earlier venues), without any of the short and austere epitaphs that made *Spoon River Anthology* compelling to readers the year before. Instead, poems like "Rain in My Heart" read like the conventional verse style that Reedy sought to discourage Masters from using back in 1914,

> There is a quiet in my heart
> Like one who rests from days of pain.
> Outside, the sparrows on the roof
> Are chirping in the dripping rain.
>
> Rain in my heart; rain on the roof;
> And memory sleeps beneath the gray
> And windless sky and brings no dreams
> Of any well remembered day.[55]

Other poems in *Songs and Satires* attempted to apply free verse to more explicitly political themes reminiscent of Masters's earlier political literature. "The Cocked Hat," for example, offered a bitter meditation of William Jennings

Bryan's legacy through the voice of a supporter mulling Bryan's place in the Wilson administration,

That's me and thousands of others like me,
And the first-rate men who were cuffed about
After the Civil War,
And most of the more than six million men
Who followed this fellow [Bryan] into the ditch,
While he walked down the ditch and stepped to the Level—
Following an ideal!

Do you remember how slim he was,
And trim he was,
With black hair and pale brow,
And the hawk-like nose and flashing eyes,
Not turning slowly like an owl
But with a sudden eagle motion?
[. . .]
Well, these fellows who marched are the cocked hat,
And I am the cocked hat and the six millions,
And more are the cocked hat,
Who got themselves despised or suspected
Of ignorance or something for being with him.
But still, he's one of the pins that's standing.
He got the money that he went after,
And he has a place in history, perhaps—
Because we took the blow and fell down
When the ripping ball went wild in the alley.[56]

Masters also returned to his interest in classical themes, which once inspired William Marion Reedy to exclaim, "damn it man you're not Doric, you're American."[57] In "Helen of Troy," Masters entirely eschewed the austere realism of *Spoon River Anthology*,

Beneath that ancient sky
Who is not fain to fly
    As men have fled?
Ah! We would know relief
From marts of wine and beef,
    And oil and bread.

Helen of Troy, Greek art
Hath made our heart thy heart,
    Thy love our love.

For poesy, like thee,
Must fly and wander free
   As the wild dove.[58]

    Songs and Satires sold well, largely on the reputation and popularity of *Spoon River Anthology*, even though its reviews were mixed. While the *St. Louis Post-Dispatch* described many of the poems as exhibiting "extreme beauty,"[59] the *Little Review* claimed that *Spoon River Anthology* proved to be "the one great book Masters had to give us."[60] A mixed review in the *New York Times* called "The Cocked Hat" "irritating and absurd."[61] The *Los Angeles Times* described Masters's new book as "incomprehensible" and criticized its "sophomoric habit" of listing material goods in a "catalog trick" that barely looked like poetry.[62] Masters appeared to many reviewers unable to reproduce the power of *Spoon River Anthology* outside of its epitaphic style. In the *Manchester Guardian*, T. S. Eliot best captured the reason for these shortcomings: "Masters . . . must have a personage, and this personage must be detached from himself in order to give his particular meditative irony its opportunity."[63] In his critique, Eliot captured the necessity of Masters's stance as an exile so as to build a "meditative irony" that inhabited characters while simultaneously studying them from a distance.

    Masters, however, blamed the mixed reviews of *Songs and Satires* on literary philistinism. Rather than recognizing that the fictional epitaphs of *Spoon River Anthology* released him from the liabilities of his conventional verse (while locking him within an easily parodied style), Masters rejected criticism of his latest work, much as he would the negative reception of all his works after *Spoon River Anthology*: "Some of the critics had sharpened their pencils for it" since they "wanted more *Spoon River*" and "turned in contempt for 'Helen of Troy.'" This, according to Masters, put him in a bind since "[i]f I had gone on in the *Spoon River* manner they would likely have said that I had but one set of strings."[64] In his frustration with the critical reception of *Songs and Satires*, Masters lamented the extent to which he would be credited for the remainder of the decade with creating a literary "revolt" against small towns in America and type-cast thereafter as the poet of rural rebellion.

CHAPTER 6

The Village Revolt

I didn't revolt against my village. The best years of
my life were spent back there in Illinois.

—Edgar Lee Masters, Interview with
August Derleth, 1939

Six years after Edgar Lee Masters published *Spoon River Anthology*, the book
editor of the *Nation* and fellow Illinoisan Carl Van Doren declared in an article
called "Revolt from the Village: 1920" that "[t]he newest style in American
fiction dates from the appearance ... of 'Spoon River Anthology,'" which
offered a "thrill" to "conventional readers," "delight" to "ironical readers," and
a "demand that pious fictions should be done away with" by readers more
"militant" in their anger at American hypocrisies.[1] In his characterization of
Masters as the vanguard of a new "style," Van Doren captured a subtle shift in
the perception of the poet's work and small-towns generally at the dawn of the
1920s. Whereas highbrow critics in the few years after the publication of *Spoon
River Anthology* perceived the "terrible truthfulness" of an amoral cosmos in the
book or understood it as a pioneer in "new movement" literature; and popular
reviewers found a moral structure that reflected populist themes that celebrated
the underdog, Van Doren characterized Masters, and authors like him, as rebels
against small towns themselves. This represented an important reconception
of the small town in popular discourse as Midwestern rural communities

ceased to be characterized as an American microcosm, and increasingly became battlefields for a short-lived culture war between the modern and the traditional, which would reappear later in the century. While critics today reject the simplistic idea of a common "revolt," and even the authors themselves denied Van Doren's terms, the persistent tradition of a literary revolt against rural communities in the 1920s marks its impact in the evolving myth of the American small town.

In Van Doren's characterization, the village rebels were literary muckrakers of retrograde America. "Where . . . were the mild decencies of Tiverton, of Old Chester, of Friendship Village?" he asked ironically, naming idyllic literary villages from earlier in the century. Now, "[t]he roofs and walls . . . were gone and the passersby saw into every bedroom; the closets were open and all the skeletons rattled undenied; brains and breasts had unlocked themselves and set the most private treasures out for the most public gaze."[2] The revolt began in Spoon River and inspired "deliberate imitations." Books like Sherwood Anderson's *Winesburg, Ohio* (1919), Floyd Dell's *Moon-Calf* (1920), E. W. Howe's *The Anthology of Another Town* (1920), Sinclair Lewis's *Main Street* (1920), and Zona Gale's *Miss Lulu Bett* (1921) capitalized on Masters's poems of small-town pathos and, taken together, represented a wholesale rejection of the idea of the rural village as the repository of simple pieties and unaffected ethics.[3] Howe and Gale were odd choices for Van Doren's "newest style" since Howe published his first novel of grim Midwestern tales, *The Story of a Country Town* (1883), nearly forty years before. And while Zona Gale's *Miss Lulu Bett* was the story of a young woman who declares her independence from the strictures of her sister's family, Gale was best known for writing in the village idyllic tradition (Van Doren used Gale's *Friendship Village* as an example of this genre in his introduction), and Van Doren noted that Gale's latest work only hinted "in a flutelike way" what other village rebels "play[ed] upon noisier instruments."[4] Van Doren made his strongest claims for the "new style" of village rebels in his review of the works of Masters, Anderson, Dell, and Lewis, and these four authors have since been canonized as members of a "village revolt," though not without controversy, even among the authors themselves.

According to Van Doren, Masters "drag[ged] . . . into the light" the "greed and hypocrisy" of a town that "clings to a pitiless decorum which veils its faults and almost makes it overlook them."[5] Indeed, the primary targets of these rebels, at least in Van Doren's terms, were the hidden faults beneath the small town's stable surface.[6] For example, Van Doren found in Sherwood Anderson's *Winesburg, Ohio*, Masters's *Anthology* "transposed" from verse to prose. And while Anderson threw "a vaguely golden mist over the village" through the story of young George Willard on the cusp of his departure from the town, according to Ronald Weber, the author intended the book to be a series of "grotesques" that exposed the "'truths' that people had allowed to define their existence, tragically limiting their embrace of life's uncertainty and development."[7] Presented in a series of short vignettes about characters on the themes of dislocation and disappointment,[8] Anderson, according to Van Doren, created a world where "there is still the individual who, perhaps all the more because of the rigid decorums forced upon him, may adventure with secret desires."[9]

Elizabeth Willard, for example, in "Mother," lives a desultory life as a proprietor of a shabby hotel and the wife of an indifferent husband, Tom, who hates the money-losing hotel and grows embittered while his youthful visions of political success curdle as younger men pass him by. Elizabeth echoes elements of Masters's populist characters in *Spoon River Anthology*, sympathetic in her plight and pathetic in her inability to understand its causes. But Elizabeth had been a bon vivant in her youth, fraternizing with out-of-town guests at her father's hotel, wearing bright colors, and once riding a bicycle in men's clothes down Main Street. As a young woman, she sought love with men who came through town, which "beg[an] with kisses and end[ed], after strange wild emotions, with peace and then sobbing repentance."[10] Anderson portrayed Elizabeth's youthful lovers as "bearded," signifying these apparitions as memories of a previous era. In the present, Elizabeth places all her hopes in her languishing son, George, for whom "she will take any blow that may befall if but this boy be allowed to express something for us both." And yet, while she prays that God "not let him become smart and successful," she also sees in him a "secret something . . . I let be killed in myself." Tom Willard, on the other hand, mouths elite opinion and chides his son for his awkwardness and apparent misanthropy. Perceiving himself a success, "although nothing he had ever done had turned out successfully," Tom demands the boy "wake up."[11] Enraged by her husband's treatment of George, Elizabeth retrieves a pair of scissors, which she holds "like a dagger" to threaten her husband,

> "I will stab him," she said aloud. "He has chosen to be the voice of evil and I will kill him. When I have killed him something will snap within myself and I will die also. It will be a release for all of us."[12]

But before she can act, George enters her room and tells her "I'm going to get out of here. . . . I don't know where I shall go or what I shall do but I am going away." Elizabeth reacts with rage,

> "You think that? You will go to the city and make money, eh? It will be better for you, you think, to be a business man, to be brisk and smart and alive?"

As he leaves, George declares his self-imposed exile, "I just want to go away and look at people and think."[13]

Later in the book, George reaches "sophistication" at the county fair, where "[g]hosts of old things creep into his consciousness":

> A door is open and for the first time he looks out upon the world, seeing, as though they marched in procession before him, the countless figures of men who before his time have come out of nothingness into the world, lived their lives again and disappeared into nothingness. . . . He knows that in spite of all the stout talk of his fellows he must live and die in uncertainty, a thing blown by the winds, a thing destined like corn to wilt in the sun.

Here, George embraces freedom in a universe devoid of overarching order, a revelation in kind with Masters's exiles in *Spoon River Anthology*. Helen White, the banker's daughter home from college, also dreams of release, "to feel and be conscious of the change in her nature." In this regard, both George's and Helen's revolt is only incidentally against Winesburg. They walk together to the edge of the fairgrounds after the fair has ended where,

> [o]n all sides are ghosts, not of the dead, but of living people. The silence is almost terrifying. One shudders at the meaninglessness of life while at the same instant . . . one loves life so intensely that tears come into the eyes.[14]

After a kiss and a jovial roll down the hill, George and Helen feel like "splendid young things in a young world" where "they had for a moment taken hold of the thing that makes the mature life of men and women in the modern world possible."[15] *Winesburg, Ohio*, in its portrayal of the lives of Elizabeth and Tom and George and Helen, is both less and more than a "revolt." Barry Gross's description of the book as "nostalgic, even elegiac" better captures the spirit of its stories.[16]

Yet in 1919, Anderson's book met receptive reviewers, who foreshadowed Van Doren's interpretation. A reviewer in the *New Republic* characterized the book as a "revolt of youth against custom-morality"[17] and the *Chicago Tribune* called it "an intensively real and sound record of small-town life."[18] The *Akron Beacon Journal* (Akron, Ohio) claimed "the same incidents could be and no doubt do happen in any small town in the country,"[19] though an incredulous review in the *New York Times* could not "believe that even a small town could produce such a large percentage of neurotics."[20] A reviewer in the *New York Herald* saw in Anderson a pale reflection of Masters:

> Write out the *Spoon River Anthology* in long hand, leave out its subtlety and humor, change its simplicity to crudity, replace inspiration with

determination, take from it, in other words, all of those intangible qualities which make it great instead of disgusting and you will have Sherwood Anderson's *Winesburg, Ohio*.[21]

Like Van Doren, this critic claimed Anderson owed a debt to Masters's book.

Other reviewers recognized in Anderson a condemnation of small towns generally, and thereby presaged Van Doren's characterization of the small town as the seat of moribund values. Writing in the *San Francisco Chronicle*, future novelist, Idwal Jones, asked, "whence come the [city's] citizens whose [death] is celebrated with the greatest splendor, lamentation, and publicity? From the small town." These exiles left home "[a]t the ominous whisper of instinct . . . from some cross-roads haunt, some village, or a county seat of such inconsequence that only the patience of the biographer could find the dot on the map." Though sometimes the prick of nostalgia sent these exiles home "on the tide of affluence, or purely at the bidding of a sentimental impulse," they stayed "only for a little while." In Jones's terms, George's departure from Winesburg is more triumphant than "elegiac." When Jones visited a town he claimed to be similar to the fictional Winesburg, he found it full of archaic tragic characters, "an old Agamemnon . . . ran a post office, a gaunt Cassandra . . . presided at accouchements, and a forlorn Medea . . . drove a thriving trade." Warming to his own literary muckraking, Jones found "[u]nderneath the placid crust of its exterior life . . . all [the] comedies, tragedies, and illicit loves . . . in 'Spoon River' or Sherwood Anderson's remarkable work."[22]

Some of the rebels Van Doren identified fit even less comfortably within his designation. Floyd Dell's *Moon-Calf* (1920) presented a "revolutionary detachment from village standards," though one "without conventional reproaches and . . . without conventional heroics."[23] Like Anderson, Dell portrayed a sensitive young man who left a Midwestern town, but Dell's dreamy, bookish Felix Fay is "happiest when he was let alone . . ., making up stories and living them," when he "lost the sense of helplessness and bewilderment that made him so miserable outside."[24] Like Anderson's George Willard, Felix dreams of escape from the rural Midwest. As he left his village he

saw in his mind's eye . . . a picture of the map on the wall of the railway station—the map with a picture of iron roads from all over the Middle West centering in a dark blotch in the corner. . . .

"Chicago!" he said to himself.

. . . [H]is tramping steps went to the rhythm of a word that said to itself over and over in his mind:

"Chicago! Chicago!"[25]

However, Dell proved uncomfortable with the characterization of his work as a kind of revolt. Felix, according to Dell, "does not hate the Middle West. . . . In fact . . . he manages to find in it the things he needs—the friendship, comradeship, love, and human education." For Dell, *Moon-Calf* was a meditation on the plight of dreamers in modern society: "What is society going to do with its moon-calves? . . . What are the moon-calves going to do with society?"[26] In this regard, Dell rejected the characterization of *Moon-Calf* as the work of a small-town rebel.

Sinclair Lewis's *Main Street* (1920) better fit Van Doren's characterization.[27] Lewis's book began with a preface that decentered Main Street from its Midwestern origins, and aimed his critique at rural communities generally:

> This is America—a town of a few thousand, in a region of wheat and corn and dairies and little groves.
>
> . . . [I]ts Main Street is the continuation of Main Streets everywhere. The story would be the same in Ohio or Montana, in Kansas or Kentucky or Illinois, and not very differently would it be told Up York State or in the Carolina Hills. . . .

From this perspective, Lewis reviewed the cultural wasteland of the American village:

> Our railway station is the final aspiration of architecture. Sam Clarke's annual hardware turnover is the envy of four counties which constitute God's country. In the sensitive art of the Rosebud Movie Palace there is a message, and humor is strictly moral.
>
> Such is the comfortable tradition and sure faith. Would he not betray himself an alien cynic who should otherwise portray Main Street, or distress the citizens by speculating whether there may not be other faiths?[28]

According to Ryan Poll, Lewis's preface transformed the Midwestern small town into a "highly mobile form that can be located anywhere," whose significance lies not in its "content" but in its "ideological form."[29] In this regard, *Main Street* lifted the Midwestern town out of any region in particular and reframed it as an ideology, where it represented traditional (or retrograde) values.[30] A cursory reading of Lewis's elevation of the Midwestern town to an archetype could lead a reader to see a similarity to Masters's idea of the town as a microcosm. But where Masters's epitaphs elided his politics, and Anderson's tales aspired to reflect universal human longings, Lewis's preface threw down a gauntlet, and his book followed a different kind of exile, a character from elsewhere, who defiantly seeks change as a means to self-actualization.

Main Street follows the young adulthood of Carol Milford who had grown up in the relatively large town of Mankato, Minnesota, attended college, trained as a librarian, lived for a time in Minneapolis, and now finds herself married to a small-town doctor, Will Kennicott, and living in tiny Gopher Prairie, Minnesota. As a newcomer, Carol is by default an internal exile, and brings an outsider's perspective to the town honed in her youth:

> From those early brown and silver days and from her independence of relatives Carol retained a willingness to be different from the brisk efficient book-ignoring people; an instinct to observe and wonder at their bustle even when she was taking part in it.[31]

But Carol soon recognizes in Gopher Prairie a canvas too small to paint her dreams of community planning, gleaned from her time at the university. Main Street itself presents a dismal view

> with its two-story brick shops, its story-and-a-half wooden residences, its muddy expanse from concrete walk to walk, its huddle of Fords and lumber-wagons, [Main Street] was too small to absorb her.[32]

Carol exhibits a naive admiration for the community's common folk, "I wonder if these farmers aren't bigger than we are? So simple and hard-working."[33] At the same time, she disdains Mrs. Lyman Cass's "plutocratic parlor" and struggles against people in the town's cliques who reject her plans for improvement.[34] Significantly, Carol's antipathy toward Gopher Prairie is both aesthetic and progressive. Mrs. Cass's parlor symbolizes both the ponderousness of Victorian class stratification and furniture design.[35] Carol's nostalgia for the simplicity of earlier generations represents an innocent pining for pioneering life, a kind of spectatorship of the past rather than connection to it; she wonders why Gopher Prairie "[c]ouldn't ... somehow ... turn ... back to simplicity," and at the same time progress in its tastes.[36] And while she finds succor with the socialist handyman Miles Bjornstam, the "Red Swede," and takes "her ration of blessed cynicism" with him,[37] her philistine husband chides her new friends in low places:

> See here, my dear, I certainly hope you don't class yourself with a lot of trouble-making labor leaders! Democracy is all right theoretically, and I'll admit there are industrial injustices, but I'd rather have them than see the world reduced to a dead level of mediocrity.[38]

Ultimately, Carol leaves Gopher Prairie to find herself in Washington, DC, though she returns "thoroughly beaten," having nevertheless "kept the faith."

Despite those who "sneer[ed] at my aspirations" she claims she will never admit that "dish-washing is enough to satisfy all women!" In an ambivalent conclusion, her husband Will Kennicott responds,

> Well, good night. Sort of feels to me like it might snow tomorrow. Have to be thinking about the storm-windows soon.[39]

In Will's tacit dismissal, Carol is encased in her exiled status, even as she accepts her permanent residency.

While Van Doren placed the start of the village revolt with *Spoon River Anthology* in 1915, the popularity of *Main Street*, its vehemence, and its explicit translation of Gopher Prairie to "Main Streets everywhere," helped Van Doren characterize Masters, Dell, and Anderson, as well as E. W. Howe and Zona Gale as part of a general "revolt." In this regard, the village "rebels" were guilty by Van Doren's association. The popularity of Lewis's *Main Street* (it sold nearly 200,000 copies during its first half-year in print) inspired Van Doren to claim that the book brought "hundreds of thousands [to] the protest against the village which these [previous] books [had] brought to thousands."[40] The village revolt therefore, in Van Doren's terms, proved to be a trend, beginning with Masters, rising through Anderson and Dell, and culminating in Lewis, a compelling narrative of a literary revolt's growth that downplayed the differences between the works themselves.[41] Lewis's novels *Babbitt* (1922), about a successful realtor who suffers ennui in the face of American conformity; *Arrowsmith* (1925), about the travails of the son of a small-town doctor who seeks to become a celebrated medical scientist; and *Elmer Gantry* (1926), about an unethical Baptist preacher, established his position as the reigning village rebel of his era.

Van Doren was not the only critic to discover signs of a "revolt" against small towns in 1921, however.[42] The popular journalist and author, William Allen White, in "The Other Side of Main Street," noticed a similar literary trend that made "the country town . . . the villain."[43] Like Masters, White was born in 1868, and, as editor of the *Emporia Gazette*, covered the rise of the Populist Party in the late nineteenth century from the center of the movement. But unlike Masters, White opposed William Jennings Bryan in 1896, published editorials wondering where Bryan acquired the funds for his whistle-stop campaign, and claimed that the Populist Party was generally "composed of dull men who really believed what [Bryan] told them."[44] But White was no organ of plutocracy, and called for a victory of "altruism" over the forces of "egoism," an embrace of the "centripetal" over the "centrifugal forces of nature," a future where "law and custom" and "the creed of the people" moved "in some small measure away from the selfishness of other generations."[45]

At the core of White's ideology was a belief that within the small town resided all the mores necessary to maintain good social order:

> Time and again we have been surprised at the charity of our people. They are always willing to forgive, and be it man or woman who takes a misstep in our town—which is the counterpart of hundreds of American towns—if the offender shows that he wishes to walk straight, a thousand hands are stretched out to help him and guide him. . . . We are all neighbours [sic] and friends, and when sorrow comes, no one is alone. The town's greatest tragedies have proved the town's sympathy.[46]

According to White, while both he and Lewis found in the small town a mold that shaped vast regions of the United States, Lewis nevertheless failed to see the "pleasant . . . side of the street" and, in this oversight, presented readers with a "picture of a maggoty mind; a snapshot from a wapperjawed camera." While no modern utopia, the "American country town . . . is much like the Utopia of the mid-Victorian dream."[47]

Whereas towns like Spoon River, Winesburg, and Gopher Prairie became communities of thwarted ambition or stifling hothouses of mediocrity in Van Doren's "revolt," White argued that Midwestern small towns were inheritors of the pioneering ideal of a town "in social commerce met," a place where "the mother moves in that small circle of friends and neighbours which circumscribes American motherhood of the best type," where "we are all workers . . ., as people are in every small town," where leisure activities are "confined . . . to baseball in the summer, football in the autumn, and checkers in the winter." In this fashion, White redeemed the small town by framing it in terms also similar to the idealized New England village in the nineteenth century, as a repository of unchanging American values. While a rage for newfangled trends from nearby cities temporarily unsettled the town's youth, "in time our social life will resume its old estate."[48] This "old estate" reflected contemporary ideals of small-town life: "grassy plots," a library, running water, schools, automobiles, and the Chamber of Commerce, that "exponent of altruism in the American small town." Comity proved to be the heart of this mid-Victorian dream, where, in White's telling, voluntary organizations drove the community's self-generating moral order, Rotarians, Masons, Knights of Columbus, Elks and churches "burning with fellowship" and, behind it all, a "collective neighborliness."[49]

White granted that *Main Street* was "a great book," even though it was written "in ignorance of the tremendous forces that make for righteousness in every American town."[50] And while the town had its elites, "they are not the whole town." While the "church crowd" might be dull, they are "essentially kind."

Laborers in White's small town have no class consciousness since "[h]ow can the . . . son of toil be class conscious when his . . . daughter is tripping the street in tricolette, and his son is sitting on the small of his back in a homemade racing car . . . ?"[51] And regarding the poor, "their sons and daughters get into high school and college and the next generation sees them in the country club."[52] For White, "[t]o fail to see the sheer power of sentiment in American life merely because you dislike sentimentality is bad art."[53] White's defense of small-town neighborliness inspired the *Des Moines Register* to ask, "Is Main Street, Iowa, a Place of Ugliness or Beauty? Which is right, White or Lewis?"[54]

In this way, White and Van Doren helped stake out the lines over which American rebellion took place in the twentieth century: were small towns and, later, modern suburbs, receptacles of values, or incubators of pathologies? Were village rebels "impatient . . . toward all subterfuges" or "wapperjawed?" The accuracy of the characterization of these writers as "rebels" is less important than the impression it left. While authors like Masters, Anderson, Dell, and Lewis did not perceive themselves as part of a singular rebellion, the appearance of their books within a few years of each other, the common Midwestern location of their subjects, and the characterization of a trend by critics like Van Doren and White, fostered the easy conclusion that something was afoot in the hinterlands. In this respect, the significance of Van Doren's characterization lies not in the motivations of the authors, but in the historical moment in which they were received.

Whose Revolt?

Needless to say, many scholars have been incredulous of Van Doren's characterization of the village revolt during this period.[55] Henry Steele Commager claimed these authors as part of a longer literary trend, starting in the 1880s, that "paralleled the political [revolt in that] . . . both were directed toward the economic malaise."[56] Henry May, conversely, discerned a short and "innocent" rebellion between 1912 and 1917, which rejected convention and celebrated the spontaneous and beautiful.[57] Ronald Weber notes that critiques of Midwestern rural life like Masters's, Anderson's, and Lewis's had "been a strain a half-century since Eggleston's *The Hoosier School-Master*."[58] Jon Lauck argues that the village rebels of Van Doren's designation "were more complicated than the thesis presumes."[59] According to the literary critic David D. Anderson, the exile's departure from the small town followed a longer-standing American compulsion "for personal advancement in an open society," that traced "the movement West beyond the Appalachians [that] began in the eighteenth and early nineteenth centuries." In these terms, George Willard's life in Winesburg taught him, and others like him, that "only they could determine the end of the search" and proved "one more manifestation of the age-old human search, American search, Midwestern search, for an ill-defined, vaguely-perceived but convincing ideal" of the "continuing unfolding myth of America."[60]

While writers before Masters mocked, pierced, and deflated the pretentions of a romanticized rural America, and while the will to escape one's birthplace can be considered a long-standing American literary theme, the common attributes of the revolt Van Doren identified fit within changing contemporary conceptions of the legacy of a Victorian ethos of progress, character, and community; this thereby encapsulated a discrete shift in some readers' conception of what constituted a just community.[61] According to Narayana Chandran, Masters's *Spoon River Anthology* "gathered around it the aura of a myth widely current in the first decade [of the twentieth century] . . . [that] celebrated the virtues of community life" and "reverse[d] all the[se] premises."[62] Anthony Channell Hilfer likewise claims that literary exposés like Masters's, Anderson's and Lewis's were precisely aimed at middle-class platitudes in light of recent trends in American culture since they "[saw] their locale as a microcosm of the nation and, provincial bourgeoises that they were, of the world." In this regard, the idea of a "revolt" became a means to explore issues significant to contemporary middle-class audiences.[63] Yet this "overall attack on middle-class American civilization"[64] was nevertheless dependent upon the older version of the mythologized small town. As the nostalgic New England village represented all that was unchanging in America, the ambivalent Midwestern small town, with its underlying secrets and sins, appeared to critics like Van Doren to be reservoirs of unplumbed truths. An attack on contemporary bromides—about the righteousness of social leaders and about the goodness of small-town life—required an already mythologized place of preternatural, but ultimately hollow, American values. This is why the relocation of the myth from the New England village to the Midwestern town proceeded along with the shift of the American "center" of the nation; by 1915, "[e]ven the East . . . usually granted the superior 'Americanism' of the Middle West."[65] This shift invited the rending of gauzy images in terms poignant to the descendants of the nineteenth-century middle class, and allowed a broader critique of middle American norms overall. As the New England village served as Eden before the fall, the Midwestern small town became the seat of a previous generation's original sins. The reconception of the Midwestern small town as the symbol of a generation's moral shortcomings was, therefore, shaped by changing norms in middle-class culture itself.[66] Barry Gross reminds us that the village rebels were not necessarily in revolt against the village, "but from the *myth* of the village as a great good place."[67] In her comprehensive and engaging entry on the "Revolt from the Village" in the *Dictionary of Midwestern Literature*, Marcia Noe argues "it cannot be denied that much negativity exists in the early-twentieth-century literature of the small-town Midwest."[68] Accordingly, Van Doren characterized these authors as rebelling against a contemporaneous notion of fatuous self-righteousness, exemplified by William Allen White's mid-Victorian dream, a place whose claims to be "simple and innocent, pure and virtuous, democratic and egalitarian" proved fraudulent once one looked under the surface.[69]

Intellectual trends provided the impetus and support for this characterization, largely by reconfiguring assumptions about human psychology. The popularization of Freud's theories of sexual repression since the 1910s provided the means by which to overturn perceived notions of the small town as a "great good place." Freud's visit to the United States in 1909 led to the dissemination of his ideas, especially after the translations of *Selected Papers on Hysteria and Other Psychoneuroses* (1909) and *Three Essays on the Theory of Sexuality* (1910). These translations, according to Richard Skues, transformed Freud's reputation from "a psychotherapist who had adopted a new method" to a psychologist with a cohesive "body of thought" regarding "neurosis, dreams, jokes, slips, [and] sexuality," at least initially among a highbrow reading public.[70] According to William Everdell, "[a]fter [Freud], self-knowledge [became] recursive, an infinite task undertaken against a fierce resistance that comes from the self. The human mind . . . is neither continuous nor whole."[71]

By the 1920s, Freud's influence continued apace. According to Russell Blankenship, writing in the 1930s, literature in the previous decade turned to the "psychological" and many of Anderson's characters, for example, "parallel cases described by scientific psychoanalysts."[72] Other contemporary critics recognized as much. For Vernon Louis Parrington, Anderson was a writer of a "single theme: the disastrous effect of frustrations and repressions . . . [d]ue to: (1) Crude, narrow environment that drives to strange aberrations; (2) Repressed instincts that break forth in abnormal action."[73] In the pages of *Reedy's Mirror*, William Marion Reedy embraced the influence of Freudian theories by printing the poet Conrad Aiken's reply to a critical review of his book *Turns and Movies* (1916). Aiken claimed, "if [my book] is decadence, then Freud is decadent, and all psychologists are decadent," thereby embracing Freud's ideas about the human unconscious as a modern form of self-abnegation in the face of trite moral sanctimoniousness.[74] Likewise, Eunice Tietjens, in Harriet Monroe's magazine *Poetry*, connected Aiken's verse to Masters's: "If . . . Masters . . . had never written, there is small doubt that *Turns and Movies* would prove ırad Aiken an authentic poet. But as it is, their unquiet ghosts stalk behind work."[75] William Marion Reedy's biographer, Max Putzel, called Aiken's poetry and Reedy's support for its Freudian undertones an "eloquent plea for a kind of poetic realism Masters had striven for, a realism that would conform not to a theory but to the newly recognized secret symbolism of man's buried life."[76] This concept of a "buried life" is a significant aspect of contemporary notions of Masters's seemingly amoral structure in Spoon River and Van Doren's village rebels generally, since Freud's theories of the sublimated id, its repression, and the everyday anxieties this repression spawned offered a revised conception of human psychology. Whereas the myth of the New England village depended upon a romantic notion of the inherent goodness of humanity in its natural state and allowed the industrial city of the nineteenth century to serve as a foil to the naturalistic village, Freud's concept of the id traced moral struggles to the repression of unconscious desires. Truth-telling, therefore, derived its power from uncovering the origins of human neuroses in the struggle between unconscious needs and the demands of a repressive society, a kind of psychological muckraking to reveal the latent causes of personal anxieties. According to Pericles Lewis, Freud "taught the twentieth century to look for hidden meanings," thereby giving intellectual heft to the exile's ability to pierce claims of moral integrity and natural goodness.[77] By the mid-1920s, Freud's theories shaped conceptions of human nature in a way that allowed a wholesale critique of pre-Freudian psychology. In 1927, even the critic Vernon Louis Parrington recognized as much when he characterized middle-aged readers as "in the unhappy predicament of being treated as mourners at their own funeral. . . . Their counsel is smiled at as the chatter of a belated post-Victorian generation that knew not Freud."[78]

By the middle of the 1920s, a largely urban, middle-class cross-section of the reading public opened a discursive space that reimagined the rural American town as the seat of contemporary anxieties, where moral hypocrisy proved to be a manifestation of social neuroses. Jon Lauck reminds us that the popularity of H. L. Mencken's articles in the *American Mercury* had "broad impact on intellectuals of the era." Mencken waged an ongoing rhetorical war against the rural "booboisie," "village editors, clubwomen, [and] Fundamentalists," that mocked them to scorn.[79] Mencken also called for a new kind of truth-teller, "emerged from the general," who had "lost [his] original certainties" and used "skepticism" to "spray acid upon all the ideas that come within his purview."[80] Lauck, channeling Christopher Lasch, traces this blanket critique of middle American backwardness to the advent of the American intellectual as a "social type," who "felt disconnected from the main traditions of American life and sought to criticize and reform them."[81] David Hollinger finds here an effort among self-anointed American intellectuals and their highbrow audience—for example, readers of the newly inaugurated *New Yorker* magazine—to reject American parochialism for the supposedly scientifically sound theories of modern psychology.[82]

Intellectuals in different fields made similar arguments. In 1923, Thorstein Veblen, University of Chicago economist and noted critic of consumer capitalism, reversed the innate "neighborliness" that William Allen White described in the American small town—"[i]ts name may be Spoon River or Gopher Prairie, or it may be Emporia or Centralia or Columbia"—and discovered, instead, naked self interest: "[a country town's] municipal affairs, its civic pride, its community interest, converge upon its real-estate values, which are invariably of a speculative character." Veblen's mixing of fictional and actual towns is telling here; he assumed his readers saw in both Spoon River and Centralia evidence of his claims. According to Veblen, the avarice at the heart of small-town life fed the moral hypocrisy exposed by Van Doren's rebels:

> One must avoid offence, cultivate good will, at any reasonable cost, and continue unfailing in taking advantage of it; and, as a corollary to this axiom, one should be ready to recognize and recount the possible shortcomings of one's neighbours [*sic*], for neighbours are (or may be) rivals in the trade, and in trade one man's loss is another's gain, and a rival's disabilities count in among one's assets and should not be allowed to go to waste.... One must be circumspect, acquire merit, and avoid offence. So one must eschew opinions, or information, which are not acceptable to the common run of those whose good will has or may conceivably come to have any commercial value.

And while "[a]ny person who ... takes his ecclesiastical verities at their face might be moved to deprecate ... these mixed motives," Veblen recognized that at the heart of neighborliness resided a "salesmanlike pusillanimity" that upheld both the moral and economic structure of small towns. Veblen's small town, then, stood "pat... somewhere about Mid-Victorian Times" in its proclamations of community values and pursuit of rapacious ends.[83] In this vein, the popularization of anthropology, especially Margaret Mead's celebration of the "primitive," advanced an attack on vestigial "Victorian" culture,[84] while Robert and Helen Lynd's *Middletown* (1929) turned the methods of social science on the Midwest. According to Henry May, for the Lynds,

> individual child-training, religion, and the use of patriotic symbols represent[ed] the past, while the future is represented by whatever is

thoroughly secular and collective, particularly in the community's work life. The town has tended to meet its crises by invoking tradition in defense of established institutions.[85]

These trends in the 1920s, especially the rise of a segment of the reading public ambivalent (or hostile) toward older perceptions of rural America, pointed to a growing divide between readers. While literary critics like Amy Lowell and Midwestern columnists like the Kansan Jay House admired Masters for different reasons between 1915 and 1917, Carl Van Doren's and William Allen White's reactions to Sinclair Lewis's *Main Street* represented the growing gulf between readers who saw American small towns as placid frauds and small-town residents who proved resentful at finding themselves the target of a culture war between the traditional and the modern.

The trope of the town's exile, then, in Van Doren's terms, became a character who pierced the pretensions of Main Street. Dreamers like Webster Ford, George Willard, and Felix Fay or malcontents like Carol Milford, and through them, authors like Masters, Anderson, Dell, and Lewis, served as a reader's interpreter of the small town, and thereby translated its dreams into symbols of repressed desires. Here, then, lay the ambivalence at the heart of the mythological Midwestern town, where a second generation of residents claimed to transform the pioneering spirit of Gallagher's "Fifty Years Ago" into William Allen White's municipality of "neighbours and friends," but the stolid surface belied antisocial unconscious desires. Thereafter, according to Russell Blankenship, even the virtues of the pioneering ethos, "its intellectual conformity, its gospel of thrift and industry, its democracy, and especially its optimism," proved to be ready targets for "ridicule" and "reasoned examination of premises."[86] This revised mythology of the frontier generation and its descendants supported a revision of the Turner Thesis itself, as Robert Dorman notes, in the hands of literary critics like Lewis Mumford, Vernon Parrington, Waldo Frank, and Van Wyck Brooks, who reimagined the Midwestern "settling out" phase and frontier communities as precursors of, in Lewis Mumford's words, "deserted villages, bleak cities, depleted soils" and "sick and exhausted souls that engraved their epitaphs in Mr. Masters's Spoon River Anthology."[87] Mumford's use of Masters's fictional characters as evidentiary symbols here is as telling as Veblen's use of Spoon River as an analogue for real towns. Both assumed their readers would recognize the reference, and understand that this fictional community proved emblematic of reality itself.

Since the rural communities that the village revolt portrayed were only incidentally Midwestern, especially after Lewis's prologue, the myth proved adaptable, a modern passion play of rapacity and repression, and a truth-revealing exile who spoke for an indolent mass. The exile on Main Street, as author or character, exposed the falsity of the previous generation's truisms, and displayed the town's anxieties for their own good. While the contours of this drama can be traced to authors that predated Masters—in the stories of Eggleston or Howe—the popularity of *Spoon River Anthology* and *Main Street* and their packaging as part of a "village revolt" by contemporary critics, mark the appeal of this kind of literary muckraking to large sections of the American reading public in the 1920s. Whether these authors saw themselves as part of a general revolt or not, and regardless of the nuanced differences in their works, the idea of a "village revolt" captured the zeitgeist of the third decade of the twentieth century with a durable formulation. For readers in the 1920s who had imbibed, likely secondhand, a little Freud, perhaps read or read about Thorstein Veblen, and likely recognized parts of Spoon River, Winesburg, or Gopher Prairie around them, Van Doren's village-in-revolt felt realistic. It seemed true that freedom was repressed by hidebound values, that sanctimoniousness covered sublimated desires, and that the darker corners of the American unconscious resided in a place quintessentially American.

What Revolt?

According to Anthony Hilfer, interest in the small town as a locus of a struggle between the traditional and the modern "fizzled out rather dismally" by the end of the 1920s.[88] Two trends, Hilfer notes, brought about this change. First, the stock market crash and subsequent economic collapse after 1929 transformed literary antipathy toward modern capitalism from "the aesthetic *vs.* the acquisitive" to the portrayal of the businessman as "objectively vicious."[89] While Masters claimed in the heady days of spring 1915 that what ailed the United States was spiritual apathy caused by the scourge of "materialism," his critique still largely depended upon a Victorian belief that character was destiny, and that a personal change-of-heart and self-knowledge could lead to individual rejuvenation and justification. By the 1930s, however, according to Hilfer, "radicals saw village rebels . . . as not exactly wrong . . . but . . . off center, irrelevant" in the face of economic collapse. Whereas the characters of the village rebels were "bourgeois inflected with a germ of revolt against dominant pieties," the literary hero of the 1930s proved to be a "rebellious working man . . . against the entire capitalist system." In this light, the "aesthetic revolt" of Van Doren's village rebels appeared to be "mere dilettantism."[90] Critics like Bernard DeVoto, in *Mark Twain's America* (1932), claimed that Eastern elites had projected their own Victorian repression onto Western pioneers and their descendants; the popularity of John Steinbeck's *The Grapes of Wrath* (1939) portrayed populist characters whose plight was structural and economic.[91] The appearance of John Reed Clubs in the 1930s, sponsored by the Communist Party USA, represented a turn in American literary trends toward more proletarian and politically activist topics. Likewise, a "return to the soil motif," exemplified by works like James Agee's nonfictional *Let Us Now Praise Famous Men* (1941) and Robert Penn Warren's *At Heaven's Gate* (1943) celebrated rural Americans as inheritors of collective "traditional wisdom."[92] For Hilfer, "the thirties had come to admire certain qualities of American life that could on a hazy day be mistaken for just those qualities the village rebels attacked."[93] In this regard, Thornton Wilder's sentimental portrayal of Grover's Corner in *Our Town* (1938), in which the deceased Emily Webb Gibbs learns from the grave the everyday joys of an average life, reflected the waning intensity for finding in the American small town "the spasmodic, the obscure, the fragmentary, [and] the failure." Whereas the village rebels, at least in Van Doren's estimation, revealed the sordidness in the small towns around them, Wilder's Emily discovered the beauty that her fellow citizens failed to recognize. In this way, Wilder's vision of Grover's Corner echoed William Allen White's own celebration of the American small town, whose only shortcomings lie in its residents' failure to appreciate it.[94]

By the 1930s, even the so-called village rebels rejected the category. Floyd Dell thought Lewis "too kind to your heroine and too cruel to the . . . Middle West." Sherwood Anderson described Lewis's prose as "dull" and "unenlightened."[95] And when August Derleth interviewed Lewis, Anderson, and Masters for the book *Three Literary Men*, each, in his own way, rebuffed Van Doren's characterization of themselves as part of a "village revolt."[96] Lewis, who eventually resettled in the Midwest, claimed "I disliked some things about village life. I dislike some things about city life, too. . . . [But] I like those people—Carol Kennicott . . . and Will Kennicott. . . . I put into my books what I saw and what I felt. I didn't think it was rebellious then. I don't think it is now, either." When Lewis asked Derleth why he remained in the Midwest and Derleth stated that he wanted to be "close to my roots," Lewis agreed, "Yes, I understand that . . . I wasn't aware of such roots then."[97] Derleth found significance in Lewis's "then," implying that his perspective on the Midwest had changed, or at least that the exile's connection to a place proved indelible, a connection that illuminated a certain nostalgia at the heart of Lewis's ambivalence. In this regard, Lewis's rejection of Van Doren's characterization of his work as part of a "rebellion," and Derleth's sympathy for this rejection, represented the influence of contemporary literary trends in the 1930s. Nevertheless, Lewis's emphatic repudiation of Van

Doren's characterization of a village revolt over fifteen years after Van Doren coined the term marked the endurance and cultural valence of the appellation.

In 1940, Derleth met with Sherwood Anderson and, ranging over a number of topics, eventually came to his place in Van Doren's village revolt. Anderson also rejected Van Doren's term, saying "[t]here wasn't anything to this revolting. . . . I saw it the way it was and put it down the way it was. . . . There's no such thing as 'revolting' or 'rebelling' or whatever it is they want to call it."[98] But while Anderson rejected Van Doren's "revolt," he accepted the idea that his portrayal of people in Winesburg represented a realistic look at Americans generally from a psychological perspective: "I'm interested in people. I want to know what makes them go. I've spent years trying to find out."[99]

Masters also took issue with Van Doren's characterization of a village revolt and his place within it. Derleth met Masters in 1939 in his apartment at the Chelsea Hotel in New York City, where the poet had moved after relinquishing his career in law to write full time. When Derleth asked the poet about the legacy of *Spoon River Anthology*, Masters rejected Van Doren's claim that he began the revolt: "I didn't revolt against my village. The best years of my life were spent back there in Illinois."[100] Nevertheless, he acknowledged that his book appeared at a time when readers sought a reformulation of the village myth:

> The people were ready for *Spoon River*. They needed that kind of book.
> They'd had their fill of moonlight and silly love stories. They'd had enough
> of sentimentality and unreality. They wanted books like *Sister Carrie* and
> *Winesburg, Ohio* and *Spoon River* and *Main Street* because they were about
> flesh and blood men and women—like the men and women they knew—the
> men and women I knew at Petersburg and Lewistown. . . .[101]

Scholars and authors have wrestled with Van Doren's characterization of a "village revolt" nearly since its inception.[102] Nevertheless, the popular and critical reception of books like *Spoon River Anthology*; *Winesburg, Ohio*; *Main Street*; *Moon-Calf*; and others, and the three-generations-long debate about the accuracy of the term, signifies its potent legacy. Not so unlike Masters himself, Carl Van Doren captured a long-simmering sentiment about the small town, a so-called "mid-Victorian dream," and provided a contemporary foil for its pretentions. In this new myth of the Midwestern small town, readers found an archetype of traditional America, one that appeared stable, moral, and—most damning—self-satisfied, but which in fact hid a churning mix of dislocation, anxiety, and avarice. As Barry Gross notes: "The city and the small town, the farm and the village, are regions of the mind as well as regions on a map."[103] A key figure in this region of the mind was the internal exile who revealed the underlying instability of Main Street. This figure, Cassandra-like, proved inexplicable to most of the other members of the community but able to reveal unappreciated forebodings to a receptive reader. In this regard, the village rebels in Van Doren's terms created a new folk tale for Americans in the twentieth century about an individual who knew the community's true nature and conspired with the audience to divulge its undisclosed secrets for the sake of self-fulfillment.

CHAPTER 7

Main Street, U.S.A.

This area will be a scaled down representation
of a typical American small town thoroughfare
at the turn of the century, complete [with]
horse-drawn (or rather pony-drawn) streetcars;
an old fashioned fire station; and shops where
merchandise can be purchased.

—*The Dispatch* (Moline, Illinois), June 6, 1955

Edgar Lee Masters never again experienced as much success as he did during the fall and spring of 1915–1916. It was not for lack of effort. After a complicated divorce from his first wife, Helen, in 1923, and a marriage to Ellen Coyne, thirty years his junior, the poet relocated to New York City, moved into the Chelsea Hotel, and continued to try to make a living as a full-time writer of poetry, drama, and biography, even hoping to break into Hollywood as an author of screenplays during the 1930s.[1] The twenty-odd books and plays he produced during these years never matched the success or influence of his small-town "epitaphy."[2] As Louis Untermeyer said, "With *Spoon River Anthology*, Masters arrived—and left."[3]

And yet a new incarnation of the mythological small town, with its drama of nostalgia and ambivalence, reappeared in popular media immediately after the Second World War. These popular portrayals of small communities in film echoed the hagiographies of small-town life by authors like William Allen White, as well as the critiques by Van Doren's "village rebels" about hypocrisy and avarice that seethed under the surface. However, where the small towns of the 1920s represented an ethical problem and public figures disagreed over the authenticity of the town's moral claims, after the Second World War, film-makers reimagined the small town as an economic problem, where the right to own a single-family home became the pressing concern. In this way, the idealized small town of the early twentieth century inspired nostalgia for its "mid-Victorian dream," but also ambivalence about whether that dream was available to prospective home owners. This ambivalence reflected an anxiety on the part of many Americans at the end of the Second World War, with memories of the Depression behind it, and fueled a nationwide impulse to build new communities that soothed these anxieties. In this way, Van Doren's characterization of a revolt by small-town truth-tellers proved adaptable to a new exile, a prodigal son, who, upon his return to town, demanded the rights of home ownership.

Three relatively recent works of scholarship help illuminate these trends in the second half of the twentieth century. Ryan Poll, in *Main Street and Empire: The Fictional Small Town in the Age of Globalization* (2012), claims that the so-called "Revolt from the Village," especially in the case of Sherwood Anderson's *Winesburg, Ohio*, offered a "modern Bildungsroman" in which a character "fixate[d]" on the "little things," static images of small-town life, that carried universal import, proved indelible, and brought a character home, either physically or psychologically. According to Poll, "the small town [was] not a space left behind, but a space to which Americans [were] invited and encouraged to return."[4] This myth of origin and return resonated after the Second World War as well and idealized a "communal" space "that foreground[ed] a sense of belonging" in the midst of the economic flux and social dislocation caused by the war. The postwar Bildungsroman revived the romanticized village by portraying a place where "individuals [were] able to return and remain in a contained locality and ideologically escape from the violences and contradictions that define global capitalism."[5] The ideal of the small town thereby re-centered the romanticized New England village first, to small towns after the war and, soon after, to the modern suburb. During the late 1940s and early 1950s, in a trend that tracked the New England village's apotheosis just as the Turnerian thesis relocated American vitality to the west, the Midwestern small town acquired a romanticized ideal at the moment its economic vitality went into eclipse. Lizabeth Cohen's *A Consumers' Republic: The Politics of Mass*

Consumption in Postwar America (2003) offers a helpful mechanism to trace the shift of the small-town myth from Main Street to the suburbs by analyzing the process by which the United States moved from a producer-focused to a marketing-focused consumer economy during the 1950s.[6] As Americans came to increasingly use consumption to define themselves, new communities became the stage on which mass consumerism operated. Finally, Grace Elizabeth Hale's *A Nation of Outsiders: How the White Middle Class Fell in Love with Rebellion in Postwar America* (2011) analyzes the cultural mechanisms by which the postwar's "romance of the outsider" provided a middle-class position from which to critique suburbia.[7] Starting in the 1950s, middle-class Americans "imagined people living on the margins . . . as possessing something vital, some essential quality that had somehow been lost from their own lives," and marked marginality as a symbol of authenticity in the face of seemingly monocultural American life. In this regard, rebellion against a perceived dominant social order provided an "imaginary resolution" to an "intractable mid-century . . . conflict" between "the desire for self-determination" and a "desire for a grounded . . . meaningful life." Like Masters's exiles, Hale's outsiders existed "simultaneously inside and outside" of the society under their skeptical eye, though as the century wore on, the small town increasingly disappeared as the target for this skepticism.[8]

In this way, the period roughly between the Great Depression and the end of the Second World War was a respite in the popular debate over the identity of the American small town. The "village revolt," then, proved to be the beginning of national argument about the extent to which the ideal community, self-contained and exemplifying contemporary ideals of the good life, harbored underlying pathologies that defined the country itself.

Homecoming

After victory in 1945, the sixteen million Americans who had served in the military during World War II were decommissioned.[9] With memories of intractable unemployment during the Great Depression, American policy-makers marshalled federal policies to prevent the economy from spiraling back into depression. The Servicemen's Readjustment Act of 1944 (popularly known as the GI Bill of Rights) inaugurated benefits to veterans who sought a college education, and also, through the Veterans Administration, smoothed the transition back to civilian life by broadening the role of the Federal Housing Authority to insure mortgages for returning soldiers.[10] This benefit, reserved primarily for white male veterans, induced banks to invest in new housing for a segment of Americans who could not have acquired mortgages before the war.[11] To foster home ownership among these select returning veterans, the federal government increased tax benefits to single-family home owners, thereby fueling a trend that privileged the creation of new, single-family, overwhelmingly white communities within commuting distance to nearby cities, rather than multifamily dwellings within an ethnically diverse urban core. According to Elaine Tyler May, for some Americans at least, it became "cheaper to buy than to rent." This change in federal policy toward single-family homes led to an explosion in housing starts in the half-decade after the war, from 114,000 in 1944 to over 1.6 million by 1950.[12]

Americans also stood on the cusp of a consumer revolution. Personal savings during this period, a practice honed during the lean years of the Great Depression, reached twenty-one percent of disposable income in 1941, up from three percent during the 1920s.[13] While the consumer economy had its origins in an earlier period of easy consumer credit during the 1920s, the advent of third-party universal credit cards after the war drove a "net increment" of spending, best represented by the ownership of household appliances like the refrigerator, which grew between 1940 and 1950 from forty-four to eighty percent. By the end of the 1950s, seventy-five percent of American households owned a car.[14]

While these statistics portray a high level of consumer confidence after the Second World War, the federal government's attempt to ease the return to civilian life reflected a latent anxiety about readjustment. Since the 1930s, family formation had been a risky proposition; the ideal of a stable household depended upon a working male who could support a dependent wife and children. The war itself forced Americans to forestall plans for family life and exacerbated this state of suspended animation. At the same time, the Great Depression and Second World War incubated contemporary ideals of family life that had remained largely static since the nineteenth century, preserved by vague notions of domestic tranquility in a nuclear family. According to Elaine Tyler May, American policy-makers cultivated this expectant waiting by "calling on the nation to support the men who were fighting to protect their families back home."[15] According to Lary May, Hollywood filmmakers during the war shifted the focus of film narratives from "struggling social injustice at home" to portraying the United States as "an innocent society that needed to be defended from foreign monopolists and tyrants."[16] In 1942, the Office of Facts and Figures sponsored a radio series that drummed up support for the war by playing upon desires for family and home:

YOUNG MALE VOICE: "That's one of the things this war's about."
YOUNG FEMALE VOICE: "About us?"

YOUNG MALE VOICE: "About *all* young people like us. About love and
gettin' hitched, and havin' a home and some kids, and breathin' fresh air
out in the suburbs . . . about livin' and workin' *decent*, like free people."[17]

The young male in this radio play, colloquially dropping his "g's," reflected
back to listeners a singular ideal of the good life. What had manifested itself as
forbearance during the Great Depression, now became sacrifice for the sake of
a "free people": love, marriage, home ownership, children, fresh air, and work;
if the sacrifice proved noble, the homecoming would be the reward.

But in 1945, the homecoming was still ill-defined. Would the social strife
and economic doldrums of the 1930s reemerge after the conflict? Would the
sweetheart still be waiting when her beau returned? Would the returning
veteran be transformed to such an extent that the payment for the sacrifice
proved empty? In an article on civilian preparations for the end of the war,
Time magazine noted, "[w]hat few seem . . . to grasp [is] that the planning and
changeover to a peace economy [will] be infinitely tougher, and politically more
explosive, than the 1940 conversion to war."[18] In another *Time* article a marine
worried "about how I'll look to them, about how much I've changed." Another
recalled a letter in which his girlfriend asked for her picture back because she
was dating another man. The marine collected all his platoon's pictures of
women and sent them to her with the note saying, "I don't remember exactly
who you are, but if your picture is among these, please pick it out and send the
rest back to me." Another, upon arriving to New York, claimed his stomach was
"all tied in knots."[19]

It was in the immediate aftermath of the Second World War that the
new American Bildungsroman, a self-actualization through return, proved
most compelling to many Americans. While Ryan Poll notes that Sherwood
Anderson's George Willard experienced nostalgia for Winesburg even as he
boarded the train to leave it, anxiety about readjustment in the aftermath of the
Second World War heightened this tension and framed the American town as
the setting where audiences exorcised these anxieties. Films like *The Best Years of
Our Lives* (1946) and *It's a Wonderful Life* (1946) reimagined the American town
as the stage for an exile's fraught return, and thereby presented Americans with
the drama of the war's aftermath within a familiar setting.[20] While a number of
scholars have situated these films within the context of the end of the Second
World War,[21] few have noted the extent to which home ownership was the crux
of these portrayals.[22]

Samuel Goldwyn took a particular interest in a script for *The Best Years of Our
Lives* after his wife showed him an article in *Time* about returning soldiers and
their anxious homecoming.[23] The script follows the travails of three returning

veterans and their readjustment to civilian life in "Boone City," a community based loosely on Cincinnati, Ohio, incidentally the same city where William Gallagher's "Fifty Years Ago" was first published over one hundred years before. While Cincinnati does not fit the definition of a small town in the traditional sense, the portrayal of Boone City exhibited many of the hallmarks of the Midwestern small town in mythological terms: a straight Main Street composed of independently owned retail establishments, home teams (baseball, football) of abiding interest to the characters, local proprietors known to the citizens, tree-lined housing districts with straight streets, large front yards, and porches. And while Boone City is full of cars, a few nightclubs, and at least two apartment buildings, it exhibits none of the alienation or population density that marked depictions of archetypal cities in, for example, contemporary film noir.

Boone City is also topographically Midwestern. The three main characters of the story fly home on a B-17 bomber, on which they take advantage of the view from the nose cone of the plane. As square plots of farmers' fields and straight roadways pass underneath, one veteran notes that they have "a nice view of the good old USA" and that below the scene "looks like we're flying by roadmap," situating Boone City within the flat, agricultural Midwest of perpendicular roadways and fields demarcated at right angles.[24]

While *The Best Years of Our Lives* reflected contemporary anxieties about readjustment generally, it emphasized the home as the debt owed for wartime service. According to Jennifer Fay, "the film explores the distance between men changed and damaged by war and a country and social order that have remained largely intact."[25] Homer Parrish, a sailor who has lost both his hands in a fire, and now adeptly uses two hooks to open beer bottles, light cigarettes, lift glasses, and eat, expects to marry his high-school sweetheart, Wilma. Fred Derry, a member of the Army Air Corp and the highest-ranking officer of the three veterans, comes from a working-class household and only wants "a good job . . . a little house for me and my wife. Give me that and I'll be rehabilitated."[26] Al Stephenson, the oldest of the three and a member of the Army Infantry, returns to the most solid home life: a wife of over twenty years, two children, and a substantial career as a banker. Al just wants his old life back. While Homer Parrish elicited the most sympathy and interest from contemporary audiences, upper-class Al and working-class Fred expressed the social and economic anxieties of viewers in the aftermath of the war.

When Al Stephenson, the banker, enters his swanky apartment building in his uniform, the doorman insists on calling up to Mrs. Stephenson, as if Al is a stranger in his own home and transformed from the elite role he played before the war. As a soldier, Al is a temporary exile and one of the uniform mass, representing returning soldiers whose homeland is ambivalent about their return. When he gives a samurai sword and Japanese flag to his son, the boy asks if he saw any of the suffering at Hiroshima and notes, "[w]e've been having lectures on atomic energy at school" and that his teacher has taught him that with atomic weapons, "we've got to find a way to live together," or else. The maid has left, and Al's daughter has gladly taken on the domestic duties after a course on "domestic science." "I don't recognize them," remarks Al, whose ideal home, as he describes it later, is "corny and Mid-Victorian."[27]

When Al arrives at his old job at the Corn Belt Loan and Trust, he returns to an institution that had been instrumental in providing loans to regular people since the nineteenth century. According to Jonathan Rose and Kenneth Snowden, until the 1930s, building and loans worked on "share accumulation" contracts, "which provided a gradual repayment mechanism through the purchase of equity shares" where shareholders pledged to purchase shares up to the amount they needed to finance their homes. Then, the borrower/shareholder paid dues into their share account, thereby creating a system in which "share accumulation . . . doubled as both a savings device and a repayment device, allowing members to easily transition from savings to borrowing when it was their turn" to do so.[28] In this way, building and loans allowed a would-be property-owner of modest means to purchase a home through a cooperative mechanism. Building and loans offered a more collective approach of buying a home than the traditional bank mortgage. And while building and loans moved to a modern system of direct-reduction loans during the Depression, in the 1940s they still resonated as an institution of shareholders whose pooled resources helped foster individual home owning for common people. The name of Al Stephenson's building and loan, the Corn Belt Loan and Trust, marked it as a Midwestern institution whose origins lay in this tradition. But when Al is promoted to vice president of small loans because "we need a man who understands soldiers' problems," he discovers that most veterans have very little collateral. Al is at first incredulous and insists to one that property for collateral is a requirement for a loan. "I haven't got any property," says the veteran. "That's why I want a loan." The veteran continues with a justification grounded in humanitarian concerns, his war experience, and an appeal to citizen rights:

> I was a sharecropper before the war like my father before me. Now I'd like a little piece of land of my own to work. With the food shortage around the world, it seems to me farming is about the most important work there is. I don't feel this is asking the bank for a handout, it's my right. At least that's what I've been told by other servicemen.

After Al is convinced and approves the loan, he is questioned by the bank president, Mr. Milton, whose assistant argues to overturn Al's decision, "no collateral, no security," to which Al argues, "his collateral is in . . . his rights as a citizen." While Mr. Milton ultimately approves the loan, he reminds Al that "this is not our money we're doling out. . . . We cannot gamble with it." Later that evening at a banquet in his honor, Al, fortified with many drinks, makes a speech in which he relates a story of an officer who directed him to take a hill: "I said no collateral, no hill. And we didn't take the hill. And we lost the war." He continues:

> I love the Corn Belt Loan and Trust. I say our bank is alive. It's human. And we'll have a line of customers asking for and receiving loans. We'll be gambling on the future of this country.

When he concludes his speech, though Al receives uncomfortable applause, he affirms his alliance with the viewing audience against the elite bankers of the town by bringing a new set of values from the war: the building and loan is "alive" and "human" and takes risks for the sake of the country's future. Al will be a banker with a conscience, and we are led to believe that he will keep his job and actualize the promise of the GI Bill by "gambling on the future of this country."[29] In this regard, Al's demand for a more humane banking system echoes Masters's own antipathy toward the "materialism" of American society, best expressed in his *New-York Tribune* interview of spring 1915. Behind both was the long-standing populist antipathy toward rapacious industrial capitalism as practiced since the Civil War, as well as an older ambivalence toward banks, whose mortgage-holding powers, along with their instability through the nineteenth and early twentieth centuries, made them the seat of economic anxiety for many Americans. In the aftermath of the New Deal and the Second World War, Al represented an enlightened member of the traditional elite, as if Ralph Rhodes, the cynical and ultimately tragic son of the banker Thomas Rhodes in *Spoon River Anthology*, had been transformed by the communal experience of war into a kind of exile from his own class, who values humanity over profit. The home, in this respect, represented a concrete manifestation of basic humanitarianism, where regular men found dignity for themselves as heads of households, and received recompense for their service to the country.

Fred Derry, a working-class character in *The Best Years of Our Lives*, encounters a similarly uncomfortable return, which is ultimately resolved with an appeal to home owning. When Fred arrives at his father's and stepmother's house under the highway, he notices that his wife, Marie, isn't home and his father informs him that "[s]he took an apartment downtown" and now has a job in a nightclub. However, "[t]here's nothing to worry about. . . . We saw her last Christmas."[30] After a short visit, Fred leaves to find Marie.

But Fred's dreams of a family and a home prove temporarily out of reach. Marie has grown cold to him and, draped over a chair and chatting on the phone with wartime boyfriends, debases Fred for his work as a soda-jerk. Eventually, she asks Fred for a divorce and disappears entirely from the film. Fred, meanwhile, reaches a breaking point. Grieving for his broken marriage and poor financial prospects, he retreats to the airplane graveyard near the Boone City airport, crawls into a decommissioned plane (symbolically called the "Round Trip?") and experiences a flashback to the battle where he lost one of his men. When his flashback is broken by a salvage worker, Fred, relieved momentarily of his grief, asks the junk man for a job. Thereafter, he learns that the abandoned bombers will be used as "material to build three fabricated houses,"[31] thereby uniting his hope for employment with his ideal of a small home for returning veterans. Like a redeemed Barry Holden, the bankrupt farmer of *Spoon River Anthology* who murders his pregnant wife over the prospect of another child, Fred Derry, though exiled from Boone City by the war, returns with a claim to a home. Al Stephenson, the redeemed member of the elite, will make sure he gets it. Thus, in the end, Al and Fred remake Boone City into a postwar reality: Al will be a banker with a conscience who helps Fred own one of the little houses he builds from planes decommissioned after the war. Fred's home will be purchased with proceeds from his new job and through a generous loan from the Corn Belt Loan and Trust, insured by the US government. Thus, in *The Best Years of Our Lives*, the crucible of war, exile, and return forged a populist-elite consensus of white, home-owning masculinity.

Contemporary reviews celebrated these themes, exemplifying the extent to which *The Best Years of Our Lives* captured postwar anxieties about returning veterans and their reception. The *Boston Globe* claimed that the film "deals with the problems that meet every type of returning veteran" and made clear that "your career in the Army isn't going to pay you dividends back home," thereby inviting returning soldiers to conceive of themselves as temporary exiles who had a right to demand the community's reward.[32] A review by Norbert Lusk in the *Los Angeles Times* celebrated the film for its "integrated perfection" by "working out the solutions of the characters under contemplation."[33] Harold Cohen, in the *Pittsburgh Post-Gazette*, summed up the social import of the film by connecting it directly to postwar worries about the nation's returning soldiers:

> Here is a photoplay of heart and substance, a document of returning soldiers so human, so heartening and so conscious of the veteran's problems it seems cut from the crosscloth that is America. There is not only glowing

entertainment in "The Best Years of Our Lives," there is also food for thought on the issues, at once grave, affecting and humorous, it presents with such understanding, sympathy and compassion.[34]

These sentiments fit broadly within Ryan Poll's conception of an American Bildungsroman and represent a moment when the popular portrayal of small-town life featured a prodigal son bringing a perspective born of a journey that reaches fulfillment only when resituated as a home owner and head of a family. This reintegration into the town, dependent upon the acquisition of a family and home, required that the community open a space for broad home ownership for returning veterans. Needless to say, the prodigal sons in *The Best Years of Our Lives* represented only a narrow slice of the American people: male, white, and war-experienced. Tellingly, the only African American character in *The Best Years of Our Lives* is a porter. In this way, the Bildungsroman of the film reimagined the drama of the exile as a means by which to build a postwar social consensus: upper-class men would become humanitarians or face the wrath of those who sacrificed for them, and working-class men would own a home in their communities. This consensus was justified by the wartime service of these men, exiled for a time from their communities, but rewarded upon their return. To help fulfill this consensus, middle-class working daughters and wives would return to their roles as homemakers or leave their husbands and face a more permanent exile.[35] According to David Culbert, "the plot of the film is carefully constructed to reveal explicit messages about class and gender, and, through explicit omission, race."[36] Both African Americans and women would challenge this consensus in the coming decades.

The same year that *The Best Years of Our Lives* was released, *It's a Wonderful Life* (1946) enacted similar themes of the postwar American Bildungsroman, but through a white, male internal exile who never left home. By 1946, Frank Capra had already established himself as a filmmaker who translated the broad sympathy for the underdog at the heart of the New Deal into popular comedies and dramas.[37] *It's a Wonderful Life* offered a nostalgic feast that extended these sentiments into the first year after the war through George Bailey, who dreamed of travel and education but could never escape Bedford Falls. While the film was something of a box office flop when it was released, it achieved a second life on American television through the second half of the twentieth century and is still part of the soft-focused nostalgia of the American Christmas season. The film itself portrayed a glossy image of the early twentieth century through a series of flashbacks to George's youth, his young adulthood, a midlife crisis, and town-assisted resolution, thereby covering the first forty-odd years of the twentieth century in a narrative that soothed contemporary anxieties about the rights of the individual and the obligations of the community through a revivification of William Allen White's notion of "neighborliness." In this way, *It's a Wonderful Life* traversed a half-century of small-town mythology while tracking the postwar anxieties of *The Best Years of Our Lives*, especially the reconciliation of individuals and their community through home ownership.

Bedford Falls, where the film takes place, is presented as a quintessential American small town, with a Main Street of local businesses and familiar faces, including Peter Bailey's building and loan, which George Bailey, the protagonist of *It's a Wonderful Life*, will save from the grasping hands of the local banker. And while Bedford Falls is set in New York state, its nineteenth-century architecture, business-lined Main Street with perpendicular side streets, its large yards and rows of residences, and its flat topography, show the influence of a half-century small-town mythology. Bedford Falls, like Lewis's Gopher Prairie, could be anywhere, but displays the contours of its mold.

The movie begins with scenes of Bedford Falls at Christmas, with overdubbed prayers for George, who has undergone a crisis and plans to commit suicide. This takes the viewer to the stars, where the heavens send a novice angel, Clarence, to save him. Thereafter, the film presents a series of flashbacks in which young George establishes his moral bona fides as a man who sacrifices himself for others: He saved his brother from drowning, he prevented the town pharmacist from accidentally prescribing poison, and most importantly, he stood up to Henry Potter, the town businessman and banker, who rides in a black carriage, dresses in an ominously nineteenth-century black suit, and, as the "richest and meanest"[38] man in town, represents over a century's worth of imagery of the powerful banker.[39] According to Brenda Wineapple, this flashback establishes character "as a set of intrinsic timeless qualities."[40] The climax of the film, then, is the test of George's character.

While the building and loan performs a service for the common people in Bedford Falls, George wants nothing to do with it. At dinner one night, viewers are introduced to the only African American character in the film, the Bailey family maid, Annie, who plays a quasi-maternal role in kind with Mammy portrayals of middle-aged African American women that stretch back to the nineteenth century.[41] Peter Bailey asks if George would consider taking over the building and loan. George tells his father that he couldn't "stand to be cooped up his whole life in a shabby little office. . . . I want to do something big, something important." To which Peter Bailey responds, "I feel we are doing something important, satisfying a fundamental urge. It's deep in the race for a man to want his own roof and walls and fireplace. And we're helping him get those things in our shabby little office."[42] Here, as in *The Best Years of Our Lives*, the home stands in for more abstract notions of male dignity and natural rights, which echoed long-standing populist notions of the small property-holder as the foundation of the republic. Peter Bailey sees his role in Bedford Falls as more than just a member of the business community; instead, the Bailey Building and Loan actualizes natural rights by providing the means to home ownership. In this regard, Peter Bailey speaks the language of the populism that shaped Masters's own moral sensibilities, romanticizing a pioneering age when community building was supposedly driven less by a profit motive, and more through a natural process of individuals "in social commerce" constructing an organic community, an ideal endangered by rapacious elites, like Henry Potter and Thomas Rhodes, whose sole motive is profit.

At his brother Harry's high school graduation party, George is reacquainted with a childhood friend, Mary Hatch, who has pined for him since childhood. And while romantic sparks fly between the two, George reasserts his plan to travel the world and then attend college. During their walk, they pass "the old Granville House,"[43] a deserted Victorian home near Mary's, which will eventually be George and Mary's home, thereby connecting the mid-Victorian dream home to the compulsion for home ownership in the twentieth century. George proposes to throw a rock through one of the windows and make a wish, but Mary stops him, saying how much she loves the old house and would like to live in it someday. When George breaks a window anyway, he tells Mary of his wish to travel and build bridges and buildings and the like. When Mary throws a stone and breaks a window, her wish proves different.

When Peter Bailey dies and it becomes clear that Henry Potter seeks to dissolve the building and loan, George is forced to take over the business in a dilemma that echoes populist Mickey M'Grew's in *Spoon River Anthology*, who had to give his college money to his bankrupt father. When Potter calls his deceased father a "starry-eyed dreamer," George makes a speech in defense of the building and loan and claims that it helps regular people to "get out of your slums, Mr. Potter."

> Doesn't that make them better citizens? Doesn't that make them better customers? Do you know how long it takes a working man to save $5000? Well is it too much to have them work and pay and live and die in a couple of decent rooms and a bath? Anyway, my father didn't think so. They were human beings to him.[44]

Echoing the banker Thomas Rhodes in *Spoon River Anthology* and reviving populist clichés about bankers that shaped Masters's own conceptions, Potter calls George's speech "sentimental hogwash."

Tellingly, Henry Potter offers rental properties ("slums") to the people of Bedford Falls, gesturing to a negative perception of urban housing after the war. The Bailey Building and Loan, on the other hand, promises home ownership for the masses. And when there is a run on the building and loan, reminding the viewer of the early days of the Great Depression, and it becomes apparent that Potter has orchestrated the run by calling in the building and loan's debts and then offering to guarantee its shares at fifty cents on the dollar, it appears imminent that the Bailey business is finished. But in a speech that separates the building and loan from Potter's bank, George reminds the shareholders that their money is not held in the safe, but used to fund their neighbors' mortgages, thereby creating a virtuous circle of investment in the community. "We've got to stick together," says George.[45] Here, then, like Masters's exiled Shack Dye, George Bailey knows what nefarious "horse-shoes . . . move" under the feet of the people of Bedford Falls, and offers an alternate, communitarian vision. In this light, George's status as a knowing exile, coupled with his populist sympathies and quasi-elite status as the proprietor of the building and loan, offers another example of the confluence of elite, populist, and exile characters in the popular media after the Second World War, as in *The Best Years of Our Lives*, hinting at the way the myths of the postwar consumer economy repackaged older, more anxious categories.

For a while, George warms to his life in Bedford Falls. He helps Giuseppe Martini, a local restaurateur, leave Potter's "slums" and move to a new subdivision, Bailey Park, made possible by mortgages provided by the building and loan. "Look at it today," says a henchman to Potter, "ninety-percent owned by the suckers who used to pay rent to you."[46] But when the building and loan receives a visit from a bank inspector, and Uncle Billy accidentally loses the deposit that would guarantee the business's solvency, George, realizing that he has given up his dreams of escape and now faces the end of the business for which he has given up those dreams, decides that he's worth more dead than alive and goes to the bridge over the river outside of town to jump.

This inaugurates a series of counterfactuals of life in Bedford Falls without George. Martini's cozy establishment becomes a honky-tonk and the formerly friendly bartender, Nick, is surly and short-tempered, snarling that "we serve hard drinks in here for men who want to get drunk fast."[47] The town is now called "Pottersville" and Main Street is covered in flashing neon lights and clubs of questionable morals, made apparent by the jazzy soundtrack that surrounds George's anguished walk through the town. The building and loan "went out of business years ago." George's childhood home is now "Bailey's Boarding House," which his mother is forced to run to make ends meet.[48] And when George goes to see Martini in Bailey Park, all the houses are gone, and only the graveyard remains. George's wife, Mary, forced to work like George's mother, is a stereotypical "old-maid" librarian, bespectacled and meek, who flees George's embrace. When the town is run by the banker's values, the community is infected by the bank's grasping immorality. The Bailey Building and Loan, on the other hand, is a humane institution; it rejects, in Masters's terms, the "hedonistic materialism" that treated "the less efficient . . . with injustice" and thereby threatened the integrity of the community.[49] When George returns to the bridge where he thought of jumping and begs, "please God, let me live again," his plea is for the community as well.[50]

When George opens his eyes, he realizes it was all an alternate reality of Bedford Falls without him and that he has returned to the world with him in it. He runs joyously home through the old Bedford Falls, wishes Merry Christmas to people on the street, and to the "movie house," the "emporium," to the building and loan, and even to Mr. Potter, who responds, "And Happy New Year to you, in jail." While George embraces his wife and children, the bank examiner is in the parlor and informs George that he is still waiting for the funds to guarantee the solvency of the building and loan. Mary, then, positions George by the Christmas tree and exclaims "It's a miracle," and opens the front door. Uncle Billy enters with George's neighbors and a basket full of donations to save the building and loan. Everyone sings "Hark, the Herald Angels Sing" and George's brother proposes a toast, "To my big brother, George, the richest man in town."[51] According to Thomas Halper and Douglas Muzzio, the film ends with George's discovery that he resides in a very special place that could be anyplace, "a compact area peopled with family, friends, and acquaintances."[52]

Ryan Poll agrees and argues that the moral of George Bailey's story lies in "the small town's foundational identity as a communal space that allows for the individual to belong."[53] To this end, *It's a Wonderful Life* "mystifies capitalism by imagining two competing forms . . . [:] benevolent capitalism . . . [,] the practice of the small town[,] and malevolent capitalism . . . [,] the practice of the city."[54] After the Second World War, the ideal of a benevolent form of small-town capitalism appeared to hang in the balance. Foreclosure had loomed over millions of homes since the 1930s, and before loan deposits were guaranteed by New Deal legislation, banks proved to be necessary institutions that inspired dread.[55] The malevolence of Henry Potter, and, in a milder form, of Mr. Milton in *The Best Years of Our Lives*, echoed long-standing populist antipathy toward American bankers while updating them to voice concerns about the viability of home ownership by "citizens" and "customers."

But the Second World War reconfigured the myth of Main Street, melding populists and exiles into prodigal sons, who, with assistance from a few enlightened elites like Al Stephenson and George Bailey, assumed the right to a "roof and walls and fireplace." Films like *It's a Wonderful Life*, according to Daniel Sullivan, offered "status, freedom, and adventure" for everyday heroes like George Bailey right in their home towns.[56] In this regard, the post-war American Bildungsroman transformed a myth of tragic populists, greedy/ hypocritical elites, and skeptical exiles into a story of "regular" Americans, a normative category that privileged white men, who sacrificed for the common good both at home and abroad, and thereby secured their right to an economic system that was "alive" and "human," since it was not too much to let a man "work and pay and live and die in a couple of decent rooms and a bath." While the federal government provided the means for home ownership after the war, the loans it insured were funneled through private institutions like the Bailey Building and Loan and the Corn Belt Loan and Trust, thereby eliding the reality of federal largess in return for the impression that the rights of home ownership required only a kind of pragmatic humanitarianism and a broad consensus. During the second quarter of the twentieth century, this ideal supported liberal politics generally while upholding anti-Communist rhetoric during the Cold War, since a just order guaranteed its righteousness through access to private property, at least for some Americans. As the economy improved after 1945, many Americans capitalized on the notion of an individual's right to home ownership, thereby enacting a new myth of the ideal community where they could kindle the "fires of love . . . that burn on warmly yet." In the midst of social and economic flux, the perceived right to own a home sustained older conceptions of individual rights and who deserved them. According to this new myth of the small town, Al Stephenson, Fred Derry, and George Bailey would rebuild their communities one house at a time.

Small-Town Simulacrum

In 1946, Edgar Lee Masters moved with his wife, Ellen, to Rydal, Pennsylvania, where Ellen had accepted a job as a professor at Ogontz Junior College. By then, Masters, now seventy-nine years old, suffered from Parkinson's disease, and became dependent almost entirely on Ellen's care. When Ellen took over as chairperson of her department, the strain of caring for Masters and tending to her professional duties proved debilitating, and she spent Christmas of 1947 in New York City, where she underwent surgery for persistent pain in her spine.[57]

Almost immediately upon her return, Masters collapsed from an unknown malady and was relocated to a convalescent home in Melrose Park, Pennsylvania. Thereafter, his writing life effectively ended. Yet the popularity of *Spoon River*

Anthology, first published nearly thirty-five years before, continued unabated. The book had been reconceived for the stage already, and plans for an operatic version were in the works.[58]

While in the nursing home, the poet soothed himself with memories of Squire Davis's farm in Petersburg, Illinois, and died in his sleep on March 5, 1950. He was buried next to his grandmother in Petersburg's Oakland Cemetery just as the nation remade the mythology of small-town life to suit its postwar purposes.[59]

After 1950, the benefits of the Servicemen's Readjustment Act and the broad desire among many Americans to own a single-family home converged to ignite an explosion in housing starts. Between 1950 and 1956, rental properties made up only one-eighth of all domestic construction, down from two-fifths during the 1920s. By 1960, one out of every four single-family homes in the United States had been built during the previous ten years. After 1960, over sixty percent of Americans claimed to own a home, up from forty percent twenty years before.[60] These homes were overwhelmingly built in new communities near urban areas, suburbs, which used relatively cheap farmland and access, at first, to commuter rail lines and, later, federally and state-funded highways, to connect new home owners to the city. Park Forest, Illinois, for example, outside of Chicago, was a planned community of 30,000 residents that included a ready-made outdoor mall to serve as a commercial and civic center. More famously, William and Alfred Levitt's "Levittown" was built in the Long Island countryside thirty miles outside of New York City and ultimately housed 80,000 residents. Later, Levittowns appeared in Bucks County, Pennsylvania, and Willingboro, New Jersey.[61] A 1950 Levittown advertisement appealed to a range of consumer visions of the good life, from accoutrements necessary for family gatherings, technological devices for home convenience, and community amenities that induced a kind of instant neighborliness:

> Does it have a fireplace? *All Levittown houses do.* Without a fireplace, you might as well stay in your apartment. You'll be missing half the fun of living in your own home.
>
> Does it have a refrigerator included in the price? And an electric range? And a Bendix? And venetian blinds? *All Levittown houses do.*
>
> Does it have the use of community swimming pools? *All Levittown houses do.* It's all right to talk about "nearness to beaches" but did you ever go to one on a hot summer Sunday? And then swore you'd never do it again?[62]

One week later, Levittown promised "a real fireplace; a 'must' in a house of your own. Can you imagine a Christmas without one?"[63]

The growth of suburban communities in the aftermath of the Second World War was further fueled by the yoking of mass consumption to the traditional American rhetoric of individual rights. As Lizabeth Cohen describes it, consumption "stood for an elaborate, integrated ideal of economic abundance and democratic political freedom, both equitably distributed, that became almost a national civil religion" and thereby connected citizen rights to home ownership and consumerism after the Second World War. A husband-breadwinner was an essential part of this new civil religion, echoing older populist notions that tied landownership to natural rights and male dignity. Elaine Tyler May notes that after the war, movies increasingly "portrayed female sexuality as a positive force only if it led to an exciting marriage; otherwise it was dangerous." Starting in the late 1940s, "subordination made the difference between good and bad female sexuality. Sexy women . . . became devoted sweethearts or wives . . . [,] those who used their sexuality for power or greed would destroy men, families, and even society."[64] Once again, federal policy proved instrumental in this regard. According to Alice Kessler-Harris, the new split-income status for spouses filing taxes allowed for the "amalgamating [of two] incomes and using a tax rate based on half the couple's total income" thereby insuring "that a couple with unequal wages paid less total tax than the two together would have paid if taxed on each income." This taxing of a family income had the effect of "lowering taxes for breadwinner husbands" by assuming that "only married couples pooled their income," though in effect, it taxed a married woman's income at a higher rate than if she filed singly. This pooling of a family income for the benefit of a male breadwinner provided "the incentive [for] married women to remain at home with their children."[65]

The advent of the suburban shopping center quickly followed these trends. Even though downtown department stores continued to attract shoppers for larger items or for shopping trips that mixed entertainment and consumption, increasingly, consumers used newly built shopping centers for goods and basic services.[66] Eventually, even large department stores opened branches in suburban outdoor shopping centers and thereby, coupled with the growth of suburban supermarkets, helped create quasi-autonomous communities on the outskirts of American cities that revolved around the growth of single-family housing. As with their origins in federal policy, these communities "rendered invisible," according to Leerom Medovoi, the ways in which race and class operated. While both prewar cities and small towns contained residents' work as well as housing, breadwinners in the suburbs commuted out of their communities and to the jobs that defined their class. Likewise, the "redlining" of suburbs by privileging white mortgage-seekers over others, further fostered the illusion that suburbs were spontaneous communities built by individual homeowners' choices.[67] When African American residents sought homes in suburban communities, the myth of the freely settled suburb came apart.[68]

During the 1950s, popular media increasingly portrayed a myth of suburban living back to Americans. Well-known television shows like *The Adventures of Ozzie and Harriet* (1952–1966), with episodes that often began in the family living room, *The Donna Reed Show* (1958–1966), which centered around the light-hearted travails of a busy housewife and her family, *Father Knows Best* (1954–1960), which featured an insurance salesman, Jim Anderson and his family, and *Leave it to Beaver* (1957–1963), which centered on the life of young Theodore "Beaver" Cleaver, offered a template for suburban life. *The Adventures of Ozzie and Harriet*, for example, began as a radio program, but smoothed much of the edginess out of its scripts in the transition to television to present a more placid portrayal of family life. This new life promised tranquility, a few hijinks, and an inward-looking perspective toward home and family, what *McCall's* magazine called in 1954 "togetherness."[69]

In 1957, the magazine *Redbook* released a thirty-minute film called "In the Suburbs" that completed the process of selling viewers' lifestyle ideals back to them.[70] Families in the film experience their share of "good moments, and others not-so good" (which amounted to home-improvement mishaps and the antics of young children), but are grateful for having escaped the city, which the film invites the viewer to "Remember?" in black-and-white: homelessness, crowds, noise, apartment living, and an overdubbed woman's voice saying "We've got to move!" "And so they joined the stream of family life in the suburbs," continues the narrator over the camera's pan of suburban homes in color. There, suburban mothers "staying home, learning new ways to run a household," realize they "could use a little extra help."[71] This is where *Redbook* came in.

Shopping malls had a special place in suburban-living-through-*Redbook*: "It's a happy-go-spending world, reflected in the windows of the new shopping centers where they go to buy." There, families busily moved in and out of shops along a pedestrian thoroughfare. "For these young adults, the shopping centers have built fountains, commissioned statues, put in restaurants . . . included banks, loan offices . . . and places to buy building materials," claimed the film, assuring viewers that all their retail needs would be met. And so would their entertainment needs: at night, the shopping center offered dancing and window-shopping, thereby completing the portrayal of the shopping center as the new community's economic and civic core, in *Redbook's* terms at least, a new Main Street for a newly idealized town.[72] And while suburban shopping centers underwent many iterations over the next fifty years—from strip malls to indoor malls to big-box retail chains along the highway—this first manifestation of a prefabricated public space at the heart of suburban communities exemplified an attempt by builders and their customers to re-create elements of the nineteenth-century town, with a pedestrian-friendly "street," lined with shops and surrounded by single-family homes detached from their neighbors by lawns and sidewalks, an integrated community of householders united around a retail core.

At the same time the suburban shopping center was idealized as a public space, small towns were reimagined in simulacrum. Long Grove, Illinois, for example, which had been an unincorporated settlement of German farmers since the 1840s, countered the encroachment of real estate developers in 1956 through articles of incorporation and later statutes that forbade neon signs and required all new retail construction to include facades that imitated architecture from the 1880s. In July 1962, the village board declared "all land . . . zoned for business within the village or any land which may in future be zoned for business" to be a historic landmark so as to "preserve and perpetuate this area as much as possible as it existed or *might have existed* in the years prior to 1890 [emphasis added]."[73] Long Grove thus by the 1960s became a weekend destination for Chicagoans and regional suburban-dwellers to shop for antiques in a town whose nineteenth-century architecture, even newly built, framed the experience. One antique proprietor updated her shop to improve its historic authenticity:

> [One] [d]elightfully important change is the Early America dining room, paneled in wood and bordered by plate rails, showing important china pieces. Along one wall stands a shiny black cook stove of grandma's day, complete with pipes and fastenings.[74]

Another shop in Long Grove promised "reproductions of colored antique glassware from West Virginia . . . as well as Early American wooden ware," thereby blurring the lines between reproduction and original.[75] In 1964, Mayor Robert Coffin looked back on the previous eight years since Long Grove's incorporation and marveled that "[we] have developed a truly unique village. In an era of monotonous one-class suburbs we have one of the few where all walks of life can live in harmony," thereby echoing William Allen White's "mid-Victorian dream" of a thriving, self-supporting, economically diverse small town.[76]

The best-known simulacrum of the Midwestern small town, "Main Street, U.S.A.," opened along with Disneyland in Anaheim, California, on June 17, 1955. As the entry point to the park, this mythological Main Street in a Midwestern mold (Walt Disney claimed that it was based on his childhood memories of Marceline, Missouri) epitomized the path of the Midwestern town from regional community in the nineteenth century to universal American town in the early twentieth century to simulacrum after the Second World War. From the town square, park-goers could visit "Frontierland" to the left (as the visitor entered the park) and "Tomorrowland" to the right, thereby creating a neat timeline from origins to the future, with a representation of a nineteenth-century Midwestern small town in between, thereby re-creating an amusement-park version of Frederick Jackson Turner's thesis of historical progress from the frontier to the future.[77] Significantly, while Main Street, U.S.A. preserved a nostalgic notion of a traditional Midwestern Main Street at the turn of the century, its placement between the frontier and "tomorrow," situated it in the near-past, and thereby eased amusement park-goers into more distant fantasies about the past and future. Richard Francaviglia notes that, architecturally, Main Street U.S.A. was "suspended between the Civil War and World War I," marking its reference to the same era of small-town tales by authors like Masters, Anderson, and Lewis.[78] But whereas these authors portrayed towns of their parents' generation, Main Street, U.S.A. felt like visiting a distant relative, familiar, yet at a remove, exhibiting comfortable traits that elicited pleasant sensations of vague recognition before the wonders of Tomorrowland. According to the key from Sam McKim's 1958 souvenir map, "Disneyland is your land. Here age relives fond memories of the past . . . and here youth may savor the challenge and promise of the future."[79]

But while "Main Street, U.S.A." imitated its Midwestern reality, instead of independent proprietors, its businesses housed the chains common to American shopping centers during the period: a "market house" by Swift, Gibson greeting cards, a Timex clock shop, an Eastman camera store, Puffin pastries, Carnation ice cream, an Upjohn pharmacy, a Pablum baby station, and a Coca-Cola "refreshment corner."[80] Here was a historic Main Street of businesses found at the local mall. The connection between the past and the present continued in the interior spaces on Main Street, U.S.A. Inside the Upjohn pharmacy, for example, visitors viewed over 1000 antiques gathered by Upjohn employees and thereby seamlessly traversed the space between the modern drug store and the independent pharmacy of yesteryear, though the soda fountain was relocated to the Carnation ice cream shop nearby.[81] Visitors to Main Street, U.S.A. understood these cues. According to the *Brooklyn Daily*, "The lure of Disneyland is immediately apparent when the visitor gets his first glimpse of Main Street, U.S.A., the area Walt Disney has re-created in the image of a small American town of 50 years gone by," thereby, as in Gallagher's poem, using a fifty-year retrospective as a marker in the mythologizing process.[82] The *Birmingham News* called it a "replica of a typical small town as it looked at the turn of the century . . . a cherished era of Americana."[83] The *Kossuth County Advance* (Algona, Iowa) drew a direct connection between Main Street, U.S.A. and its own Main Street: "Here we find the familiar buildings like the Old Opera House," which looked to the reviewer like the local theater in Algona.[84]

But for other visitors, Disneyland typified mass culture's vast phoniness. In the June 7, 1958, issue of *The Nation*, Julian Halevy united "Disneyland and Las Vegas" in a critique of the "revolving . . . barrel of fun" that had become the nation.[85] Both, it seemed, exposed "a growing need in the United States to escape from reality."[86] Disneyland, for Halevy, was the place where "the universe, and all man's striving for dominion over self and nature, have been reduced to a sickening blend of cheap formulas packaged to sell," a festively hued version of Joseph Conrad's Congo Free State:

> Romance, Adventure, Fantasy, Science are ballyhooed and marketed: life is bright-colored, clean, cute, titivating, safe, mediocre, inoffensive to the lowest common denominator, and somehow poignantly inhuman[,] [an adventure into] the heart of darkness where Mr. Disney traffics in pastel-trinketed evil for gold and ivory.[87]

For Halevy, both Disneyland and Las Vegas numbed "social anxiety," and offered spaces where "secret longings" were "pseudo-satisfied." Both were also the future: "as conformity and adjustment become more rigidly imposed on the American scene, the drift to fantasy release will become a flight. So make your reservations early."[88] Here, Halevy reprised the role of the exile on Main Street from Masters's Spoon River, where the reader's eyes followed the perspective of an outsider, and thereby saw the depth of the illusion that called itself true. In this way, Halevy uncoupled the exile from the postwar consensus of movies like *It's a Wonderful Life* and echoed Masters's 1915 warning against "materialism," while at the same time giving voice to highbrow antipathy for popular culture in the postwar era. Whereas Masters's dead were messengers of the last generation's moral shortcomings, Halevy spoke with an exiled voice about the present and future, disdainful of Disneyland kitsch and reflecting a broader critique of mass culture generally during the second half of the twentieth century. This, then, reflected a reemergence of the muckraking social critique that Van Doren found in the "revolt from the village."

A trip to Main Street, U.S.A. was meant to be a homecoming, where the default American town of the past was nineteenth-century and Midwestern. But the Disney simulacrum of Main Street, with its pastiche of "Midwesterness" and contemporary consumer culture, ossified the image of the American small town for the remainder of the century. While during the first half of the twentieth century, the small town was a contested space, where public figures like William Allen White and Sinclair Lewis argued over characterizations of small towns as a proxy for broader debates about the traditional versus the modern, by the end of mid-1950s, this culture war shifted to a conflict between notions of mass culture and individual integrity.

Exile Universal

As the suburbs expanded and the Midwestern small town congealed in memory, a counter-discourse reimagined the idea of "togetherness" as a cover for social alienation. Grace Elizabeth Hale characterizes this alienation amid togetherness as part of a "romance of the outsider," a new myth for the postwar era, where white, middle-class Americans sought to reconcile two seemingly incongruent ideals: an organic community and autonomous individuality.[89] The attempt to reconcile the individual and the community can be traced back, in broad terms, to earlier myths about American organic compacts, to Ralph Waldo Emerson's nostalgic history of Concord, or to William Gallagher's pioneers and, later, to William Allen White's small town imagined as a gathering of individuals for the promotion of the common good. During the fifty years after the Second World War, this "romance" proved particularly compelling to middle-class Americans as a way to characterize individual choice as manifestations of inviolable identity, which mass culture threatened to "alienate." While alienation in the economic sense during the nineteenth century referred to the effects of capitalism on the relationship between a worker and work, in the romance of the *outsider*, as Hale uses the term, alienation threatened an indelible inner uniqueness that struggled to actualize itself in the world, and thereby to achieve individual "authenticity." As C. Wright Mills put it in *White Collar: The American Middle Classes* (1951), "[n]ow there are no centers of firm and uniform identification. Political alienation and spiritual homelessness are widespread."[90] Applied in this way, the romance of the outsider by the 1950s fed popular forms of psychology, literature, media, and fashion, since flourishing meant finding one's inner-self manifest in the community, or conversely, *against* the community when it demanded sublimation of the authentic self.[91]

While the theories of Sigmund Freud shaped highbrow notions of human nature during the early twentieth century, by the 1950s, a simplistic understanding of Freud began to shape popular culture: repression caused anxiety, conformity was a form of repression, and therefore, liberation from enforced conformity proved curative. The psychologist Robert Lindner, for example, who found a popular audience with his writings on juvenile delinquency, argued in *Prescription for Rebellion* (1952) that signs of social deviancy in modern America were neurotic manifestations of a repressive conformist culture. In fact, according to Lindner, the idea of "social adjustment," which he called "the lie that binds," promised "happiness," but ultimately proved to be "malicious," "biologically false," and a "psychologically harmful" stance that ultimately "disarms mankind."[92] According to one review of the book, "Lindner rides to death the rather popular contemporary thought . . . that to conform is to lose one's individuality, one's birthright to rebel."[93] The title of an earlier work by Lindner, *Rebel Without a Cause: The Hypnoanalysis of a Criminal Psychopath* (1944), proved inspirational for the later film of teenage angst. Lindner's *Must You Conform?* (1956) offered a question with an obvious answer.

Postwar ideas of self-actualization through rebellion also entered the public consciousness through popular media. Holden Caulfield, the prep-school exile who negotiated a New York City full of "phonies" in J. D. Salinger's *The Catcher in the Rye* (1951), seemed to be a unlikely hero at first, but Salinger's book became a best-seller soon after its release.[94] Sloan Wilson's Tom Rath, an adulterous, money-obsessed, psychologically scarred, suburban-dwelling veteran played the role of one of Caulfield's elite phonies in *The Man in the Gray Flannel Suit* (1956) and wonders, "if it were legitimate to wish on a painted star," as he passes through Grand Central Station, only to conclude "it would be all right to make a phony wish, so he wished he could make a million dollars."[95] Thus, Caulfield and Rath respectively echoed the exiled and cynical elite characters of Masters's Spoon River, displaying a return of the anxiety over whether received opinion proved hollow and a materialistic outlook proved to be the only realistic one. Popular nonfiction echoed these themes. David Riesman's *The Lonely Crowd: A Study of the Changing American Character* (1950) claimed alienation was produced by modern bureaucracies that transformed "inner directed" Victorians into "other directed" social climbers, where "manipulation" of others became the means to success and personal integrity proved malleable to ambition.[96]

While intellectuals like C. Wright Mills, David Riesman, and Robert Lindner hoped that their writing would prove a counterforce to mass culture, Hollywood dramas of fulfillment-through-rebellion filled the space that theories about alienation opened. In this regard, the idea of a self-contained municipality, a small town or suburb stuck in its ways, sometimes served as a proxy for mass culture, thereby providing a familiar narrative that took its cue from the tradition of the "village rebels." Two examples from mid-century embraced this romance of the outsider and applied it to varied locales: the film *All That Heaven Allows* (1955) tells the story of an affluent widow whose staid suburban life is turned upside down when she falls in love with her gardener; *Rebel Without a Cause* (1955) tracks a disaffected teen through Los Angeles as he struggles to define himself against parents, community, and peers.

In *All That Heaven Allows* (1955), Cary Scott sees her staid suburban life in Stoningham turned upside down when she falls in love with her gardener, Ron Kirby. Ron is an unaffected natural man, a flannel-shirt-wearing, short-on-words, strong-of-arm character, who hand-feeds deer on his country property and lives by the adage "to thine own heart be true." Ron has already converted one of his wealthy acquaintances, a former advertising executive who now reads *Walden*, to his unaffected lifestyle. And while the narrative of star-crossed lovers is an old one, *All That Heaven Allows* explores two divergent "lifestyles" as manifestations of mass culture's effect on individual identity. Cary's manicured suburban existence is exemplified by her lawn and garden, where Ron makes a living tending her trees. Not only is Cary ignorant of the types of trees and bushes she has in her yard, but also, at the beginning of the movie, she doesn't even know Ron's name.[97] In this way, Cary resides in her home without really knowing its details and rhythms and is thereby alienated from the life she lives. Cary is elite, but exiled and unfulfilled. Ron, on the other hand, owns a tree farm where he not only knows the trees he raises, but also cares for them himself, and uses them to actualize his will to commune with nature; here, then, is a populist-exile whose freely chosen lifestyle is a manifestation of his inner self. In this way, Ron and Cary represent the indelibility of the two kinds of exiles in Masters's Spoon River, those at peace and those unfulfilled. Ron represents a free spirit like Russian Sonia, who knows the underlying hypocrisies of received opinion. Cary, like Webster Ford and Herbert Marshall, pines for release. Within Ron's converted old-mill-cum-cottage, he regales Cary with his unassuming and fun-loving mode of living, easygoing friends, and hikes in the countryside. In this way, Ron is at one with his surroundings; his work, life, and personal philosophy are an integrated whole.

According to Salomé Aguilera Skvirsky, Ron's virtue derives from his rejection of the "consumerism of the country club set . . . *on principle*" through "freely chosen actions."[98] Ron, then, embraces his exile status; it is, in effect, self-made. Ron's simple flourishing and honesty to himself and others attracts Cary away from the empty pretentions of the suburb she inhabits. But when Cary agrees to marry Ron, she must overcome the disdain of her high-class friends and children and, through rebellion, fully become herself.

When she at first rejects Ron upon her children's urging, Cary begins to suffer severe headaches. Her children, representing the status quo in the film, try to soothe Cary's anguish by buying her a new television. In this way, according to Sharon Willis, *All That Heaven Allows* frames "the family's difficulties in the well-worn pop Freudian clichés of the period" about the soullessness of mass culture. In one scene, Cary's bereft image in the blank television screen characterizes her status for her children as a "useful ... image, and an image borrowed from the idealized repertoire of television."[99] However, Cary's doctor, who knows of Cary's affair with Ron and senses that Cary's ailment is existential rather than physical, gives her advice that Webster Ford might approve:

> there's nothing organically wrong with you, Cary. You're punishing yourself for running away from life. The headaches are nature's way of making a protest. You expect me to give you a prescription to cure life? If you loved him you'd go to him, in spite of the town, the children, and everything.[100]

When Cary finally turns her back on the suburb, her disapproving friends, and even her ambivalent children, she awakens Ron with a kiss and the promise that she is finally "home."[101]

Whereas Cary Scott seeks escape from the stultifying conformity of suburban life, teenage Jim Stark must overcome parents and peers; but like Cary, he must also to his own heart be true. Since its release, *Rebel Without a Cause* (1955) has served as a kind of ur-text for teenage rebellion in the twentieth century, where all the symbols of elite power stand opposed to a misunderstood and exiled group of young people.

Rebel Without a Cause pits Jim and his friends Plato and Judy against both mindless teenage toughs and parents who abandon them to the streets of Los Angeles. Jim, Plato, and Judy form an exile collective in the film, challenging their parents' emotional abuse and their peers' absurd rituals. Judy withstands her father's cruelty and rejects the gang's hierarchy by siding with troubled Jim. Plato, deserted by his elite parents and rejected by his peers, finds a surrogate family in Jim and Judy. Jim, played by James Dean, serves as the center of this rebel collective and achieves a kind of populist masculinity by overcoming his father's neutered deference to his mother and by winning at a tragic game of "chicken," where he and a rival, Buzz, race stolen cars toward a cliff's edge, resulting in Buzz's death.[102] According to Will Scheibel, Jim's iconic status as teen rebel derived from Dean's ability to pantomime exile with a "body [that] does not conform to the world around him, ... [whose] hesitant performance ... constantly calls attention to itself, oscillating between tough, cool composure and awkward, painfully insecure affectation."[103] Thus, Dean encoded the posture of young rebel masculinity onto the culture for the rest of the twentieth century.

Tragedy transforms this exile collective when the gang comes after Jim, and Plato retrieves his mother's gun to protect his friend, only to be killed by the police, making him a martyr to society's hypocrisy, stupidity, and self-righteousness. In the end, Jim introduces Judy to his parents in a feeble attempt to enact a middle-class ritual in the aftermath of Plato's death, ending the film with the realization that they cannot escape the debased world, but at least they can live with their exile bona fides intact. And they still have each other.[104]

Released a month after James Dean's death in a car wreck, *Rebel Without a Cause* established the actor as an icon for young male rebellion and a template for teen angst generally for much of the second half of the twentieth century.[105] *Life* magazine noted that Dean, a native of Indiana, was raised by guardians who were tolerant of his eccentricities. After high school, Dean moved permanently to California, thereby conflating art and reality in the popular conception of the actor, an exile from the heartland who personified the rebellion he portrayed.[106]

Films like *All That Heaven Allows* and *Rebel Without a Cause* reprised many of the literary ploys of Masters's *Spoon River Anthology*. All recruited the audience to the side of those who were on, but not of, Main Street, and showed them its sordid pettiness through the eyes of a rebel-exile. And like the exiles of Masters's Spoon River, these rebels touched upon larger economic and social injustices in only individual terms (and on racial injustice not at all), thereby making the moral hypocrisy of Cary's Stoningham and the oppressive norms of Jim's middle-class Los Angeles the product of individual ignorance and avarice, best countered by a wise few who served as the viewer's proxy. But unlike Masters's book, which provided no explicit moral system and whose exiles often suffered for their rejection of the status quo, these mid-century exiles achieved self-actualization through each other: Cary, a symbol of suburban alienation, moved in with Ron; Jim and Judy, symbols of teenage angst, ultimately found solace together, all contrary to the revelation of Spoon River's Herbert Marshall, whose love aspired to the stars, though they "want us not." Thus, these films hinted at the popular media's resolution to the "romance of the outsider." Both Ron and Cary and Jim and Judy overcame alienation through a fellow exile, a community of two, a happy ending that pointed toward a newly made familial, and perhaps even a home-owning, future. Masters's exiles either embraced or were broken by their status. Mid-century Hollywood, on the other hand, created a durable narrative that imagined alienation as a temporary phase, overcome with a soul mate who provided the means of self-actualization, and thereby perpetuated the myth of the ideal American household by making the exile part of its creation.

While the drama of elite, populist, and exile continued to shap
narratives at mid-century, the small town became increasingly
conceive of as the universal home against which to rebel. According
Johnson, in 1920, about 34 percent of Americans lived in rural cou
of those who did not live in small towns were likely only a generation or two
removed from them. However, starting in the 1930s, upward trends toward
urban and, later, suburban residency tracked a decline in rural populations as
a percentage of the population overall for the next forty years.[107] This decline
had its origins in long-term changes in the US economy from agricultural to
industrial production, supercharged by the Second World War, which moved
employment opportunities into cities, and, later, a shift to a service economy,
which ultimately hollowed out businesses on Main Street. Also after 1950,
small towns that were once a half-day's trip from a city when they were built,
themselves became increasingly suburbanized with the advent of the federal
highway system, fundamentally changing their character.[108] While some suburbs
sought to maintain the "small town" integrity of their downtowns, and a few
even went as far as Long Grove, Illinois, to maintain the illusion of a nineteenth-
century community, when suburbs expanded to surround small towns, they
transformed them in such a way that any illusion of municipal and economic
integrity could no longer be maintained.[109] By the 1970s, the rural population
of the United States hovered at around 16 percent of the total population. This
was a result not only of out-migration, but also the transformation of many small
towns on the outskirts of American cities into suburbs.[110] These trends, coupled
with a shift of population growth to sun-belt states, increasingly removed the
small Midwestern town from living memory for many Americans.[111]

Changes in the public discourse around race and social justice also made
the small town an untenable location to exorcise national anxieties. Towns like
Spoon River, Winesburg, and Gopher Prairie were almost completely devoid
of African American characters, as were most popular portrayals of small towns
in the decade after the Second World War, a time when formal and informal
rules of segregation upheld the illusion of small towns as representative of the
whole. But, by the late-1950s and early-1960s, new images of American towns,
real places like Little Rock and Greensboro, made the post-Victorian concerns
of Webster Ford and George Willard appear increasingly fey. The fraught years
between 1955 and 1970 of activism, legislative progress, urban riots, police
violence, and "long, hot summers" accentuated not only the sheer whiteness
of the myth of the American small town, but also, with its gloss of postwar
nostalgia, made it appear increasingly callow. While echoes of the nostalgia
and ambivalence mythology continued to feature in some American films—
for example, *In the Heat of the Night* (1967), about an African American police

officer from Philadelphia who investigates a murder in rural Mississippi,[112] or *The Last Picture Show* (1971), about a dying Texas town in the 1950s,[113]— small towns in late-twentieth-century portrayals appeared increasingly exotic, defined by their isolation and idiosyncrasies and no longer representative of the whole.[114]

A Secondary Life

During the twentieth century, poets continued to find inspiration in Masters's *Spoon River Anthology*. Sterling Brown's *The Last Ride of Wild Bill and Eleven Narrative Poems* (published posthumously in 1975) included parts of Brown's Slim Greer Sequence, where, in "Slim Greer in Hell," hell turned out to be Dixie, positioning Brown's character as a truth-teller who uncovers the sordidness underlying a seemingly respectable surface.[115] Melvin B. Tolson modeled his *A Gallery of Harlem Portraits* (published posthumously in 1980) on Masters's *Spoon River Anthology*, with each poem titled after the subject-character.[116] Greg Kuzma, according to Joanna Lloyd, experimented "with personae, with prose poetry, with place, and with evocations of pain" in "Nebraska" (1977) and *Village Journal* (1978).[117] Kuzma's "Lunch Break at Vien Dong" takes an exile's purview similar to Masters's: "As I sit and wait with my daughter/ my father comes and sits down in my body./ He is dead a year and a half, but he is on the move."[118] And, in George Saunders's *Lincoln in the Bardo* (2017), the dead speak to each other and the reader as they watch Lincoln mourn for his son. This, according to Michiko Kakutani, "creates a kind of portrait of an American community—not unlike the one in Edgar Lee Masters's . . . 'Spoon River Anthology.'"[119]

While writers of highbrow literature continued to find vitality in Masters's poetry, the setting of Masters's book congealed into an amusement park simulacrum for popular audiences during the late twentieth century. Places like Long Grove, Illinois, and Main Street, U.S.A. fostered this trend, giving an antique sheen to the idea of the Midwestern small town. This glossy image made simulacra of its residents as well, dressed in charming old clothes, going about their seemingly simple lives. Costumed types on Main Street in Disneyland, parasol in hand or straw hat on head, enforced this perception, as did the immaculate and charming buildings from the "1880s" in Long Grove, where visitors were invited to imagine themselves in placid olden times.

In the last third of the twentieth century, *Spoon River Anthology* increasingly came to be popularly perceived as a collection of poems from a distant time about a distant place. Nevertheless, the poetry of Edgar Lee Masters achieved a second life for popular audiences on the stage and in classrooms. During this period, *Spoon River Anthology* upheld the small-town simulacrum by explicitly situating itself in a Midwestern small town circa 1890, while, at the same time, undermining it by revealing desires, anxieties, fears, and foibles of a seemingly modern type, opposed to the nostalgic simulacra of Main Street, U.S.A. In this light, *Spoon River Anthology* in its late-century context implied that beneath vast historical differences, humans remained essentially the same. Even though Masters wrote historically on the cusp of modern American culture, where consumerism, psychological repression, and social alienation had already arisen as topics of anxiety among the middle class, to readers in the last third of the twentieth century, Spoon River's residents existed in a time and place that seemed very far away, yet exhibited concerns close to home, at odds with the contemporary simulacrum of the Midwestern small town of yesteryear. In this way, the dramas and dilemmas, little tragedies, and absurd revelations experienced by the citizens of Spoon River began to feel timeless.

Here, then, was a seeming psychological astuteness of Masters's work: characters who existed in a distant America nevertheless suffered fortune's slings and arrows in a way familiar to modern readers. *Spoon River Anthology* felt real in William Marion Reedy's terms, but doubly so, in spite of historical context, since the tribulations of Spoon River's ghosts offered the impression that even in America's distant past, people were like you and me.

This effect, however, was a result of the small-town simulacrum of the mid-twentieth century, which transformed the Midwestern small towns of the relatively recent past into charming landscapes of a timeless America. When readers recognized the contours of their lives in Masters's Spoon River, the jarring contrast between the simulacrum and familiar reality created the sensation that Masters had revealed timeless truths about people's lives.

While dramatic versions of *Spoon River Anthology* were produced before Masters's death, and radio versions of the poems were made in the 1930s,[120] one of the first national radio productions of the poems, "Epitaphs," appeared as part of the CBS Radio Workshop series in 1957. Produced with orchestral scoring by Wolfgang Franco and narration by William Conrad, later a star of the 1970s TV detective drama *Cannon*, this radio play claimed that Masters's book was "barely remembered today," but in its time, had opened contemporary authors' minds "to the vast dimensions . . . of our land and its people." Conrad compared writers like Lewis, Anderson, Hemingway, and Sandburg to the "quiet, bespectacled partner of Clarence Darrow" and dedicated the broadcast to a "new generation" who had likely not heard of the poet. This began a trend of rediscovering Edgar Lee Masters that continued throughout the second half of the twentieth century. While *Spoon River Anthology* had never been out of print, historicizing the poetry became part of a reconception of the book, from a truth-telling exposé in the terms of the 1920s to a kind of time capsule of a bygone America.[121]

The best-known theatrical adaptation of *Spoon River Anthology* was Charles Aidman's 1963 Broadway version. Aidman, a California actor (but a native Midwesterner), first produced his dramatic version at Theater West in Hollywood before bringing it to Broadway.[122] His adaptation of *Spoon River Anthology* is still likely the most reproduced, and its version of the book has had perhaps the greatest influence on the way Masters's poetry is collectively received. While the 1957 CBS radio production treated the book in pseudo-scholarly terms, with an authoritative-sounding narrator and an orchestral score that emulated the soundtracks of contemporary films, the Aidman version of *Spoon River Anthology* surrounded the poems in mid-century conceptions of American folk culture, relocating it in a kind of timeless American past, vaguely Midwestern, and, as drama, in kind with the play *Our Town*.

A preview piece of the Aidman adaptation that appeared in the *New York Times* in 1963 characterized the play as the fulfillment of Masters's "long . . . romance with the theater" and supported this contention with mention of his early play *Maximilian* (1902), as well as the poet's attempts to profit from screenplays during the 1930s.[123] Another review that year described Aidman's production as experimental and "offbeat," noting especially that the book was never meant to be performed. The reviewer also wondered if the poems "might have been the inspiration for . . . 'Our Town,'" and repeated Van Doren's argument that Sherwood Anderson, Sinclair Lewis, "and other historians of the prairie land" owed their inspiration to Masters.[124] In this sense, the review furthered the popular misconception that *Spoon River Anthology* was a rediscovered piece of literature, a lost inspiration of better-known works, and, lately, largely forgotten. Harold Taubman's review in the *New York Times* described Aidman's stage version as evoking the "sights, sounds and smells of a prairie town of half a century ago," with actors dressed "like country folk" in "homespun," creating "a brooding and loving American folk poem."[125] This reference to the book as a product of folk culture proved to be a legacy of Aidman's production, with its guitar-and-banjo score and folk songs that echoed the Americana revival of the early 1960s.[126] As the play was reproduced nationwide, it elicited similarly nostalgic reactions; it was "small-town Americana of another era,"[127] which portrayed an "America of innocence . . . before Vietnam, before Watergate." It was "Walt Whitman, Thornton Wilder, and the Reader's Digest" rolled into one, as "American as green apple pie and old cemeteries."[128] Over fifteen years after its first production, Aidman's *Spoon River Anthology* was still a play of "old folks tunes,"[129] "fiddle music and guitar playing and a square-dancing sequence," and "very real people from the 1890–1910 time frame."[130]

This is not to say that all productions of the Aidman adaptation of *Spoon River Anthology* were necessarily so nostalgic, but a review of newspapers in the fifteen-odd years after the play's Broadway production shows overwhelmingly that the popular dramatic version of the book ossified an image of Spoon River as an old-timey place with residents situated in a quaint setting. This was likely due to the folk music score and attendant homespun-and-string-tie costuming in these productions, which framed the poems in a way that was comfortably old-fashioned.

While the Aidman version of *Spoon River Anthology* continued to be performed throughout the late twentieth century, excerpts from the book increasingly became part of the high school literature curriculum. Since the 1950s, English educators had been sensitive to contemporary concerns about modern alienation and adolescent disaffection. Perhaps as importantly, literature teachers sought compelling readings for their charges, especially as their population of students expanded in the 1950s and 1960s. Through their lessons, the poems of *Spoon River Anthology* became canonized as not only "village revolt" literature, but also convenient representatives of the struggle between the individual who sought self-actualization and the society that prevented it. With the growth of publicly funded secondary education nationwide as a result of rising birth rates after the Second World War, poems from Masters's *Spoon River Anthology* formed part of a literature curriculum that treated literature as a means to student self-understanding through self-expression. In the high school classroom, Masters became a handy resource by which students could discover themselves.

Before the Second World War, American high schools served primarily in college preparatory or vocational capacities. However, after the Second World War, following trends that began in the 1930s, larger proportions of students remained in high school, a trend that continued with the rising population of baby-boomer students in the 1960s. After the Second World War, literature educators aimed their curricula at "fostering good living" since "scholarship for its own sake . . . proved extraneous to the single purpose of helping the student achieve a socially adequate and personally satisfying life in a democracy."[131] Accordingly, literature educators developed two responses to the ever-larger proportion of the population in their classrooms. First, they aimed literature education at "adolescent problems,"[132] namely by seeking works that spoke directly to a student's condition. But this pursuit of relevant literature came up against an English teacher's desire to introduce students to "great" literature at a time when an exposure to the literary canon was still considered an essential part of a literature curriculum. Edgar Lee Masters fit this second aim as well since, by the 1950s, the "revolt from the village" had become accepted as a discrete literary moment of the period between the wars. Likewise, Masters offered a relatively easy introduction to modern poetry, since his poems were written in free verse, without rhyme, marking them as "modern." But they were also more comprehensible and seemingly personal than works by poets like Ezra Pound, T. S. Eliot, and H. D. Also, educators sought to "focus on language and communication skills," which in the classroom translated into the recitation of poetry, an analysis of its meaning, and a public presentation of this analysis.[133] Later in the twentieth century, "communication skills" also came to mean the reproduction of a particular style of creative writing. In this regard, Edgar Lee Masters's poetry offered a handy opportunity for students to practice recitation, analysis, and, later, composition based on *Spoon River Anthology*'s epitaphs. Masters's poems were short, their language was relatively simple, their subjects were interesting, and the premise that their speakers wrote from the grave proved compelling to young people. One teacher in 1954 noticed that after a panel of students chose selections from *Spoon River Anthology* for a round of memorized recitation, one of her students took to carrying the book with him every day and reading it during study hall.[134]

Teachers who read Masters with their students asked their classes to interpret his poetry from the context of their own lives. This was an easy form of analysis for students new to literature since historical interpretation required background reading, and a closely read interpretation of style and structure required training that many students lacked, and teachers lacked the time to teach. In 1961, Mary Snouffer and Patricia Rinehart of Prince George's County, Maryland, found that Masters's poetry proved useful "for the reluctant" since many of their working-class students had little experience with poetry (less than a third had parents who had graduated from high school). According to Snouffer and Rinehart, "these boys lack[ed] 'social polish' . . . [and] had shown little awareness of or interest in community, state, or national problems. They and their peers enjoyed a social status peculiar to themselves." However, Masters's characters encouraged students to identify their "counterparts in real life, selecting national as well as local figures," which had to be "handled deftly by the teacher so that restraints did not dampen the fresh enthusiasm." Accordingly, "this activity revealed personal reactions not only to the poems but also to actual experiences," and according to one student "I would like to hear some more of *them* poems about people."[135] In 1968, Howard Decker, of Morton Township High School in Illinois, found that Masters's poems "fascinated most of my students and bored none." To capitalize on this interest, Decker "killed" his students in various ways (trampling in a fire, mysterious disease, and so forth) and asked them to write their own epitaphs. Decker's students treated the process as an exercise in self-revelation; they "seemed to draw from within themselves—to reveal their secrets and emotions. Almost every writer seemed to be saying: 'This represents me—not a cliché, not a phony front, but me!'" For Decker, Masters inspired student verse that exhibited "a touch of the vices and a liberal sprinkling of power and sincerity that so often lie dormant within the hearts and minds of adolescent writers."[136] In 1971, Lois Le Bloch, of Centennial High School in Champaign, Illinois, faced students who "lacked oral ability and dramatic experience" and were therefore "entirely normal and not yet up to *Hamlet*," but found in *Spoon River Anthology* a collection "perfectly suited to oral interpretation." However, Le Bloch's students found Masters's work compelling not for its "literary innovation," but because it offered "significant and timeless comment on the larger society." In this way, Le Bloch echoed many of the goals of literature teachers who sought to introduce "great" literature through an intimate connection to students' lives. Whereas Masters's work was a product of the history of the Midwest in the late nineteenth century and the poet's reflection upon this history in the early twentieth century, and its impact played out against changes in American intellectual sensibilities in the 1920s, his aspiration to create a microcosm of humanity worked with teachers' goals to offer literature that seemed timeless and, therefore, forever relevant. Masters's epitaphs traversed two generations, back to a time and place increasingly historical for readers, which nonetheless spoke intimately to the present about shared struggles. According to Le Bloch, students found themselves in Masters's characters, or tried on new identities for size,

> A boisterous member of each class picked drunken Deacon Taylor[,] while optimistic and attractive girls favored Lucinda Matlock and Anne Rutledge. Other students wanted to be unusual or difficult characters completely different from themselves (like the village atheist, Elsa Wertman, and "Indignation" Jones).[137]

In 1971, A. L. Reynolds of Rochelle Township High School in Illinois was inspired to teach *Spoon River Anthology* when he overheard students "commenting about the people and events that were taking place in their own town." Accordingly,

> [t]he poetry in *Spoon River* appeals to adolescents, especially those from small towns who know by experience many aspects of small-town life that can be seen in Masters's work. . . . Students frequently frown at sing-song rhymes about places that are remote from them; *Spoon River* is in free verse

... [and] presents common everyday problems of living that students can immediately apply to their lives.[138]

This was a common theme among teachers. Rosemary Adam of Claremont High School in Claremont, California, claimed, in 1981, "[m]y high school students really respond to this book of soap-opera-like situations. The characters never cease to surprise and delight."[139] When asked in 1985 to write epitaphs of relatives after reading *Spoon River Anthology*, Kristin Leedom of Alexandria, Virginia, noticed,

> One student confessed to feeling uneasy writing about his "Pop-Pop" and would not show the poem to his mother because he felt almost "sacrilegious." Another student chose not to have her poem included in the class anthology ... [because it] showed how she, the younger sister, felt she could not match the accomplishments of her older sister.

When students were asked to write their own epitaphs, a "quality of sadness," like Webster Ford's, appeared: "Many regretted letting their youth pass without taking time to enjoy life."[140] In 1989, Jo Buckner of Oak Hill Junior High in Morganton, North Carolina, noticed that her students enjoyed, like many of the dead of Spoon River, "telling all" from the grave.[141]

Within seventy-five years of the publication of *Spoon River Anthology*, Masters's work became a generally common feature in high school classrooms. A survey of forty-two popular high school anthologies undertaken by Arthur Appleby in 1990 showed that Masters appeared somewhat regularly in junior-year American literature surveys, less than Emily Dickinson, Robert Frost, Walt Whitman, Langston Hughes, and Gwendolyn Brooks, about the same as T. S. Eliot, and more frequently than W. H. Auden, Dylan Thomas, Ernest Hemingway, and Sherwood Anderson. Sinclair Lewis did not make the list.[142]

It appears at first difficult to historically account for Edgar Lee Masters's continued life as a poet in American high schools. While his contemporaries counted him as part of the "new movement" in poetry, critical hindsight often characterized him as a regional poet who, with a little luck and prodding from William Marion Reedy, caught an early wave of modernist verse in the middle of the second decade of the twentieth century. Anthologies are a peculiar medium, however, in which authors are chosen for what they represent or how they can be used to make a larger point, and Masters worked well in this regard. When teachers made lessons that included Edgar Lee Masters, they justified his place in the curriculum because his short epitaphs were a convenient introduction to modern poetry for recalcitrant students; their postmortem laments were interesting, and their style appeared easy to imitate for novice poets.

But educators also recognized that *Spoon River Anthology* invited students to meditate on their own lives. In this regard, another legacy of the book was its continuing power to make complex what was remembered in a superficial fashion. As the lived reality of small Midwestern towns disappeared from American popular memory, and the mythology of small towns grew increasingly facile, Masters's poetry in the hands of high school teachers and their students undermined saccharine and two-dimensional portrayals. William Marion Reedy celebrated *Spoon River Anthology* for exposing with "terrible truthfulness" the lives of its characters. Masters claimed that readers turned to him in their fatigue over "sentimentality and unreality." *Spoon River Anthology* frustrated easy communal memories of rural America with stories of moral hypocrisy, economic struggle, everyday fortitude, and the sense of being an exile in one's own community. Schoolteachers, then, and their students, preserved Masters's claim to present life in all its complexity in one fictional town.

Conclusion

It is tempting to think of history in terms of turning points. And while turning points are convenient for counterfactual bull sessions that pose the question, "What would have happened if . . . ?" professional historians are rightly suspicious of the idea. Change is complicated and legacies are messy.

I have tried to balance this book between treating *Spoon River Anthology* as a product of its time and arguing that it is of particular historical significance. On the one hand, *Spoon River Anthology* grew out of a disparate set of trends: the settlement patterns of the Midwest; the pioneering legacy and the myths around it; the political geography of Illinois, especially the central part of the state during and after the Civil War; the idea of the Midwest as the first truly American fruit of the frontier; the rise of the Populist Party; the influence of Populism on the Democratic Party between 1896 and 1908; the literary scene in Chicago during the ten years before and after 1900; *Reedy's Mirror* and *Poetry* magazine; Squire Davis, Lucinda, Emma, and Hardin Masters; and, ultimately, Masters's recollection of it all. *Spoon River Anthology* was more genealogical than revolutionary.

But Masters's contemporaries read in his book a turning point. Critics like William Marion Reedy, Harriet Monroe, Amy Lowell, and Ezra Pound claimed that Masters revealed a hitherto untreated literary subject: the American small town as microcosm, displaying all the pathos and comedy that human life had to offer. And while there were many authors before the twentieth century who used the Midwestern small town as a subject for literary treatment, Carl Van Doren's claim that *Spoon River Anthology* began a "revolt" against small-town life became part of the book's history and thereby shaped its future, since it proved compelling to critics, popular reviewers, and readers thereafter. After this so-called revolt was overtaken by new literary trends during the 1930s, there arose a conception of a canon of writers who, in hindsight, captured a moment when an older generation's bromides were questioned through representations of the American small-town. Thus, the small Midwestern municipality became a synecdoche for the modern nation, at least for a little while.

In this regard, the historian faces the dilemma of taking contemporaries at their word as a way to illuminate the context in which they wrote or using the power of hindsight to interrogate their claims. I have mostly chosen the former in this book and sought to explore Masters's historical context and the contemporaneous reception of *Spoon River Anthology*. While it is too much to say that films like *It's a Wonderful Life* and *The Best Years of Our Lives* owed their themes specifically to *Spoon River Anthology*, both drew from the same cultural spring that portrayed a quintessential American community in certain recognizable ways—as a series of single-family homes laid out along a grid pattern of straight streets, with a retail thoroughfare at its center, a Main Street; and residents who struggled with their individual desires and the mores of their community, who faced economic rapacity and moral hypocrisy, and, ultimately, achieved happiness, if they were lucky, within the confines of a place that could be anyplace. These portrayals owe their backdrop to the small towns founded in the Midwest in the nineteenth century. One hundred years later, the physical attributes of these towns, and a simplistic memory of their people, became a symbol for a bygone America.

But by the second half of the twentieth century, the small-town synecdoche for the national whole no longer held up. Demographic trends, new communities, and an expansion of what was popularly conceived of as "American" made a myth of the small town as either a microcosm or universal municipality increasingly untenable. Was America best represented by its cities, its suburbs, or its little towns? Was any particular location more American than another? By the latter half of the twentieth century, largely because of an expanded, and increasingly fractious, public discourse about who was a representative American, it became impossible to make a credible claim for any representative region, municipality, or identity.

But small towns did not disappear from popular portrayals in the late-twentieth century. Films like *Breaking Away* (1979), in which Dave, a high-school student and amateur cyclist in Bloomington, Indiana, fantasizes about

Italian cycling and, along with his working-class friends, beats the local university team in a bicycle race, echoed the populist sympathies of *Spoon River Anthology*. *Footloose* (1984), where Chicagoan Ren McCormack moves to rural Utah and teaches the town to appreciate rock music and dancing, challenged the efficacy of moral elites. Both portrayed small towns in ways that echoed the themes of Masters and the "rebels" against the staid conformity of Carl Van Doren's estimation, yet also promoted self-actualization-through-rebellion in a way that shows the extent to which the themes of movies like *All That Heaven Allows* continued to resonate. Likewise, *Back to the Future* (1985), in which teenager Marty McFly time-travels back to Hill Valley, California, in 1955 to save his mother and father from a local bully, revisited some of the themes of *Rebel Without a Cause*, with a fair dose of nostalgia and not nearly as much angst, and again raised up the exile, in this case, a high-schooler from the 1980s, in the face of peer oppression and parental moral shortcomings. *Heathers* (1988), a black comedy about an oppressive clique of high-school students, their rebellious friend, Veronica, and her psychopathic boyfriend, J.D., takes place in "Sherwood," Ohio, likely a nod to Sherwood Anderson and *Winesburg, Ohio*, and features a languid rebel who apes James Dean's style. But none of these films consciously established their small communities as necessarily microcosmic, in Masters's terms, or universal, in Lewis's. Instead, they foreshadowed two broad trends in the portrayal of small towns in popular culture that became increasingly defined at the millennium: small towns were either exotic or surreal.

Garrison Keillor's radio show, *A Prairie Home Companion* (1974–2016), represented one of the longest-running examples of the "exotic" Midwestern small town. Keillor's performances of folksy American music and his portrayal of Lake Wobegon, Minnesota, as a kind of timeless community of ironic and humorous residents echoed both the simulacrum of Disneyland, U.S.A. and Aidman's dramatic version of *Spoon River Anthology*. Tellingly, Keillor's show was initially rejected by NPR for national syndication. While in hindsight this might appear to have been a mistake considering the show's eventual popularity, NPR's president at the time, Frank Mankiewicz, feared that the way in which *A Prairie Home Companion* portrayed small towns might alienate rural residents and "cement our status as elitist" since the show seemed to condescend to small communities in its idealization of their timeless charm.[1] Likewise, films like *Fargo* (1996) and *Three Billboards Outside Ebbing, Missouri* (2017), incidentally both starring Frances McDormand, portrayed their respective communities in Minnesota and Missouri as insular and unusual, full of stereotypes of regional proclivities and accents. Each film revolves around a murder whose mystery is wrapped in the mores of the community where it takes place. In the case of Ethan and Joel Coen's *Fargo*, it is the supposedly overweening niceness of the upper Midwest; in Martin McDonagh's *Three Billboards*, it is the turgid conformity and latent violence of small towns in the lower Midwest. In both, Frances McDormand plays a populist-exile, not so unlike the populist exiles of *It's a Wonderful Life* and *The Best Years of Our Lives*, who marshals egalitarian righteousness to undercover a community's hidden crimes. At the same time, McDormand's characters in both films personify the eccentric quirks of each community—in the case of *Fargo*, a persistent Minnesota friendliness that veils a flinty determination, and in the case of *Three Billboards*, a hard-scrabble compulsion to seek justice in spite of a Missouri town's corrupt legal structures. Conversely, the narrative conceit of Bill Dubuque and Mark Williams's Netflix series *Ozark* (2017, 2018, 2020) about the Byrde family, Chicago suburbanites, who are forced to move to the Ozarks to launder money for a drug cartel, depends upon the juxtaposition between the suburban Byrdes and the colorful locals around them. While Masters's Spoon River included various grotesqueries, the poet's microcosm invited reflection from contemporary readers, who were expected to find someone familiar in the town. *Ozark,* instead, invites spectatorship from the audience and positions its viewers to be sympathetic with the Byrdes, urbane exiles, who are entertained or dismayed by the antics of the rural residents they encounter.

In the decades before and after the millennium, popular media also portrayed small towns as places where the surreal and freakish happened. David Lynch's television series *Twin Peaks* (1990), about a murder and demonic possession of a small town in the Pacific Northwest, and Gary Ross's *Pleasantville* (1998), about two siblings who are transported to a black-and-white 1950s television sit-com "Pleasantville" and colorize it as they teach the citizens about sex, modern art, and love, are examples of the surreal-small-town from late in the twentieth century. More recently, the popular Netflix series *Stranger Things* (2016, 2017, 2019), by Matt and Ross Duffer, portrays a nostalgic Hawkins, Indiana, whose affliction by a portal to a sinister alternate dimension and exploitation by a hidden government lab further situate the small town as a community with secrets; these just happen to come from another world. Nevertheless, the local exile, Joyce Byers, and the populist sheriff, Jim Hopper, as well as children who play truth-tellers in the face of local incredulity and elite conspiracy, mark the continued resonance of similar themes that shaped Masters's own characterization of rural life one hundred years before, but while Webster Ford's apparition on the Spoon River proved prophetic, the supernatural happenings in *Stranger Things* exemplify the town's difference from the rest of the country. HBO's series *The Outsider* (2020) repeats these themes almost in duplicate, where a supernatural "grief eater" inhabits the bodies of citizens in a rural Cherokee City, Georgia, and is hunted by a local investigator, Ralph Anderson, a populist character in flannel, and an African American investigator, Holly Gibney, a stranger in town, who first uncovers the underlying evil that afflicts Cherokee City.[2] In each example, the supernatural plays a key role in characterizing the small town; the exile's embrace or defeat of the supernatural drives the narrative to its conclusion.[3]

In these examples, the small town continues to play a role as a representative place in American popular mythology, though one that is distant from the lives of everyday Americans. By contrast, in the nineteenth century, in the face of middle-class anxiety about changes in American cities, the small town was a refuge for all that was abiding and good. In the early twentieth century, in the aftermath of the so-called closing of the frontier and the growth of the economic and social influence of the Midwest, the small town was imagined again as a representative, but contested, place, where conceptions of the traditional and the modern, the Victorian and the Freudian, struggled to lay claim to the reality of the place itself. By the early twenty-first century, the American small town was reimagined in a fashion that reflected contemporary anxieties, as a place where localism abided in an increasingly interconnected society, an insular place of charming peculiarities or backward notions, and sometimes a place where the supernatural emerged from the nearby woods, symbolically uniting media portrayals of retrograde superstitions in rural America with supernatural events. In each of these cases, while the small town was emphatically portrayed as elsewhere, it still represented a kind of core constituency, a portion of the nation that laid claim to national originality and an essential "Americanness," a kind of native tribe still living by traditional ways in the interior. This population was sometimes marshaled by politicians for their own ends, as seen by Barack Obama's comparison of Main Street and Wall Street in 2008, or, later, in appeals to make the nation "great again" that proved politically potent in the Midwest during the 2016 election. In this regard, the nostalgia and ambivalence that Americans felt toward small towns continued to resonate in new ways. Inevitably, the small town will continue to play a role in the nation's conception of itself, and, as in Masters's day, it will likely be a contested space between those who find in it a bulwark of tradition and those who see it as a roadblock to progress. But Edgar Lee Masters did not conceive his "rampant yokelisms" in these terms. Neither should we.

Spoon River Anthology's legacy lies neither in its resonance in the popular media during the mid-to-late twentieth century, nor in the newer versions of myth-making in the twenty-first century. Instead, the book's continued sale and its ongoing use in classrooms represents its abiding significance as a key piece of American literature. In fact, as the small town undergoes future mythological manifestations, *Spoon River Anthology*'s poignant portrayals of modern anxieties wrapped in a seemingly old-fashioned community will likely continue to surprise and engage. I have treated *Spoon River Anthology* like a historical subject, with origins that explain a moment of influence, and a dénouement that illuminates the ways in which times change. But *Spoon River Anthology*'s significance lies not only in its history but also in its enduring life as a book that people read.

Notes

Introduction

1. Thoreau, *Walden*, 118.

2. John Timberman Newcomb places Masters within a broader movement of early modernist poets who overcame a nadir in poetry reading in the United States through free verse, vernacular language, and an urban focus. However, as I note later, Masters was a generation older than most modernists and embedded in his poetry themes that reflected the difference. In this regard, though Masters borrowed elements of early modernist poetry and was embraced by poets and editors sympathetic to modernist verse, he does not neatly fit within Newcomb's characterization. See Newcomb, *How Did Poetry Survive?*

3. Herbert K. Russell notes that "*Spoon River Anthology* was reported to have sold 80,000 copies in its first year alone ... although Masters's own words indicate that this figure is too high," Russell, *Edgar Lee Masters*, 2.

4. Baym, *Norton Anthology of American Literature*, vii–xi.

5. James Engelhardt, email to author, March 7, 2017.

6. Russell, *Edgar Lee Masters*, 1.

7. "Virginian" and "Calvinism" are Masters's own terms. Masters, "The Genesis of Spoon River," 38–55.

8. Burgess, "Edgar Lee Masters," 71.

9. Burgess, "Ancestral Lore in *Spoon River Anthology*," 186.

10. Ibid., 204.

11. Burgess, "*Spoon River*," 348, 363.

12. John E. Hallwas, "Introduction," *Spoon River Anthology: An Annotated Edition* (Urbana: University of Illinois Press, 1992), 21, 27, 69.

13. Primeau, *Beyond Spoon River*, xi.

14. Russell, *Edgar Lee Masters*, 8.

15. Espada, "Through Me Many Long Dumb Voices," 52–58, 53.

16. From Eliot's "Whispers of Immortality." McCue, "T. S. Eliot, Edgar Lee Masters and Glorious France," 45–73, 52.

17. Scott Herring. "Spoon River Anthology's Heterosexual Heartland." *Literature Compass.* vol. 3, issue 3 (2006): 256–269.

18. VanWagenen, "Masters Vs. Lee Masters," 679–698, 680.

19. Avădanei, "Wilder Masters," 106–115, 106.

20. See Russell's entry on *Spoon River Anthology* in the *Dictionary of Midwestern Literature* vol. II (Bloomington: Indiana University Press, 2016), 813.

21. Barker and Sabin, *The Lasting of the Mohicans*, 5–14.

22. Meer, *Uncle Tom Mania*, 8.

23. Richards, *Life*, 300.

24. "We cannot only have a plan for Wall Street. We must also help Main Street." Sen. Barack Obama, "Obama Calls for Help on Main Street," September 19, 2008, *Associated Press.* https://www.youtube.com/watch?v=mAIxlK8EPA8. Accessed August 25, 2020.

25. The nod to Whitman here is intentional. Masters's exiles work much like Whitman's bard persona, whereby a knowledgeable eyewitness to the world serves as an authority for the reader.

Chapter 1. Origin Stories

1. See Williams, *The Country and the City*, 13–34. Williams traces this dichotomy back to Hesiod and, later, to the classical era: "Thus the contrast within Virgilian pastoral is between the pleasures of rural settlement and the threat of loss and eviction. This developed, in its turn, into a contrast already familiar from some earlier literature, in times of war and civil disturbance, when the peace of country life could be contrasted with the disturbance of war and civil war and the political chaos of the cities," 17. For the resonance of this tradition in the Midwest, see Barillas, *The Midwestern Pastoral*, especially 11–55.

2. For other examples of idyllic New England villages in the late-eighteenth and early-nineteenth centuries, see Herron, *The Small Town in American Literature*, 28–70.

3. Noah Webster, *An American Dictionary of the English Language* (New York: White & Sheffield, 1841), 906, 847, 148.

4. Burrows and Wallace, *Gotham*, 576.

5. Ibid., 638.

6. Halttunen, *Confidence Men and Painted Women*, 102.

7. Kasson, *Rudeness & Civility*, 174; Shamir, *Inexpressible Privacy*, 38.

8. Burrows and Wallace, *Gotham*, 726.

9. Gilfoyle, *City of Eros*, 92–113. Jewett's real name was Dorcas Doyen.

10. See Cohen, *The Murder of Helen Jewett.*

11. *Sentinel and Democrat [Untitled]*, from an article in the *Boston Statesman* summarizing an article in the *New York Sun.*

12. *The York Gazette*, "The Murder of Helen Jewett."

13. Patricia Cline Cohen, *The Murder of Helen Jewett*; Elliott Gorn, *The Manly Art: Bare-Knuckle Prize Fighting in America*, 28.

14. Cohen, *The Murder of Helen Jewett*, 335.

15. Quoted in Halttunen, *Confidence Men*, 2.

16. See Lippard, *The Quaker City*.

17. Wood, "'Build, Therefore, Your Own World,'" 32–50, 32.

18. Ibid., 46.

19. Wortham-Galvin, "The Fabrication of Place in America," 21–34, 24.

20. Lance Banning (paraphrasing Joyce Appleby) claims that Jefferson's notion of the agriculturalist as natural citizen was based on "the prospect of an expanding, improving, commercial mode of agriculture [which persuaded Jefferson] that the bulk of the American people could enjoy . . . unprecedented social and economic independence." See Lance Banning, "Jeffersonian Ideology Revisited: Liberal and Classical Ideas in the New American Republic," *William and Mary Quarterly*, vol. 43, no. 1 (Jan. 1986): 3–19, 14, 5.

21. Ralph Waldo Emerson, "A Historical Discourse: Delivered Before the Citizens of Concord, 12th September, 1835. On the Second Centennial Anniversary of the Incorporation of the Town" (Concord, MA: G. F. Bemis, 1835).

22. In the ten years between 1820 and 1830, Boston's population grew by nearly a third; see Peterson, *The City-State of Boston*, 175. By 1835, the textile production factories of Lowell, Massachusetts, which helped fuel the economic growth of Boston, had been in existence for fifteen years.

23. Cabot, *A Memoir of Ralph Waldo Emerson*, vol. I, 191.

24. Emerson, *The Complete Works*, vol. XI, 29–30.

25. Ibid., 37.

26. Ibid., 43.

27. Ibid.

28. Ibid., 47.

29. Ibid., 73.

30. Ibid., 75.

31. "Cultivators of the earth are the most valuable citizens. They are the most vigorous, the most independent, the most virtuous, and they are tied to their country, and wedded to its liberty." Letter to John Jay, August 23, 1795, Jefferson, *Memoir, Correspondence, and Miscellanies*, 291.

32. Ibid., 83.

33. See, for example, Demos, *A Little Commonwealth*; Boyer and Nissenbaum, *Salem Possessed*; Thatcher Ulrich, *A Midwife's Tale*.

34. Henry Wadsworth Longfellow's *The Courtship of Miles Standish* (1848) portrays the New England countryside of the past in similarly nostalgic terms.

35. Fuller, *Summer on the Lakes in 1843*, 37–39.

36. *Vermont Christian Messenger*. "New England Villages, &c."

37. "The Two Neighbors," *The Brooklyn Daily Eagle and Kings County Democrat*, March 25–26, 1847, pg. 1, cols. 1 and 2.

38. Ibid.

39. *Vermont Christian Messenger*, "New England Villages, &c."

40. Whitman called his students "clowns and country bumpkins[,] flat-heads ... coarse, brown-faced girls, dirty, ill-favoured young brats, with squalling throats and crude manners ... bog-trotters, with ... disgusting conceit." Arthur Golden, "Nine Early Whitman Letters, 1840–1841," *American Literature*, vol. 58, no. 3 (Oct. 1986): 348.

41. Walt Whitman, "Letters from a Travelling Bachelor." October 14, 1849. Jason Stacy, ed. *The Walt Whitman Archive.* https://whitmanarchive.org/published/periodical /journalism/tei/per.00297.html. Accessed September 11, 2016.

42. While Long Island inhabitants were diverse from its earliest days, eastern Long Island, where Whitman visited on this assignment, was generally believed to be still inhabited by the descendants of Puritan villagers who settled there in the 1650s. See Whitaker, *History of Southold, L.I.*, 25.

43. Williams in *The Country and the City* notes that the idea of a "golden age" of rural repose that shaped contemporary critiques of urban life had a long pedigree. See pages 35–46.

44. See "Sunday Dispatch," *Walt Whitman Archive.* https://whitmanarchive.org /published/periodical/journalism/tei/per.00353.html. Accessed September 17, 2019.

45. The Long Island rail line from Brooklyn to Greenport was completed in 1844. See Fischler, *Long Island Rail Road*, 17.

46. Walt Whitman, "New York Dissected." August 23, 1856. Jason Stacy, ed., *The Walt Whitman Archive.* Ed Folsom and Kenneth M. Price, gen, ed. http://www .whitmanarchive.org. Accessed September 18, 2016.

47. See Downing's plan for a "A Suburban Cottage for a Small Family," in *Cottage Residences*, 35–49.

48. French, "The Cemetery as Cultural Institution," 37–59, especially 48–49.

49. "For the Evening Post," *New York Evening Post*, March 17, 1842, pg. 2, col. 3.

50. Quoted in Shamir, *Inexpressible Privacy*, 189.

51. Ralph Waldo Emerson, *Emerson's Complete Works: Miscellanies* (Boston: Houghton Mifflin Company, 1883), 170.

52. Downing, *Rural Essays by A.J. Downing*, 124.

53. Ibid., 125.

54. Ibid., 127, 130.

55. Ibid., 128, 126.

56. Ibid., 129.

57. Shamir, *Inexpressible Privacy*, 178–179.

58. Thoreau, *Walden*, 90.

59. Shamir, *Inexpressible Privacy*, 97.

60. Warren, *History of the Harvard Law School*, 294.

61. Parker, "The Origin, Organization and Influence," 17.

62. Ibid., 23.

63. Ibid., 59.

64. Ibid.

65. Ibid., 62.

66. Ibid.

67. Ibid., 63.

68. Ibid., 65.

69. See Novick, *That Noble Dream*, 61–86.

70. Channing, "Town and Country Government" in *Johns Hopkins University Studies*, 7–8.

71. Ibid., 23.

72. Ibid., 32.

73. Ibid., 54.

74. According to Channing, "The argument that because a New England town and a Germanic village were each surrounded by a defensive wall, the one is descended from the other, proves too much. A similar line of argument would prove the origin of New England towns to be the Massai enclosure of Central Africa." Channing quoted in Novick, *That Noble Dream*, 88.

75. Channing, *A Short History of the United States*, 23–24, 31–33; *The United States of America, 1765–1865*, 37; and *A History of the United States vol. I 1000–1660*, 421, 427, 526–527.

76. Applegate, *The Most Famous Man in America*, 299.

77. Beecher, *Norwood*, 1.

78. Applegate, *The Most Famous Man in America*, 377.

79. Beecher, *Norwood*, 7.

80. Ibid., 8.

81. Twelbeck, "Eden Refound(ed)," 65–67.

82. Brown, *Meadow-Grass*, 1–18.

83. Jewett, *The Country of Pointed Firs*, 2.

84. Deland, *Old Chester Tales*, 3.

Chapter 2. The Premodern Midwest

1. Venable, *Beginnings of Literary Culture in the Ohio Valley*, 436. Gallagher was a booster for Midwestern literature throughout his career and advocated their publication in periodicals. See Gallagher, "A Periodical Literature for the West."

2. *Louisville Daily Courier*, "New Song for the West." For information on Peters and Webster, publisher of Gallagher's poem and accompanying sheet music, see Osborne, *Music in Ohio*, 512. For dedication of the poem to the descendants of Israel Ludlow, see Garrard, *Memoir of Charlette Chambers*, 57.

3. *Times-Picayune*, "Concert at the Washington Armory Hall."

4. *Louisville Daily Courier*, "New Song from the West."

5. *Brooklyn Daily Eagle*, "Fifty Years Ago," *Springfield Express*, October 9, 1847, pg. 1, col. 1.

6. *Joliet Signal*, "Fifty Years Ago." The *Signal* inaccurately ascribes the poem to "Br Wm. G. Gallagher."

7. For a discussion of Gallagher's attempt to portray the Midwest in literary terms distinct from the traditions of the East and of Europe, see Watts, *An American Colony*, 148–153. For a discussion over Midwestern anxiety over change in nineteenth- and

twentieth-century Midwestern authors like Hamlin Garland, Sinclair Lewis, and Edgar Lee Masters, see Barillas, *The Midwestern Pastoral*, 52.

8. Masters, *Across Spoon River*, 4.

9. Russell, *Edgar Lee Masters*, 13–14; Burgess, "The Maryland-Carolina Ancestry of Edgar Lee Masters," 53.

10. US Census, "Illinois," 1850, Table II, 713.

11. I draw much of the information in this section from Etcheson's *The Emerging Midwest*, 4.

12. Ibid., 5.

13. Finley, *The Autobiography of James B. Finley*.

14. "Butternut," coined for the means by which some individuals dyed their clothing, was a popular term for Upland Southerners in the Ohio River Valley and Lower Midwest throughout the nineteenth century. During the Civil War, it became a term of derision in Illinois for individuals who supported the Southern cause. See McPherson, *Battle Cry of Freedom*, 31. For a contemporary source, see "The Threat on the Polls," *Chicago Tribune*, November 8, 1864, pg. 2, col. 2.

15. Buck, *Illinois in 1818*, 58.

16. Abraham Lincoln's parents followed a similar route to central Illinois. See White, *Lincoln*, 20–40.

17. Davis, *Frontier Illinois*, 84 and 125. For a biography and history of one of these families and their chain migration settlement pattern, see Ostermeier, "Biography," *Borderlands*. https://whiteside.siue.edu/omeka/biography.html. Accessed May 5, 2017.

18. Davis, *Frontier Illinois*, 113.

19. See Etcheson, *Emerging Midwest*, 3.

20. Davis, *Frontier Illinois*, 93; also see Gregory H. Nobles (cited in Davis, 441), "Straight Lines and Stability: Mapping the Political Order of the Anglo-American Frontier," *Journal of American History*, June 1993, who argues that structured settlement was perceived as a bulwark against anarchy in the West, 34.

21. Buck, *Illinois in 1818*, 60, 84.

22. Dana, *Geographical Sketches of the Western Country*, 143.

23. Buck, *Illinois in 1818*, 60.

24. See Davis, *Frontier Illinois*, 220–234.

25. One marker of Southern influence was ongoing support for a slave economy among some Illinoisans. For example, enslavers who entered the state often reclassified enslaved African Americans as indentured servants whose contracts extended throughout their natural life. Also, in 1823, a failed referendum nearly revised the Illinois constitution to allow slavery in the state.

26. Davis, *Frontier Illinois*, 191.

27. The history of settler colonialism and the genocide of native peoples in the Midwest is most recently told in Ostler, *Surviving Genocide*.

28. Kryczka, "Captive Audiences," 10.

29. Davis, *Frontier Illinois*, 207.

30. Ibid., 234.

31. Cronon, *Nature's Metropolis*, 59.

32. Ibid., 60, 64.

33. Ibid., 67.

34. Ibid., 68–70.

35. Ibid., 68.

36. Cayton and Onuf, *The Midwest and the Nation*, 27.

37. See Campanella, *Lincoln in New Orleans*. A contemporary source cites Alton and Chicago as "convenient sites" for boat building, representing the importance of these two port towns, one on the Mississippi, the other on Lake Michigan, as early as 1837: Mitchell, *Illinois in 1837*, 59.

38. Davis, *Frontier Illinois*, 236–237. Davis analyzed advertisements for towns between 1835 and 1838 and found that access to timber, navigable water, and rich soil proved to be consistent selling points.

39. Masters, *Across Spoon River*, 66.

40. Davis, *Frontier Illinois*, 235.

41. In this regard, Davis quotes a contemporary source: "On rivers, and marshes, the western side is esteemed healthier than the eastern side; as the prevailing winds during the summer and autumn months are from the west." Oliver and Sabin, *Eight Months in Illinois: With Information to Emigrants*, (Detroit: Gale/Sabin Americana, 2012, originally published in 1843), quoted in Davis, *Frontier Illinois*, 459.

42. Davis, *Frontier Illinois*, 235.

43. Mitchell, *Illinois in 1837*, 116.

44. Ibid., 117.

45. Ibid., 124.

46. Ibid., 115–130.

47. Davis, *Frontier Illinois*, 236–238.

48. *The History of Menard and Mason Counties, Illinois*, 239.

49. Cayton and Onuf, *The Midwest and the Nation*, 44, 50–51.

50. Davis, *Frontier Illinois*, 237–238.

51. Perkins, *Border Life*, 60.

52. Ibid., 165.

53. Ibid., 168.

54. Mitchell, *Illinois in 1837*, 72. For a modern and balanced history of the so-called Black Hawk War and its dire effect on the Sauk, see Jung, *The Black Hawk War of 1832*, and Owens, *Mr. Jefferson's Hammer*.

55. Kryczka, "Captive Audiences."

56. Masters, *Across Spoon River*, 5.

57. Farnham, *Life in Prairie Land*, 269–274.

58. Ibid., 155–156.

59. Atherton, *Main Street on the Middle Border*, 65.

60. Henry Wadsworth Longfellow, "The Village Blacksmith," McGuffey, *McGuffey's Fifth Eclectic Reader*, 154–155.

61. Atherton, *Main Street on the Middle Border*, 67, 71.

62. Ibid., 72.

63. Miller and Ruggles, *The History of Menard and Mason Counties, Illinois*, ii.

64. Ibid., 747–748.

65. Ibid., 100.

66. Rowe, "The Republican Rhetoric," 672.

67. Heerman, "In a State of Slavery," 114–115.

68. Ibid., 118.

69. Ibid.,121.

70. Miller and Ruggles, *The History of Menard and Mason Counties, Illinois*, 737.

71. Ibid., 747.

72. Ibid., 808.

73. Ibid., 860.

74. Masters, *Across Spoon River*, 5.

75. Herbert K. Russell, introduction to Masters, *Lincoln: The Man*, xiv.

76. Masters, *Across Spoon River*, 56.

77. Kleen, "The Copperhead Threat in Illinois," 74.

78. Menard County was created out of Sangamon County in 1839. During the following presidential elections, the party who won in Menard County was: 1840, Whig; 1844, Whig; 1848, Whig; 1852, Democrat; 1856, Democrat; 1860, Democrat.

79. Masters, *Across Spoon River*, 21.

80. *Joliet Signal*, "The Presidential Proclamations."

81. *Salem Weekly Advocate*, "Untitled."

82. *Woodstock Sentinel*, "Martial Law Declared."

83. *Mattoon Gazette*, "The President on the War," and "Extract from a Speech of Robert Davis."

84. Christian, Montgomery, Clark, Cumberland, Jasper, and Crawford Counties. See Kleen, "The Copperhead Threat in Illinois." 77.

85. Sebastian, "A Divided State," 381–394, 381.

86. Historians debate whether antiwar Democrats actually formed a real and organized threat through conspiracies and secret societies like the Knights of the Golden Circle, or were, instead, beneficiaries of low Republican turnout in the off-year election of 1862 and victims of conspiracy theorizing and war hysteria. See Klement, *The Copperheads in the Middle West*, 134–169; Weber, *Copperheads*, 73–102; Neely Jr., *Lincoln and the Democrats*, 45–75.

87. Quoted in Bahde, "'Our Cause Is a Common One,'" 75.

88. *Mattoon Gazette*, "Copperhead and Butternut Pins."

89. *Mattoon Gazette*, "Review of Dr. A. L. Keller's Speech."

90. In this regard, the antidraft violence in Detroit in 1863 mirrored that of other cities, most prominently, New York City. See Kundinger, "Racial Rhetoric" and Cook, *Armies of the Streets*.

91. *Mattoon Independent Gazette*, "Copperfaces and Copperheads."

92. *Centralia Sentinel*, "How They Write."

93. Bahde, "'Our Cause Is a Common One,'" 76.

94. Ibid., 81.

95. *Mattoon Gazette*, "Billy Shot."

96. Kleen, "The Copperhead Threat in Illinois," 71–72.

97. Ibid., 88.

98. Masters, "The Genesis of Spoon River," 40–41.

99. Masters, *Across Spoon River*, 44.

100. Ibid., 24.

101. Russell, *Edgar Lee Masters*, 15.

102. Masters, *Across Spoon River*, 77.

103. Ibid., 80.

104. Frank Klement argued that Illinois Copperheads "justi[fied] their wartime views and activities" with a renewed critique of "Wall Street . . . the ascendancy of industrialism," and a claim to be the "disciples of Jeffersonianism"; see *The Copperheads in the Middle West*, 251. Ronald Formisano, however, argues that Klement's claim that Illinois agrarian politics grew from "Butternut Democracy" ignores the fact that most of the support for issues like the maintenance of Greenbacks came from central Illinois; see "The Concept of Agrarian Radicalism," 27. Whatever the case, Petersburg, Illinois, lies within the central Illinois zone that Formisano includes as the locus of "agrarian radicalism" in the 1870s, a region that also saw some of the greatest conflict between antiwar Democrats and Republicans between 1862 and 1864; see Sebastian, "A Divided State." See also Bahde, "'Our Cause Is a Common One'"; and Kleen, "The Copperhead Threat in Illinois."

105. Masters, *Lincoln: The Man*, 123, 232.

106. Sutton, "The Illinois Central," 281.

107. Cronon, *Nature's Metropolis*, 74.

108. See Wilentz, *Chants Democratic*, 193. For an argument about the ways in which Populism in the late-late-nineteenth century proved contrary to Jeffersonian ideals, see Goodwyn, *The Populist Moment*, 4.

109. Ibid., 4.

110. Michael Kazin notes that "Populists continued to assume, as did their Jeffersonian and Jacksonian forebears, that 'the plain people,' meant those with white skin and a tradition of owning property on the land or in a craft." Kazin, *The Populist Persuasion*, 41.

111. See Postel, *The Populist Vision*, for the most recent synthesis of Populism.

112. Dunning, ed., *The Farmers' Alliance History*, 323.

113. Peterson, *The Jefferson Image*, 257.

114. Davis, *A Political Revelation*, 111.

115. The Chicago Stock Exchange was created in 1882.

116. Masters, *The New Star Chamber*, 63.

117. Masters, *Across Spoon River*, 56.

118. Ibid., 10–11.

119. Ibid., 8, 45.

120. Ibid., 57, 10.

121. See, for example, Hooper, *Adventures of Captain Simon Suggs*. Among the "realists" of the late-nineteenth century, Ronald M. Grosh also lists George Washington Cable, Rebecca Harding Davis, John W. DeForest, Mary E. Wilkins Freeman, Sarah Orne Jewett,

David Ross Locke, Elizabeth Stewart Phelps, and Harriet Beecher Stowe. Grosh, "Early American Realism I," 132–144, 133.

122. Eggleston, *The Hoosier Schoolmaster*, 30.

123. Herron, *The Small Town in American Literature*, 203.

124. Quoted in Parrington, *Main Currents in American Thought I*, 289.

125. Grosh, "Early American Realism," 134. See also Jay Martin, *Harvest of Change in American Literature, 1865–1914* (New York: Prentice Hall, 1967).

126. Holman, *A Certain Slant of Light*, 51.

127. Howe, *The Story of a Country Town*, 1.

128. Weber, *The Midwestern Ascendancy*, 37.

129. Smith, *Virgin Land*, 245.

130. Fred Lewis Pattee, a professor of literature at Pennsylvania College in 1915, called Garland's book "the complete triumph of dialect and of local color." Pattee, *A History of American Literature since 1870*, 307.

131. For the connections between the literature of the Old Southwest and, later, the Midwest and Turner's thesis, see Smith, *Virgin Land*, 193–194, 250–260.

132. Garland, *Main-Travelled Roads*, 221.

133. Ibid., 235.

134. Ibid., 236.

135. Ibid., 263.

136. Ibid., 209.

137. Ibid., 214–215.

138. Bray, *Rediscoveries*, 74.

139. See Brown, "The Popular, The Populist, and the Populace," 89–110.

Chapter 3. Frontiers

1. Russell, *Edgar Lee Masters*, 31.

2. As quoted in ibid., 30.

3. Masters, *Across Spoon River*, 140.

4. Pacyga, *Chicago: A Biography*, 71.

5. Boston University, "Population History of Chicago from 1840–1990." http://physics.bu.edu/~redner/projects/population/cities/chicago.html. Accessed September 25, 2016.

6. Pacyga, *Chicago: A Biography*, 57–58.

7. Ibid., 71.

8. Olmstead quoted in Miller, *American Apocalypse*, 12.

9. Ibid., 12–13.

10. Ibid., 13.

11. Ibid., 18.

12. See Wilentz, *The Rise of American Democracy*, especially 413–423.

13. Pacyga, *Chicago: A Biography*, 196.

14. Ibid., 198–200.

15. "Red War," *Chicago Tribune*, July 26, 1877, Vol. XXXII, 1, col. 3.

16. See Green, *Death in the Haymarket* and Hirsch, *After the Strike*.

17. *Chicago Tribune*, "Uncle Sam Awards the World's Fair Prize."

18. Gustaitis, *Chicago's Greatest Year, 1893*, 15.

19. Burg, *Chicago's White City of 1893*, 83–84.

20. Masters, *Across Spoon River*, 163.

21. Russell, *Edgar Lee Masters*, 35–36.

22. George R. David, Dedication Address, 198.

23. *Chicago Tribune*, "Ready for the World." May 2, 1893, Vol. LII, No. 2, col. 1.

24. Quoted in Russell, *Edgar Lee Masters*, 36.

25. Ida Tarbell made similar claims for the power of the frontier in her biography of Abraham Lincoln, first published in serial in *McClure's Magazine* starting in 1894. *The Life of Abraham Lincoln*; for example, see 66–70.

26. Turner, "The Significance of the Frontier," 119–227.

27. Ibid.

28. Ibid.

29. Smith, *Virgin Land*, 252, 253.

30. *Chicago Tribune*, "Ready for the World."

31. McVey, "The Populist Movement," 144.

32. See McMath Jr., *American Populism*, 143–180.

33. Masters, *Across Spoon River*, 177.

34. Ibid., 178.

35. Ibid., 179.

36. Kazin, *A Godly Hero*, 55.

37. Masters, *Across Spoon River*, 209.

38. Ibid., 210.

39. Ibid., 212. See: Jason Stacy, "Popucrats: Producerist Populism and the Formation of Midwestern Political Identity in the 1890s," *The Making of the Midwest: Essays on the Formation of Midwestern Identity, 1787–1900*, Jon Lauck, ed. (Hastings, Nebraska: Hastings College Press, 2020).

40. Quoted in Russell, *Edgar Lee Masters*, 39.

41. Quoted in Ravitz, *Clarence Darrow*, 97.

42. Farrell, *Clarence Darrow*, 48.

43. See Morton, "A Victorian Tragedy."

44. Farrell, *Clarence Darrow*, 76–77.

45. Masters, *Across Spoon River*, 270–271.

46. *New York Times*, "Spoon River Poet Called Great," 7–8.

47. Russell, *Edgar Lee Masters*, 49.

48. *U.S. Ex Rel. Turner v. Williams* (1904), "Find Law." http://caselaw.findlaw.com/us-supreme-court/194/279.html. Accessed October 4, 2016.

49. Jefferson Club Jackson Day Banquet Program, Auditorium Hotel, Chicago, January 8, 1908, New York Public Library Digital Collections. https://digitalcollections.nypl.org/items/510d47db-8fc0-a3d9-e040-e00a18064a99#/?uuid=510d47db-8fc5-a3d9-e040-e00a18064a99. Accessed August 7, 2019.

50. Masters, *Across Spoon River*, 283.

51. Russell, *Edgar Lee Masters*, 34–45.

52. Duffey, *The Chicago Renaissance in American Letters*, 53–54. For a more recent history of the Chicago Renaissance, see Olson, *Chicago Renaissance*.

53. Duffey, *The Chicago Renaissance in American Letters*, 55–56.

54. Masters, *Across Spoon River*, 336.

55. Ibid., 337.

56. Duffey, *The Chicago Renaissance in American Letters*, 143.

57. Read, *I Remember*, 230.

58. Masters, *Across Spoon River*, 153.

59. Read, *I Remember*, 200–201.

60. The short-lived Flash Press of 1840–41 is a notable exception. See Timothy Gilfoyle, Patricia Cline Cohen, and Helen Lefkowitz Horowitz, *The Flash Press: Sporting Male Weeklies in the 1840s* (Chicago: University of Chicago Press, 2008).

61. For a lively portrayal of the libertine culture of Chicago writers during this period, see Kramer, *Chicago Renaissance*, especially 66–81 and 185–200.

62. Read, *I Remember*, 27–28.

63. Masters, "The Genesis of Spoon River," 45.

64. Burnham, "Introduction," *After Freud Left*, 3.

65. Ibid., "Transnationalizing," 26.

66. Duffey, *The Chicago Renaissance in American Letters*, 144.

67. Ross, "Freud and the Vicissitudes," 165.

68. Ibid., 166.

69. Woolf, "Mr. Bennett and Mrs. Brown," 2–3. George V ascended to the throne in May 1910.

70. Skues, "Clark Revisited," 70.

71. Bennett, "Is the Novel Decaying?" 4.

72. Hynes, "The Whole Contention," 34–44, 38.

73. Woolf, "Mr. Bennett and Mrs. Brown," 20.

74. Lewis, *The Cambridge Introduction to Modernism*, 61.

75. Woolf, *Granite and Rainbow*, 152.

76. Masters, *Across Spoon River*, 285.

77. Russell, *Edgar Lee Masters*, 59.

78. Masters, *The New Star Chamber*, 9.

79. Russell traces two of these plays, *Eileen* and *The Locket*, to Masters's unhappy love affair with Tennessee Mitchell, 59.

80. Masters, [pseudonym Dexter Wallace] "Ballade of Dead Republics," *The Blood of the Prophets* (Chicago: The Rooks Press, 1905), 99.

81. Ibid., 106.

82. Newcomb, *How Did Poetry Survive?*, 9.

83. Ibid., 19.

84. Putzel, *The Man in the Mirror*, 193.

85. Newcomb, *How Did Poetry Survive?*, 26.

86. Masters, *Across Spoon River*, 282.

87. Reedy, *The Law of Love*, 1, 136.

88. Putzel, *The Man in the Mirror*, 193.

89. Ibid., 159.

90. Ibid., 194.

91. Ibid., 195.

92. Masters, *Across Spoon River*, 325.

93. Hansen, *Midwest Portraits*, 246.

94. Mackail, *Select Epigrams from the Greek Anthology*, 4–5.

95. Putzel, *The Man in the Mirror*, 195.

96. Masters, *Across Spoon River*, 284.

97. Quoted in Russell, *Edgar Lee Masters*, 62.

98. Masters, *Across Spoon River*, 330–331.

99. Library of Congress, "Chronicling America." http://chroniclingamerica.loc.gov/lccn/sn83045487/. Accessed October 10, 2016.

100. Masters, *Across Spoon River*, 334.

101. Ibid., 336.

102. Ibid., 337.

103. Knapp, *Ezra Pound*, 35.

104. Pound, "A Few Don't by an Imagiste," 200.

105. Ibid., 205.

106. Flint, "Imagisme," *Poetry*, 198.

107. Masters, "For a Dance," *Reedy's Mirror*.

108. Quoted in Russell, *Edgar Lee Masters*, 67.

109. Masters, *Across Spoon River*, 339.

110. Masters, "The Genesis of Spoon River," 41.

111. *Chicago Tribune*, October 1, 1904, col. 2.

112. Quoted in Russell, *Edgar Lee Masters*, 67.

113. Masters, "The Genesis of Spoon River," 48–49.

114. Masters, "Future Poets."

115. Kennon, "Spoon River Cemetery."

116. Monroe, "Our Contemporaries," *Poetry*, 42–44.

117. Monroe, "Comments and Reviews," *Poetry*, 280. For a discussion on the publication of *Spoon River Anthology* from the perspective of *Poetry* magazine, see Williams, *Harriet Monroe and the Poetry Renaissance*, 111–112.

118. Masters, *Across Spoon River*, 345.

119. Kennon, "Bohemia—Dartmoor—Spoon River."

120. Reedy, "The Writer of Spoon River."

121. Ibid.

Chapter 4. Rampant Yokelisms

1. Masters, "The Genesis of Spoon River," 38–55.

2. Louis Untermeyer divided Masters's types differently, "In the first of these, we have the power of plain statement . . . ; the second and largest division has disillusion as its

motive; the third lifts both statement and disillusion to a plane of exaltation." While I agree that these traits broadly characterize the citizens of Spoon River, Masters's activist literature published only a few years before *Spoon River Anthology*, and his work as a labor lawyer throughout the period, incline me to divide his characters broadly by social classes—populist and elite—which nonetheless exhibit Untermeyer's characteristics, and "exiles," who offer the poet's perspective on the lives of Spoon River from an ironic remove. See Untermeyer, *American Poetry since 1900*, 120.

3. Or consider the Oracle of Delphi's prediction that King Croesus of the Lydians would "destroy a mighty empire" if he attacked the Persians, which ultimately turned out to be true since the king, upon attacking the Persians, ultimately caused the destruction of his kingdom. Herodotus, *The Histories of Herodotus*, 19.

4. Masters's reference here is to the myth of Daphne and Apollo. See Ovid, *The Metamorphoses*, 44.

5. "HERE my last words, and the most baffling,/ Here the frailest leaves of me, and yet my strongest-lasting,/ Here I shade down and hide my thoughts—I do not expose them,/ And yet they expose me more than all my other poems." Walt Whitman, "Calamus," *Leaves of Grass* [1860], 377, *The Walt Whitman Archive*, Gen. ed. Ed Folsom and Kenneth M. Price. http://www.whitmanarchive.org. Accessed May 28, 2020.

6. Masters, "The Genesis of Spoon River," 38–55.

7. Hallwas, "Masters and the Pioneers," 392.

8. Burgess, "Spoon River," 347–363; Hallwas, "Two Autobiographical Epitaphs," 28–36; Hurt, "The Sources of the Spoon," 403–431.

9. Masters, *Lincoln: The Man*, 495–496.

10. *The Walt Whitman Archive*, Gen. ed. Ed Folsom and Kenneth M. Price. http://www .whitmanarchive.org. Accessed May 14, 2020.

11. K. Narayana Chandran describes the exiles in Spoon River in similar terms, but frames them as rebels for a slightly different cause, "What distinguishes these [most disillusioned of voices] from those of their kinsmen is their passion and the dream: passion to preserve the sanctity of individual freedom and self-respect; the dream of a pastoral abode less vitiated by the factory machine and man-made systems of social and political oppression." Chandran, "Revolt from the Grave," 441.

12. Henderson, "Spoon River Anthology," 147.

13. Ross, "Freud and the Vicissitudes of Modernism," 165.

14. Ibid., 145.

Chapter 5. Reception

1. This initially put Bryan, as Wilson's Secretary of State, in a precarious political position, though he eventually supported the Federal Reserve System when it was placed under greater government control.

2. Masters, *Across Spoon River*, 325–326.

3. Ibid., 340.

4. Ibid., 344.

5. Masters was forty-six in 1914 compared with Stevens, who was thirty-five, Sassoon, who was twenty-eight, and Wattles, who was twenty-six.

6. Newcomb, *How Did Poetry Survive?*, 5.

7. Masters, *Across Spoon River*, 347.

8. Lowell, "In a Garden," 38.

9. Munich and Bradshaw, "Introduction," *Amy Lowell*, xi.

10. Ibid., xii.

11. Lowell, *Tendencies in Modern American Poetry*, 140.

12. Ibid., 142.

13. Ibid.

14. Ibid., 153.

15. Ibid., 158.

16. Ibid., 174, 182, 183.

17. Ibid., 176, 183.

18. Ibid., 177.

19. Pound, "Webster Ford," 11.

20. Brooks, *Letters and Leadership*, 15–16.

21. Ibid., 7.

22. Gilman, "The Book of the Month," 271.

23. Shanafelt, "Tubs, Archaic Decencies," 790. Shanafelt published twelve poems in *Poetry* magazine between 1913 and 1937 and appeared in *The New Poetry: An Anthology*, which was edited by Harriet Monroe and Alice Corbin Henderson and included prominent modernists like H. D., Amy Lowell, T. S. Eliot, and Edgar Lee Masters, among others. *The New Poetry* was published by Macmillan, the same company that published *Spoon River Anthology*.

24. Braithwaite, *Anthology of American Verse for 1915*, 241.

25. Dell, "A Winged Word," 320; Dell's letter was in response to a critique of his review in *The New Republic*, "Spoon River People," April 17, 1915.

26. Rittenhouse, "Poetry and Democracy," 142.

27. *New York Times*, "Spoon River Poet Called Great."

28. James, *The Proceeding of the First Annual Meeting*, 4.

29. *New York Times*, "Spoon River Poet Called Great."

30. Ibid.

31. *Evening Public Ledger*, "Spoon River Folks."

32. *Battleboro Daily Reformer*, "Spoon River Anthology. Edgar Lee Masters," June 15, 1915, 2, col. 4.

33. Chandran, "Revolt from the Grave," 445. Chandran also argues that "[i]n representing this revolt in poetic terms, there of course lurked the inevitable hazard of the *Anthology* teeming with the populist mumbo-jumbo, anachronistic appraisals of the past in the reformist jargon, and worse still, aspersions cast on the present and the living in the out-worn romantic idiom," 438.

34. Woolf, "Mr. Bennett and Mrs. Brown," 20.

35. Masters, "What Can Poetry Do?"

36. *Topeka Daily Capital*, "On Second Thought," June 3, 1915, 4, col. 4.

37. House was also elected mayor of Topeka in 1915.

38. *Salina Evening Journal*, "Out Here in Kansas."

39. *Republican Register*, "On Second Thought."

40. *Topeka Daily Capital*, "On Second Thought."

41. *New York Times*, "A Human Anthology of Spoon River."

42. *Guthrie Daily Leader*, "Spoon River Anthology."

43. *New York Times*, "A Year's Harvest in American Poetry."

44. *St. Louis Post-Dispatch*, "Spoon River Anthology."

45. *Press and Sun-Bulletin*, "The Spoon River Dead."

46. Russell, *Edgar Lee Masters*, 95.

47. *New-York Tribune*, "Hudson River Anthology."

48. *New-York Tribune*, "Subfluminal Anthology."

49. Likely Asafoetida.

50. *New-York Tribune*, "Anthracite Anthology."

51. *New-York Tribune*, "Fox Meadow Tennis Club Anthology." June 22, 1915, pg. 9, col. 1.

52. Russell, *Edgar Lee Masters*, 82.

53. Ibid.

54. Masters, "The Genesis of Spoon River," 33–55.

55. Masters, "Rain in My Heart," *Songs and Satires*, 31.

56. Masters, "The Cocked Hat," *Songs and Satires*, 10–12.

57. Masters, "The Altar," Reedy quoted in Russell, *Edgar Lee Masters*, 67.

58. Masters, "Helen of Troy," *Songs and Satires*, 70.

59. *St. Louis Post-Dispatch*, "New Books."

60. Zwaska, "Modernity Exposed," 12.

61. *New York Times*, "Songs and Satires by Mr. Masters."

62. *Los Angeles Times*, "Verse and Books of Fiction."

63. Quoted in Patterson, "The American Legacy of Prufrock," 68; also quoted in Russell, *Edgar Lee Masters*, 108.

64. Masters, *Across Spoon River*, 374.

Chapter 6. The Village Revolt

1. Van Doren, "Contemporary American Novelists," 407–412. Van Doren revisited this theme in "On Hating the Provinces," in *The Roving Critic* (Port Washington, NY, Kennikat Press, Inc., 1923). See also Brooks, *Letters and Leadership*.

2. Van Doren, "Contemporary American Novelists," 407.

3. Van Doren also included F. Scott Fitzgerald's *This Side of Paradise*.

4. Van Doren, "Contemporary American Novelists," 411.

5. Ibid., 407.

6. Needless to say, entire populations and regions were left out of the idea of a village revolt. Authors like Masters, Anderson, Lewis, Hale, and Dell, and propagators of the idea of a "revolt," like Van Doren, proved almost entirely blind to African Americans,

for example. In fact, the villages they supposedly revolted against reflected the rise of the "sun-down town" during the late-nineteenth and twentieth centuries. The wave of lynching in the Midwest during this period was almost entirely absent from these meditations on the indignities of small-town life. See Loewen, *Sundown Towns*, 90–116. See also Madison, *Lynching in the Heartland*; Pfeifer, *Lynching beyond Dixie*.

7. Weber, *The Midwestern Ascendancy in American Writing*, 105, 104.

8. A number of Anderson's stories had appeared previously as stand-alone short fiction in journals like *Masses* and *Seven Arts*. See ibid., 106.

9. Van Doren, "Contemporary American Novelists," 409. Russell Blankenship likewise claims that "[t]he only vestige of the frontier [in *Winesburg, Ohio*] . . . was a unified society held together by standardized thinking."

10. Sherwood Anderson, *Winesburg, Ohio Authoritative Text Background and Contexts, Criticism*, Charles E. Modlin, Ray Lewis White (New York: W. W. Norton & Co., 1996), 20–21. Original publication, 1919.

11. Ibid.

12. Ibid., 20.

13. Ibid., 22.

14. Ibid., 130–136. Ryan Poll offers a very useful interpretation of the ambivalent undertones to George Willard's departure in *Main Street and Empire: The Fictional Small Town in the Age of Globalization* (New Brunswick, NJ: Rutgers University Press, 2012), 44.

15. Ibid.

16. Gross, "In Another Country," 101–111, 105.

17. Quoted in ibid., 101–111, 103.

18. *Chicago Tribune*, "'Winesburg, Ohio,' [Huebsch]."

19. *Akron Beacon Journal*, "Sketches of Life in a Small Town."

20. *New York Times*, "Winesburg, Ohio."

21. *New York Herald*, "A Gutter Would Be Spoon River."

22. Jones, "'Winesburg, Ohio' Sundry Tales."

23. Van Doren, "Contemporary American Novelists," 411.

24. Dell, *Moon-Calf*, 30.

25. Ibid., 394.

26. Dell quoted in Broun, "Books."

27. Lewis rejected Van Doren's claim himself, especially that he was inspired by Masters. See Lingeman, *Sinclair Lewis*, 185.

28. Sinclair Lewis, *Main Street: The Story of Carol Kennicott* (New York: Harcourt, Brace, and Howe), 1920, v.

29. Poll, *Main Street and Empire*, 37.

30. Books like *Adventures of Huckleberry Finn*, notwithstanding. Twain's setting forty-odd years before the book's publication put its moral critique at a remove, though its skepticism of contemporary religious discourse proved poignant.

31. Sinclair Lewis, *Main Street* (Mineola, NY: Dover Publications, 1999), 6. Originally published in 1920.

32. Ibid., 29.

33. Ibid., 51.

34. Ibid., 152.

35. Lewis, according to James Shortridge, took "aim squarely at the values of the town aristocracy," a class that maintained the staid hypocrisies of Gopher Prairie and policed the borders of accepted decorum. Shortridge, *The Middle West*, 43–44.

36. Lewis, *Main Street*, 151.

37. Ibid., 116.

38. Ibid., 180.

39. Ibid., 400.

40. Van Doren, "Contemporary American Novelists," 410. See Hutchinson, *Rise of Sinclair Lewis, 1920–1930*, 9. For the impact of Lewis's *Main Street*, see Miller, *New World Coming*, 64, cited in Poll, *Main Street and Empire*, 38. *Main Street* was also chosen unanimously by a three-judge panel to receive the Pulitzer Prize in 1921, though the decision was ultimately overturned since the book was deemed undermining of the prize's "wholesomeness" requirement.

41. Neither Howe nor Gale fit easily into this trajectory, especially since both had published successful novels before Masters. Van Doren also discussed Fitzgerald's *This Side of Paradise* at the end of his review.

42. Shortridge also notes that "the initiation of a change from ebullient self-assurance to doubt and defensiveness can be dated rather precisely at 1920." *The Middle West*, 39.

43. White, "The Other Side of Main Street," 7–19.

44. *Emporia Gazette*, October 12, 1896, pg. 2, col. 2; *Emporia Gazette*, "History Repeated," 2–3.

45. White, *The Old Order Changeth*, 69.

46. White, *In Our Town*, 19. A reader of White's book scrawled in the margins "your [sic] a liar W" and crossed out "help him" and replaced it with "drag him down." While it is impossible to date this marginalia, White's portrayal of small-town ethics, and this reader's rejection of its claims, exemplifies the antipathy expressed by Van Doren's village rebels to a romanticized vision of small-town life. For White's fictional versions of the small Midwestern town as the ideal American community, see *The Court of Boyville* (1899), *A Certain Rich Man* (1909), and *In the Heart of a Fool* (1918).

47. White, "The Other Side of Main Street," 7. Vernon Louis Parrington best summarized White's conception of this mid-Victorian dream as "(1) A land of economic well-being, uncursed by poverty and unspoiled by wealth; (2) a land of 'folksiness'—the village a great family of neighborliness, friendliness, sympathy; (3) Primarily middle-class, and therefore characteristically American, wholesome, and human; (4) The home of American democracy, dominated by the spirit of equality, where men are measured by their native qualities." Parrington, *Main Currents in American Thought*, 373–374.

48. White, *In Our Town*, 332, 79, 81.

49. White, "The Other Side of Main Street," 8.

50. Ibid.

51. Ibid., 19.

52. Ibid.

53. Ibid., 18.

54. *Des Moines Register*, "Is Main Street, Iowa, a Place of Ugliness or Beauty?"

55. It is impossible here to thoroughly discuss the half-century of scholarship that interrogates the idea of a village revolt. The "Revolt from the Village" entry by Marcia Noe in *Dictionary of Midwestern Literature: Vol. II: Dimensions of Midwestern Literary Imagination* (Philip A Greasley, ed.) provides an excellent review of this scholarship.

56. Commager, *The American Mind*, 248.

57. I am indebted to Marcia Noe's interpretation of May's "innocent rebellion" here, from *Dictionary of Midwestern Literature*, Vol. II, 738.

58. Weber, *The Midwestern Ascendancy in American Writing*, 162.

59. Lauck, "The Myth of the Midwestern," 43. Also see Lauck's *From Warm Center to Ragged Edge*, 11–37, and Lasch, *The New Radicalism in America, 1889–1963*.

60. Anderson, "The Midwestern Town in Midwestern Fiction," 27–43.

61. In this regard, I am more concerned with how these works were received in light of intellectual trends in the third decade of the twentieth century. Admittedly, these were largely driven by influential critics, like Van Doren and H. L. Mencken, who were inclined to interpret Midwestern literature from a perspective that privileged an urbane perspective.

62. Chandran, "Revolt from the Grave," 439.

63. Hilfer, *The Revolt from the Village: 1915–1930*, 5. John Timberman Newcomb notes that topics of interest to poets and audiences shifted from the rural and romantic to the urban and modern between 1910 and 1925. According to Newcomb, these poems of "urban modernity" sought "meaning from the city's welter of discordant material, but not by effacing anxieties over emotional dispossession and social heterogeneity. Instead, they posit ironic forms of coherence built from the jagged contradictions of experience in the twentieth-century metropolis." While Masters's poems were set in a rural community, *Spoon River Anthology*'s sensitivity to irony and "jagged contradictions" appealed also to the readers of the avant-garde, urbane verse that Newcomb describes. See Newcomb, *How Did Poetry Survive?*, 147–179.

64. Hilfer, *The Revolt from the Village: 1915–1930*, 5.

65. Ibid.

66. It seems that *Spoon River Anthology*, at least in one instance, provided the means for this kind of revolt as well. One student at Grinnell, Marguerite Merryman, published a series of poems based on her hometown in the college's literary magazine *Junto* and was sued by her former teacher for $5000 in 1926. "Sues Student Writer: Former Teacher Objects to Amateur 'Spoon River Anthology' at Grinnell," *Lincoln Star Journal* (Lincoln, Nebraska), January 26, 1926, 1, col. 6.

67. Gross, "The Revolt That Wasn't," 5.

68. Noe, "Revolt from the Village," 741.

69. Gross, "The Revolt That Wasn't," 4–8, 5.

70. Skues, "Clark Revisited," 75–76.

71. Everdell, *The First Moderns*, 140.

72. Blankenship, *American Literature as an Expression*, 650, 672.

73. Parrington, *Main Currents in American Thought, vol. III*, 370.

74. Aiken, "Poet Aiken's Reply," 260.

75. Tietjens, *Turns and Moves and Other Tales*, 99–100.

76. Putzel, *The Man in the Mirror*, 33.

77. Lewis, *The Cambridge Introduction to Modernism*, 24.

78. Parrington, *Main Currents in American Thought, vol. III*, 401.

79. Lauck, "The Myth of the Midwestern Revolt," 44. Also see Lauck's *From Warm Center to Ragged Edge*, 11–37.

80. Nathan and Mencken, *The American Credo*, 10.

81. Lauck, "The Myth of the Midwestern Revolt," 45. Also see Lauck's *From Warm Center to Ragged Edge*, 11–37. Also see Lasch, *The New Radicalism in America, 1889–1963*.

82. David A. Hollinger, "Ethnic Diversity, Cosmopolitanism, and the Emergence of the American Liberal Intelligentsia," *American Quarterly*, vol. 27, no. 2 (May 1975), in Lauck, "The Myth of the Midwestern 'Revolt from the Village,'" 45.

83. Thorstein Veblen, "The Country Town," *The Freeman*, July 11, 1923, 417–420, and July 18, 1923, 440–443, quoted in Veblen, *Absentee Ownership and Business Enterprise in Recent Times*, 142–165. For a historical analysis of Veblen's arguments, see Atherton, "The Midwestern Country Town," 73–80.

84. Mead, *Coming of Age in Samoa*, 85–109. Also see Lauck, *From Warm Center to Ragged Edge*, 19.

85. May, "Shifting Perspectives on the 1920s," 405–427, 408.

86. Blankenship, *American Literature as an Expression*, 650.

87. Lewis Mumford as quoted in Dorman, *Revolt of the Provinces*, 6, 84–85. See Dorman on the regionalist overturning of the Tunerian thesis, 84–85. For Mumford, see *The Golden Day*. New York: Boni and Liveright, 1926, 107.

88. Hilfer, *The Revolt from the Village: 1915–1930*, 220.

89. Ibid., 244.

90. Ibid., 245.

91. Ibid., 67, 247.

92. Ibid., 245–246, 247.

93. Ibid., 247.

94. Thomas Halper and Douglas Muzzio note that during the 1930s and 1940s, cinematic portrayals such as *Boys Town* (1938), *Mr. Deeds Goes to Town* (1936), *Four Daughters* (1938), and the movie adaptation of *Our Town* (1940) offered similarly optimistic portrayals of the moral integrity of small-town life. *Fury* (1936), directed by Fritz Lang, offered a notable exception. See Halper and Muzzio, "It's a Wonderful Life," 1–21, 6–8.

95. Quoted in Weber, *The Midwestern Ascendancy in American Writing*, 160–161.

96. Thanks to Jon Lauck for drawing attention to this useful book in "The Myth of the Midwestern 'Revolt from the Village,'" 43.

97. Derleth, *Three Literary Men*, 13.

98. Ibid., 34.

99. Ibid., 36.

100. Ibid., 49.

101. Ibid., 40.

102. Derleth notes that Lewis rejected the term soon after Van Doren coined it. See ibid., 12–13.

103. Gross, "In Another Country," 111.

Chapter 7. Main Street, U.S.A.

1. Russell, *Edgar Lee Masters*, 260–261. Masters even wrote a second collection of epitaphs entitled *The New Spoon River* when the town had slowly been encroached upon by Chicago. Masters, *The New Spoon River*.

2. William Marion Reedy likely coined the term *epitaphy* in his editorial of 1914 where he revealed Masters's identity. Reedy, "The Writer of Spoon River."

3. Untermeyer, *American Poetry since 1900*, 123. Untermeyer continued, "[After 1915,] [m]onologue after tiresome monologue issued from him, he began to give erudite explanations of the metrical construction of his essentially casual lines, he came to distrust those critics who hailed his work as anything less than a *Comédie Humaine*. In short, he began to take himself and his art with pontifical seriousness."

4. Poll, *Main Street and Empire*, 46.

5. Ibid., 50–51.

6. Cohen, *A Consumers' Republic*, 292–295.

7. Hale, *A Nation of Outsiders*, 1.

8. Ibid., 51.

9. Kennedy, *Freedom from Fear*, 637.

10. May, *Homeward Bound*, 151.

11. Cohen, *A Consumers' Republic*, 122.

12. May, *Homeward Bound*, 151.

13. Cohen, *A Consumers' Republic*, 71.

14. Ibid., 22, 123–124. Cohen notes that Diners Club cards first appeared in 1949, soon followed by American Express, Bank of America, and Chase Manhattan cards in the next decade.

15. May, *Homeward Bound*, 60.

16. Lary May, *The Big Tomorrow*, 140.

17. Quoted in Elaine Tyler May, *Homeward Bound*, 51.

18. *Time Magazine*, "The American Mood," 19.

19. *Time Magazine*, "The Way Home," 17.

20. According to Robert Schultz, "[p]opular films, as other historical artifacts and documents, are created under specific historical conditions and they embody aspects of those conditions. In contrast to other culture texts, however popular films are created to make money from ticket sales to diverse audiences. To do so, they must speak to the social experiences and concerns of those audiences. The commercialism of film, then,

makes the medium a significant index of ideas extant in mass discourse, and the dominant ideologies encoded in popular films reveal large-scale social patterns." Schultz, "Celluloid History," 41–63, 43.

21. See Fay, "Democratic Film and the Aesthetics of Choice," 169–192; Culbert, "*The Best Years of Our Lives*," 227–253; Wineapple, "The Production of Character," 4–11; Valenti, "The Theological Rhetoric," 23–34; Sullivan, "Sentimental Hogwash?," 115–140; Costello, "The Pilgrimage and Progress of George Bailey America," 99, 31–52; Halper and Muzzio, "*It's a Wonderful Life*," 1–21.

22. Lary May traces this trend toward equating home ownership with rights to the advent of the idea of the "American Way," a process by which "grassroots reform and class conflict came to be stigmatized as unpatriotic. The result was that a republican nationalism that pervaded the nation for a hundred years was delegitimized. In its place, freedom was identified less with public life and an autonomous civic sphere than with a consumer culture identified with the rise of the 'white suburban home' undergirded by anxiety." May, *The Big Tomorrow*, 141.

23. Culbert, "*The Best Years of Our Lives*," 227–233, 227–228. The article supposedly read by Goldwyn's wife, as described by Culbert, was published in June 1944 but also sounds similar to "The Way Home," from the August 1944 issue of *Time* magazine.

24. Wyler, et al., *The Best Years of Our Lives*.

25. Fay, "Democratic Film and the Aesthetics of Choice," 178.

26. Wyler, et al., *The Best Years of Our Lives*.

27. Ibid.

28. Rose and Snowden, "The New Deal," 548–566, 549–550.

29. Wyler, et al., *The Best Years of Our Lives*.

30. Ibid.

31. Ibid.

32. *Boston Globe*, "Esquire Theater."

33. *Los Angeles Times*, "'Best Years' Applauded in New York."

34. *Pittsburgh Post-Gazette*, "The New Films."

35. For the shifting conceptions of women and work between the Second World War and the years immediately thereafter, see Elaine Tyler May, *Homeward Bound*, 56–62.

36. Culbert, "*The Best Years of Our Lives*," 229.

37. See *Mr. Deeds Goes to Town* (1936), *Mr. Smith Goes to Washington* (1939), and *Meet John Doe* (1941). Peter Valenti, "The Political Rhetoric of 'It's a Wonderful Life,'" 23–34, 23.

38. Capra et al., *It's a Wonderful Life*.

39. See, for example, the political cartoons "General Jackson Slaying the Many Headed Monster," from 1836, https://www.loc.gov/pictures/resource/cph.3a05364/, and "Commercial Might Versus Divine Right," from 1902, https://www.loc.gov/pictures/resource/ppmsca.25637/. Accessed September 13, 2019. The anachronism here placed Potter out of his times and therefore preserved Capra's film from accusations of purveying a leftwing critique of modern capitalism.

40. Wineapple, "The Production of Character," 5.

41. See, for example, Cheryl Thurber, "The Development of the Mammy Image and Mythology." *Southern Women: Histories and Identities*, Virginia Bernhard, Betty Brandon, Elizabeth Fox-Genovese, Theda Perdue, eds., (Columbia: University of Missouri Press, 1992).

42. Capra et al., *It's a Wonderful Life.*

43. Ibid.

44. Ibid.

45. Ibid.

46. Ibid.

47. Ibid.

48. Ibid.

49. Masters, "What Can Poetry Do for Our Republic?"

50. Capra et al., *It's a Wonderful Life.*

51. Ibid.

52. Halper and Muzzio, "*It's a Wonderful Life*," 3.

53. Poll, *Main Street and Empire*, 50.

54. Ibid., 49. Notably, Poll's argument here echoes Thorstein Veblen's uncovering of the acquisitive capitalism beneath the town's seeming comity, exemplifying the extent to which the ideology of the "village revolt" has come to shape received opinion, even nearly one hundred years after it appeared.

55. The dread of banks, of course, has a longer history before this period, stretching back to the 1830s. See, for example, Harry L. Watson, *Liberty and Power: The Politics of Jacksonian America*, (New York: Hill and Wang, 1990).

56. Sullivan, "Sentimental Hogwash?," 123.

57. Russell, *Edgar Lee Masters*, 354.

58. Ibid.

59. Ibid., 355, 357–359.

60. Cohen, *A Consumers' Republic*, 122–123.

61. James Patterson, *Grand Expectations: The United States, 1945–1975* (Oxford: Oxford University Press, 1996), 73.

62. "Don't Have the Wool Pulled!," *New York Daily News*, May 6, 1950, pg. 213.

63. "Drop the Gun, Louie," *New York Daily News*, May 13, 1950, pg. 229.

64. May, *Homeward Bound*, 54.

65. Alice Kessler-Harris, *In Pursuit of Equality: Women, Men, and the Quest for Economic Citizenship in 20th-Century America* (Oxford: Oxford University Press, 2001), 195–196.

66. Cohen, *A Consumers' Republic*, 269.

67. Medovoi, *Rebels*, 95.

68. See Sugrue, "Crabgrass-Roots Politics," 551–578.

69. Miller, "Family Togetherness and the Suburban Ideal," 393–418, 394.

70. See Cohen, *A Consumers' Republic*, 194–195.

71. Arcamone, Ward, and Spielvogel, *In the Suburbs*. See "In the Suburbs (1957)," https://building.youtube.com/watch?v=QFk5y5C82tk. Accessed August 28, 2019.

72. Ibid.

73. *Arlington Heights Herald*, "Long Grove Clings to 19th Century."

74. *Daily Herald* (Chicago, Illinois), Emma Keiler, "Long Grove Antique Shops."

75. Ibid.

76. Ibid., "Plan Board Head Resigns." Rachel Price similarly argues that "[t]he pastoral image of the village functions . . . as a kind of simulacrum, an ideal that still permeates the American cultural imagination." See "Beyond 'Main Street': Small Towns in Post-'Revolt' American Literature" (doctoral dissertation, University of Arkansas, 2016), i, 95.

77. See Jon Storbeck, "Windows on Main Street, U.S.A., at Disneyland Park," *Disney Parks Blog.* https://disneyparks.disney.go.com/blog/2014/03/windows-on-main-street-u-s-a-at-disneyland-park-sam-mckim/. Accessed August 29, 2019.

78. Francaviglia, "Main Street U.S.A.," 141–156, 145.

79. For a high-resolution image of McKim's 1958 map, see Caroline Chamberlain, "Disneyland's Evolution through Maps," KCRW, Santa Monica, CA. http://blogs.kcrw.com/dna/wp-content/uploads/2015/05/FunMap-1958i.jpg. Accessed May 28, 2020.

80. Each of these establishments is labeled on McKim's 1958 map.

81. Neuman, "Disneyland's Main Street," 83–97, 84.

82. *Brooklyn Daily*, Gladys M. Sullivan, "Vacation at Disneyland."

83. *Birmingham News*, "Leaving for Yesterdays and Tomorrows."

84. *Kossuth County Advance* (Algona, Iowa), "Disneyland Fascinating for Adults."

85. Julian Halevy, "Disneyland and Las Vegas," 510.

86. Ibid., 511.

87. Ibid.

88. Ibid., 513.

89. Hale, *A Nation of Outsiders*, 5.

90. Mills, *White Collar*, 332.

91. See Medovoi on "identitarianism" in the 1950s, Medovoi, *Rebels*, 49–51, specifically, 50.

92. Lindner, *Prescription for Rebellion*, 12–14.

93. "Book Notices," *Journal of Clinical Psychology*, vol. 9, no. 2, April 1953, 204–205, 204.

94. See Cohen, *A Consumers' Republic*, on J. D. Salinger's *Catcher in the Rye*, 13–34. Also see Medovoi, *Rebels*, 73–85.

95. Wilson, *The Man in the Grey Flannel Suit*, 77. Also see Hale, *A Nation of Outsiders*, 31.

96. Riesman, *The Lonely Crowd*, 133–186. Also see Hale, *A Nation of Outsiders*, 39.

97. Fenwick et al., *All That Heaven Allows*.

98. Skvirsky, "The Price of Heaven," 90–121, 95.

99. Willis, "The Politics of Disappointment," 131–175, 143.

100. Fenwick et al., *All That Heaven Allows*.

101. Ibid.

102. Ray, Stern, and Weisbar. *Rebel Without a Cause*.

103. Scheibel, "Rebel Masculinities of Star/Director/Text," 125–140, 130.

104. Ray, Stern, and Weisbar, *Rebel Without a Cause*.

105. The demographic category of a teenager is a relatively modern one. See Fasick, "On the 'Invention' of Adolescence," 6–23.

106. Scheibel, "Rebel Masculinities of Star/Director/Text," 131.

107. Johnson also notes two periods of population growth in rural counties 1970s and again in the 1990s, though the percentage of Americans living in rural co continued to decline overall as the population of the United States grew. John "Demographic Trends," 8. See https://scholars.unh.edu/cgi/viewcontent.cgi?art_cie =1004&context=carsey. Accessed May 28, 2020.

108. See, for example, the interactive map of the growth of Chicago suburbs at the online *Encyclopedia of Chicago*. http://www.encyclopedia.chicagohistory.org/pages/1756.html. Accessed September 13, 2019.

109. Incidentally, Masters's sequel to *Spoon River Anthology*, *The New Spoon River* (1923), portrayed a town under threat from encroachment by Chicago.

110. Johnson, "Demographic Trends," 8.

111. See Glaeser and Tobio, "The Rise of the Sunbelt." https://www.hks.harvard.edu /sites/default/files/centers/taubman/files/sunbelt.pdf. Accessed June 1, 2020. Glaeser and Tobio note that rising productivity, and the growth of housing after 1970, contributed to the population shift to the Sun Belt.

112. Based on John Ball's novel of the same name (1965).

113. Based on Larry McMurty's book of the same name (1966).

114. Consider examples where small towns were portrayed as increasingly cute or ominous but ultimately novel rather than universal: *Breaking Away* (1979), *Footloose* (1984), *Back to the Future* (1985), *Twin Peaks* (1990–1991), *Fargo* (1996), *Pleasantville* (1998), *Stranger Things* (2016).

115. Brown, *The Last Ride of Wild Bill*. See "Slim in Hell," 37–40. Brown recognized Masters's often overt racist statements when he said, "Just think for a minute, how the negroes excel,/ Can you beat them with a banjo or a broiling pan?" in *Toward the Gulf* (1918), and responded that this line was "hardly worthy of the poet of Spoon River." Quoted in Mark Jeffreys, "Irony without Condescension: Sterling A. Brown's Nod to Robert Frost," in Mishkin, ed., *Literary Influence and African-American Writers*, 2015, 212.

116. Tolson, *A Gallery of Harlem Portraits*.

117. Lloyd, "Nebraska: A Poem by Greg Kuzma," 361–363, 361.

118. Kuzma, "Lunch Break at Vien Dong," 405.

119. Kakutani, "Review: 'Lincoln in the Bardo.'" https://www.nytimes.com/2017/02/06 /books/review-george-saunders-lincoln-in-the-bardo.html. Accessed January 29, 2020.

120. For example, *Santa Ana Register*, "Homer Canfield's Radiolog"; *The Nebraska State Journal*, "Spotlight Features"; and *Courier-Journal*, "Behind the Microphone."

121. Froug, "Epitaphs (Spoon River Anthology)."

122. Aidman, *Spoon River Anthology*.

123. Richard Shepard, "Masters' Unfulfilled Romance with Theater to Be Realized," *New York Times*, September 27, 1963, pg. 19, col. 3–4.

124. *Daily News*, "Spoon River Anthology."

125. Howard Taubman, "The Theater, 'Spoon River Anthology'; Adaptation of Masters Portraits at Booth," *New York Times*, September 30, 1963, 23, col. 2–4.

126. For a history of the mid-century folk revival, see Cantwell, *When We Were Good,* especially 189–241.

127. *The Record,* "Masters Elegies in Deft Staging."

128. *Fort Lauderdale News,* "New Spoon River Anthology."

129. *The Herald,* "MCC Stages Epic."

130. *Great Falls Tribune,* "'Spoon River Anthology' Is After-Dessert Treat."

131. "Progressive Education Association, Commission on Second School Curriculum," quoted in Applebee, *Teaching and Reform in the Teaching of English,* 139.

132. Ibid., 139.

133. Ibid., 140.

134. Baloyan, "Enjoying Literature," 310.

135. Snouffer and Rinehart, "Poetry for the Reluctant," 44–46, 45–46.

136. Decker, "Poetry-Writing," 849–851, 850.

137. Lois E. Le Bloch, "A *Spoon River* Experience," *Illinois English Bulletin,* vol. 59, no. 1 (October 1971): 1–5.

138. Reynolds, "'Kyle Creek' and 'Spoon River Anthology,'" 5–16. This is likely Alfred Reynolds, who is listed in the 1971 Rochelle High School yearbook as an English Teacher.

139. Adam, "Our Readers Write?," 60–68, 66.

140. Leedom, "Writing Assignment of the Month," 6.

141. Buckner, "Explore Cultural Values!," 52–56, 53.

142. Applebee, "A Study of High School Literature Anthologies," 24. Emily Dickinson: 138; Robert Frost: 101; Walt Whitman: 64; Langston Hughes: 53; Gwendolyn Brooks: 34; T. S. Eliot: 29; Edgar Lee Masters: 28; W. H. Auden: 27; Dylan Thomas: 25; Ernest Hemingway: 15; Sherwood Anderson: 13.

Conclusion

1. See Cokie Roberts et al., 102.

2. In Stephen King's novel on which the series is based, Holly is a Lithuanian-American character.

3. William Barillas notes that there is a strain of the supernatural that runs from the talking dead in *Spoon River Anthology* to George Bailey's fantastical trip to a Bedford Falls without him and, from there, into the late twentieth century. According to Barillas, these include not only *Back to the Future* and *Pleasantville* but also "*Field of Dreams, Groundhog Day, Edward Scissorhands,* and *Peggy Sue Got Married.*" These examples, "deal with alienation and repression in small towns, and their narrative hinges on one magical transformation—dead baseball players showing up in Iowa or contemporary teenagers being pulled into a 1950s TV sitcom, for example—they stem, historically, from *It's a Wonderful Life* and thereby . . . *Spoon River [Anthology],*" note to Jason Stacy, April 13, 2020.

Bibliography

Primary Sources

Adam, Rosemary. "Our Readers Write: What Is a Sure-Fire Work of Literature for Non-Sure-Fire Students?" *The English Journal*, vol. 70, no. 1 (January 1981), 60–68.

Aidman, Charles. *Spoon River Anthology*. New York: Samuel French, 1966.

Aiken, Conrad. "Poet Aiken's Reply," *Reedy's Mirror*, 26 (April 13, 1917), 260.

Akron Beacon Journal. "Sketches of Life in a Small Town," June 14, 1919, pg. 4, col. 4–5.

Anderson, Sherwood, and Charles Baxter, eds. *Collected Stories*. New York: Library of America, 2012.

——. *Winesburg, Ohio Authoritative Text Background and Contexts, Criticism*. Charles E. Modlin, Ray Lewis White. New York: W. W. Norton & Co., 1996.

Arcamone, Carlo, Tracy Ward, and Bert Spielvogel. *In the Suburbs*. Chicago: *Redbook Magazine*, 1957.

Arlington Heights Herald (Arlington Heights, Illinois). "Long Grove Clings to 19th Century, Quaint Charm Kept Intact," August 2, 1962, pg. 18, cols. 1–5.

Baloyan, Mary. "Enjoying Literature More through Dynamic Groups," *The English Journal*, vol. 43, no. 6 (September 1954), 310.

The Battleboro Daily Reformer. "Spoon River Anthology. Edgar Lee Masters," June 15, 1915, pg. 2, col. 4.

Baym, Nina, ed. *The Norton Anthology of American Literature: American Literature between the Wars vol. D*. New York: W. W. Norton & Company, 2003.

Beecher, Henry Ward. *Norwood; or, Village Life in New England*. New York: Charles Scribner & Company, 1868.

Bennett, Arnold. "Is the Novel Decaying?" *The Register*, August 25, 1923.

Birkbeck, Morris. *Letters from Illinois, by Morris Birkbeck... Third Edition*. London: Taylor and Hessey, 1818.

Birmingham News. "Leaving for Yesterdays and Tomorrows," Lily May Caldwell, October 30, 1955, pg. 85, col. 1–2.

Blankenship, Russell. *American Literature as an Expression of the National Mind*. New York: Cooper Square Publishers, 1931.

Boston Globe. "Esquire Theater, 'The Best Years of Our Lives,'" December 26, 1946, pg. 2, col. 2–4.

Braithwaite, William Stanley. *Anthology of American Verse for 1915*. New York: Gomme & Marshall, 1915.

The Brooklyn Daily Eagle and Kings County Democrat. "Fifty Years Ago," August 20, 1847, pg. 1, col. 1.

———. "The Two Neighbors," March 25, 1847, pg. 2, cols. 1 and 2.

Brooks, Van Wyck. *Letters and Leadership*. New York: B. W. Huebsch, 1918.

———. "The Literary Life in America." *America's Coming-of-Age*. New York: B. W. Huebsch, 1915.

Brooklyn Daily. Gladys M. Sullivan, "Vacation at Disneyland," April 12, 1957, pg. 21, col. 1.

Broun, Heywood. "Books," *New-York Tribune*, November 12, 1920, pg. 10, cols. 7–8.

Brown, Alice. *Meadow-Grass: Tales of New England Life*. Boston: Copeland and Day, 1896, 1–18.

Brown, Henry, 1789–1849. *The History of Illinois, from Its First Discovery and Settlement, to the Present Time*. Neal A. Maxwell Institute for Religious Scholarship at Brigham Young University, 1844.

Brown, Sterling Allen. *The Last Ride of Wild Bill, and Eleven Narrative Poems*. Detroit: Broadside Press, 1975.

Buck, Solon Justus. *Illinois in 1818*. Springfield: The Illinois Centennial Commission, 1917.

Buckner, Jo. "Explore Cultural Values in Your Own Community through Literature!" *The Examined Life: Family, Community, and Work in American Literature*, Jim Wane Miller, Barry M. Buxton, eds. Boone, NC: Appalachian Consortium Press, 1989, 52–56.

Cabot, James Elliot. *A Memoir of Ralph Waldo Emerson, vol. I*. Boston: Houghton, Mifflin and Company, 1895.

Capra, Frank, et al. *It's a Wonderful Life*. Hollywood, California: Paramount Pictures, 2016. Original release 1946.

Centralia Sentinel. "How They Write: Patriots vs. Copperheads," July 9, 1863, pg. 1, col. 4.

Channing, Edward. *A History of the United States vol. I, 1000–1660*. New York: The Macmillan Company, 1906.

———. *A Short History of the United States for School Use*. New York: The Macmillan Company, 1908.

———. "Town and Country Government in the English Colonies of North America," *Johns Hopkins University Studies in Historical and Political Science*, Herbert B. Adams, ed. Baltimore, MD: N. Murray, 1884.

———. *The United States of America, 1765–1865*. New York: Macmillan and Co., 1896.

Chicago Tribune. "Epoch in Human Progress," May 2, 1893, vol. LII, no. 2, col. 1.

―――. Image, November 2, 1964, pg. 148, cols. 3–4.

―――. "A Little about the Movies in your Neighborhood." January 6, 1956. pg. 26, col. 1.

―――. "Ready for the World," May 2, 1893, vol. LII, no. 2, col. 1.

―――. "Reign of Terror," June 22, 1877, vol. XXXII, pg. 6, col. 2.

―――. "The Threat on the Polls," November 8, 1864, pg. 2, col. 2.

―――. "Uncle Sam Awards the Word's Fair Prize to the Fairest of All His Daughters," February 25, 1890, vol. L.

―――. "'Winesburg, Ohio,' [Huebsch]," June 8, 1919, pg. 53, col. 1.

Courier-Journal (Louisville, Kentucky). "Behind the Microphone," May 14, 1939, pg. 45, col. 4.

Daily Herald (Chicago, Illinois). Emma Keiler, "Long Grove Antique Shops Ready for Spring Season," March 5, 1959, pg. 57, cols. 1–2.

―――. (Chicago, Illinois), Emma Keiler, "Plan Board Head Resigns Over Park District Defeat," November 5, 1964, pg. 29, cols. 3–4.

Daily News (New York, New York). "'Spoon River Anthology,' Vivid, Offbeat Theatrical Experiment," September 20, 1963, pg. 26, cols. 1–3.

Dana, Edmund. *Geographical Sketches of the Western Country Designed for Emigrants and Settlers: Being the Result of Extensive Researches and Remarks.* Cincinnati: Looker, Reynolds & Co., 1819.

Darrow, Clarence, and S. T. Joshi, eds. *Closing Arguments: Clarence Darrow on Religion, Law, and Society.* Athens: Ohio University Press, 2005.

David, George R. Dedication Address. *World's Columbian Exposition Illustrated,* vol. II, no. 8 (October 1892).

Davis, James H. *A Political Revelation.* Dallas: The Advance Publishing Co., 1894.

Decker, Howard F. "Poetry-Writing: A 'Killing' Assignment." *The English Journal,* vol. 57, no. 6 (September 1968), 849–851.

Deland, Margaret. *Old Chester Tales.* New York: Harper and Brothers, 1898.

Dell, Floyd. *Moon-Calf.* New York: Alfred A. Knopf, 1920.

―――. "A Winged Word," *Poetry,* vol. 6, no. 6 (September 1915).

Des Moines Register. "Is Main Street, Iowa, a Place of Ugliness or Beauty?" August 21, 1921, pg. 30, cols. 1–6.

Downing, Andrew Jackson. *Cottage Residences: Or, A Series of Designs for Rural Cottages and Cottage Villas, and Their Gardens and Grounds.* New York: Wiley and Putnam, 1842.

―――. *Letters and Leadership.* B. W. Huebsch, 1918.

―――. *Rural Essays by A.J. Downing,* George William Curtis, ed. New York: Leavitt & Allen, 1853.

Dunning, N. A., ed. *The Farmers' Alliance History and Agricultural Digest.* Washington, DC: The Alliance Publishing Company, 1891.

Eggleston, Edward. *The Hoosier Schoolmaster: A Story of Backwoods Life in Indiana.* New York: Grosset and Dunlap, 1913.

Emerson, Ralph Waldo. *The Complete Works*, vol. XI. New York: Houghton, Mifflin and Company, 1904.

Emporia Gazette. "History Repeated," October 23, 1896, pg. 2, cols. 2–3.

Evening Public Ledger. "Spoon River Folks," May 18, 1915, pg. 8, col. 3.

Farnham, Eliza Woodson. *Life in Prairie Land*. New York: Harper & Brothers, Publishers, 1847.

Fenwick, Peg, et al. *All That Heaven Allows*. New York: Criterion Collection, 2001. Originally released in 1955.

Finley, James B. *The Autobiography of James B. Finley or, Pioneer Life in the West*, W. P. Strickland, ed. Cincinnati: R. P. Thompson, 1856.

Flint, Frank Stewart. "Imagisme," *Poetry: A Magazine of Verse*, vol. I, no. 6 (March 1913), 198–200.

Fort Lauderdale News (Fort Lauderdale, Florida). "New Spoon River Anthology Portrays America of Innocence," May 1, 1973, pg. 23, cols. 1–4.

Frederick, John T. "The First Person Plural," *The Midland*, vol. 1, no. 1 (January 1915).

French, Stanley. "The Cemetery as Cultural Institution: The Establishment of Mount Auburn and the 'Rural Cemetery' Movement," *American Quarterly*, vol. 26, no. 1 (March 1974), 37–59.

Froug, William. "Epitaphs (Spoon River Anthology)," *CBS Radio Workshop. The Theatre of the Mind: Original Radio Broadcasts*, Volume 5. Chicago: Dreamscape Media, 2016.

Fuller, Margaret. *Summer on the Lakes in 1843*. Boston: Charles C. Little and James Brown, 1844.

Gale, Zona. *Friendship Village*. New York: Macmillan, 1908.

———. *Miss Lulu Bett*. New York: D. Appleton and Co., 1920.

Gallagher, William. "A Periodical Literature for the West: What Has It Been? What Ought It to Be?" *Western Literary Journal and Monthly Review*, vol. 1, no. 1 (1844).

Garland, Hamlin. *Main-Travelled Roads*. Boston: The Arena Publishing Company, 1891.

Garrard, Lewis H. *Memoir of Charlotte Chambers*. Philadelphia: TE and PG Collins, 1856.

Gilman, Lawrence. "The Book of the Month: Moving-Picture Poetry," *The North American Review*, vol. 202, no. 2 (August 1915).

Great Falls Tribune (Great Falls, Montana). "'Spoon River Anthology' Is After-Dessert Treat of GFHS's Dinner-Theater Production This Week," October 21, 1979, pg. 57, cols. 1–4.

Guthrie Daily Leader. "Spoon River Anthology," September 30, 1915, pg. 4, col. 6.

Halevy, Julian. "Disneyland and Las Vegas," *The Nation*, June 7, 1958.

Hansen, Harry. *Midwest Portraits: A Book of Memories and Friendships*. New York: Harcourt, Brace, 1923.

Hatcher, Harlan. *Creating the Modern American Novel*. New York: Williams and Norgate, 1936.

Henderson, Alice Corbin. "Spoon River Anthology, by Edgar Lee Masters," *Poetry: A Magazine of Verse* (June 1915).

The Herald (Crystal Lake, Illinois). "MCC Stages Epic in Biographical Form," November 29, 1979, pg. 9, cols. 1–2.

Herodotus. *The Histories of Herodotus*, Book I, Henry Cary, trans. New York: D. Appleton and Company, 1904.

The History of Menard and Mason Counties, Illinois. Chicago: O. L. Baskin & Co. Historical Publishers, 1879.

Hooper, Johnson Hones. *Adventures of Captain Simon Suggs, Late of the Tallapossa Volunteers*. Philadelphia: T. P. Peterson, 1848.

Howe, E. W. *The Story of a Country Town*. Atchison, KS: Howe & Co., 1883, 1.

Illinois in 1837: A Sketch Descriptive of the Situation, Boundaries, Face of the Country. Philadelphia: S. Augustus Mitchell, 1837.

James, George Francis. *The Proceeding of the First Annual Meeting of the National Conference on University Extension*. Philadelphia: J. B. Lippincott Company, 1892.

Jefferson, Thomas. *Memoir, Correspondence, and Miscellanies, from the Papers of Thomas Jefferson, vol. I*. Thomas Jefferson Randolph, ed. Boston: Gray and Bowen, 1830.

Jewett, Sarah Orne. *The Country of Pointed Firs*. New York: Houghton Mifflin, 1896.

Joliet Signal. "Fifty Years Ago," December 14, 1847, pg. 1, col. 2.

———. "The Presidential Proclamations," September 30, 1862, pg. 3, col. 2.

Jones, Idwal. "'Winesburg, Ohio' Sundry Tales of an Ohio Small Town Life by Sherwood Anderson." *San Francisco Chronicle*. pg. 6, cols. 5–6.

Kelley, E. E. "Concerning Ed Howe." *Topeka Daily Capital*, January 22, 1921. pg. 4, col. 5.

Kennon, Harry B. "Spoon River Cemetery," *Reedy's Mirror*, July 3, 1914.

Kossuth County Advance (Algona, Iowa). "Disneyland Fascinating for Adults as well as Younger Generation," T. H. Chrischilles, March 5, 1957, pg. 35, cols. 1–3.

Kuzma, Greg. "Lunch Break at Vien Dong," *Midwest Quarterly*, vol. 52, issue 4 (Summer 2011), 405–407.

Lasch, Christopher. *The New Radicalism in America, 1889–1963: The Intellectual As a Social Type*. New York: Norton, 1986.

Le Bloch, Lois E. "A *Spoon River* Experience," *Illinois English Bulletin*, vol. 59, no. 1 (October 1971).

Leedom, Kristen P. "Writing Assignment of the Month," National Council of Teachers of English, vol. 2, no. 3 (January 1985).

Lewis, Sinclair. *Main Street*. Mineola, NY: Dover Publications, 1999, 6 (first published in 1920).

Lindner, Robert. *Prescription for Rebellion*. New York: Reinhart & Co., 1952.

Lippard, George. *The Quaker City: or The Monks of Monk Hall*, David Reynolds, ed. Amherst: The University of Massachusetts Press, 1995 (first published in 1844).

Los Angeles Times. "'Best Years' Applauded in New York," November 29, 1946, pg. 13, col. 1.

———. "Comment and Opinion," September 26, 1915, pg. 49, col. 4.

———. "Dramatic Tension High in 'Black Rock' Story." February 10, 1955, pg. 53, cols., 2–3.

———. "Verse and Books of Fiction: 'Songs and Satires,'" April 9, 1916, pg. 52, cols. 1–2.

———. "'Winesburg, Ohio,'" June 15, 1919, pg. 58, col. 1–3.

Louisville Daily Courier. "New Song for the West," June 11, 1846, pg. 2, col. 7.

Lowell, Amy. "In a Garden," *Des Imagistes: An Anthology*. New York: Albert and Charles Boni, 1914.

————. *Tendencies in Modern American Poetry*. New York: The Macmillan Company, 1917.

Mackail, J. W. *Select Epigrams from the Greek Anthology*. New York: Longmans, Green, and Co., 1911.

Masters, Edgar Lee. *Across Spoon River: An Autobiography*. Urbana: University of Illinois Press, 1936.

————. "Future Poets," *Reedy's Mirror*, June 19, 1914.

————. "The Genesis of Spoon River," *The American Mercury*, January 1933.

————. *Lincoln: The Man*. New York: Dodd, Mead & Company, 1931.

————. *The New Spoon River*. New York: Boni and Liveright, 1924.

————. *The New Star Chamber, and Other Essays*. Chicago: Hammersmark Pub. Co., 1904.

————. *Songs and Satires*. New York: Macmillan and Company, 1916.

————. *Spoon River Anthology: An Annotated Edition*. John Hallwas, ed. Urbana: University of Illinois Press, 1992.

————. "What Can Poetry Do for Our Republic?" *New-York Tribune*, June 13, 1915, pg. 22, col. 1–7.

————. *Whitman*. New York: Charles Scribner's Sons, 1937.

Mattoon Gazette. "Billy Shot," February 24, 1864, 2.

————. "Copperhead and Butternut Pins," April 4, 1863, pg. 2, col. 2.

————. "Extract from a Speech of Robert Davis, at Hickory Grove, Bond County, Illinois," pg. 2, col. 5.

————. "The President on the War," September 9, 1863, pg. 2, col. 3.

————. "Review of Dr. A. L. Keller's Speech Delivered Before a Meeting of Copperheads of Sullivan, Moultrie County, Ill., January 8th, 1863," March 14, 1863, pg. 1, col. 5.

Mattoon Independent Gazette. "Copperfaces and Copperheads: From the St. Paul Press," March 28, 1863, pg. 1, col. 4.

McGuffey, William Holmes. *McGuffey's Fifth Eclectic Reader*. New York: American Book Company, 1879.

McVey, Frank L. "The Populist Movement," *Economic Studies*, vol. I, no. 3 (August 1896).

Mead, Margaret. *Coming of Age in Samoa: A Psychological Study of Primitive Youth for Western Civilization*. New York: William Morrow Company, 1927.

Miller, R. D., and James M. Ruggles. *The History of Menard and Mason Counties, Illinois: Containing a History of the Counties—Their Cities and Towns, &C., Portraits of Early Settlers and Prominent Men, General Statistics, Map of Menard and Mason Counties, History of Illinois, Illustrated, History of the Northwest, Illustrated, Constitution of the United States, Miscellaneous Matters, &C., &C., &C*. Mt. Vernon, IN: Whippoorwill Publications, 2000.

Mills, C. Wright. *White Collar: The American Middle Classes*. Oxford: Oxford University Press, 1951.

Mitchell, S. Augustus. *Illinois in 1837; A Sketch Descriptive of the Situation . . . Agricultural Productions . . . Manufactures, &C. of the State of Illinois . . . Together with a Letter on the Cultivation of the Prairies, by the Hon. H. L. Ellsworth. To Which Are Annexed the Letters from a Rambler in the West. [By Samuel A. Mitchell. With a Map.]*. Philadelphia: S. A. Mitchell, 1837.

Monroe, Harriet. "Our Contemporaries," *Poetry: A Magazine of Verse*, vol. 5, no. 1 (October 1914).

Nathan, George Jean, and H. L. Mencken. *The American Credo: A Contribution toward the Interpretation of the National Mind.* New York: Alfred A Knopf, 1921.

Nebraska State Journal. "Spotlight Features," May 14, 1939, pg. 39, col. 3.

New York Evening Post. "For the Evening Post," March 17, 1842, pg. 2, col. 3.

New York Herald. "A Gutter Would Be Spoon River," June, 1, 1919, pg. 57, cols. 1–2.

New York Times. "A Human Anthology of Spoon River," July 18, 1915, pg. 65, cols. 1–4.

———. "Masters' Unfulfilled Romance with Theater to Be Realized," September 27, 1963, pg. 19, col. 3–4.

———. "Songs and Satires by Mr. Masters," May 1916, pg. 200, cols. 1–3.

———. "Spoon River Poet Called Great: Famous English Critic Lifts Edgar Lee Masters from Chicago Obscurity to the High Peak of Parnassus," April 5, 1915, pg. 7, col. 1.

———. "Winesburg, Ohio," May 31, 1919, pg. 12, col. 8.

———. "A Year's Harvest in American Poetry," November 28, 1915, pg. 68, col. 1–4.

New-York Tribune. "Anthracite Anthology," August 15, 1915, pg. 7, col. 1.

———. "Fox Meadow Tennis Club Anthology," June 22, 1915, pg. 9, col. 1.

———. "Hudson River Anthology," July 15, 1915, pg. 7, col. 1.

———. "Subfluminal Anthology," September 24, 1915, pg. 7, col. 1.

Novick, Peter. *That Noble Dream: The 'Objectivity Question' and the American Historical Profession.* Cambridge: Cambridge University Press, 1988.

Ostler, Jeffrey. *Surviving Genocide: Native Nations and the United States from the American Revolution to Bleeding Kansas.* New Haven, CT: Yale University Press, 2020.

Ovid. *The Metamorphoses,* vol. I, books I–Viii, Henry T. Riley, trans. Philadelphia: David McKay Publisher, 1899.

Packard, Vance. *The Hidden Persuaders.* New York: David McKay, 1957.

Parker, Joel. "The Origin, Organization and Influence of the Towns of New England," *Massachusetts Historical Society,* January, 1866.

Parrington, Vernon Louis. *Main Currents in American Thought.* New York: Harcourt, Brace and Company, 1927, 1930.

Partisan Review. "Our County and Our Culture," vol. 19, no. 3 (May–June 1952).

Pattee, Fred Lewis. *A History of American Literature Since 1870.* New York: Appleton-Century Company, 1915.

———. *The New American Literature, 1890–1930.* New York: The Century Co., 1930.

Pittsburgh Post-Gazette. "The New Films: 'Best Years of Our Lives' at Fulton; Senator Gets 'It's a Joke, Son,'" March 6, 1947, pg. 11, cols. 1–2.

Post-Standard (Syracuse, New York). "Suspense and Superb Acting in 'Bad Day at Black Rock,'" February 26, 1955, pg. 2, cols. 6–7.

Pound, Ezra. "A Few Don't by an Imagiste," *Poetry: A Magazine of Verse,* vol. I, no. 6 (March 1913).

———. "Webster Ford," *The Egoist,* vol. II, no. 1 (January 11, 1915).

Press and Sun-Bulletin (Binghamton, New York). "The Spoon River Dead Tell Their Life Stories," July 9, 1915, pg. 14, col. 1–2.

Ray, Nicholas, Stewart Stern, and David Weisbart. *Rebel Without a Cause.* Los Angeles: Warner Bros. Entertainment, 2005. Originally released in 1955.

Read, Opie. *I Remember, by Opie Read*. New York: R. R. Smith, 1930.

The Record (Hackensack, New Jersey). "Masters Elegies in Deft Staging," September 30, 1963, pg. 53, cols. 6–7.

Reedy, William Marion. *The Law of Love: Being Fantasies of Science and Sentiment Inked into English to Cheer up the Gloomsters*. East Aurora, New York: The Roycrofters, 1905.

———. "The Writer of Spoon River," *Reedy's Mirror*, November 30, 1914.

The Republican Register (Washington, Kansas). "On Second Thought," November 27, 1914, pg. 5, col. 2.

Reynolds, A. L. "'Kyle Creek' and 'Spoon River Anthology,'" *Illinois English Bulletin*, vol. 59, no. 1 (October 1971), 5–16.

Richards, Keith. *Life*. New York: Little, Brown, 2010.

Riesman, David. *The Lonely Crowd: A Study of the Changing American Character*. Garden City, NY: Doubleday & Company, 1950.

Rittenhouse, Jessie B. "Poetry and Democracy," *Bulletin of the American Library Association*, vol. 10, no. 4 (July 1916).

Salem Weekly Advocate. "Untitled," November 6, 1862, pg. 1, col. 2.

Salina Evening Journal (Selina, Kansas). "Out here in Kansas," July 10, 1914, pg. 4, col. 2.

Santa Ana Register (Santa Ana, California). "Homer Canfield's Radiolog," February 12, 1938, pg. 3, col.3.

Scanlan, Charles Martin. *Indian Massacre and Captivity of Hall Girls: Complete History of the Massacre of Sixteen Whites on Indian Creek, Near Ottawa, Ill., and Sylvia Hall and Rachel Hall As Captives in Illinois and Wisconsin During the Black Hawk War, 1832*. Bowie, MD: Heritage Books, 2002.

Sentinel and Democrat (Burlington, Vermont). "Untitled," April 22, 1836, pg. 2, col. 6.

Shanafelt, Clara. "Tubs, Archaic Decencies, and the 'Spoon River Anthology,'" *The North American Review*, vol. 202, no. 720 (November 1915).

Skvirsky, Salomé Aguilera. "The Price of Heaven: Remaking Politics in *All that Heaven Allows, Ali: Fear Eats the Soul,* and *Far from Heaven*." *Cinema Journal* 47, no. 3: 90–121.

Snouffer, Mary S., and Patricia Rinehart. "Poetry for the Reluctant," *The English Journal*, vol. 50, no. 1 (January 1961), 44–46.

St. Louis Post-Dispatch. "New Books for the Week at the Public Library," June 3, 1916, pg. 8, col. 2.

———. "Spoon River Anthology," June 12, 1915, pg. 5, col. 2.

Tarbell, Ida. *The Life of Abraham Lincoln*. New York: Lincoln Memorial Association, 1899.

Thoreau, Henry David. *Walden*. New York: Thomas Y. Crowell & Co, 1910.

Tietjens, Eunice. "*Turns and Moves and Other Tales in Verse* by Conrad Aiken," *Poetry Magazine*, November 1916, 99–101.

TIME Magazine. "The American Mood," vol. 44, no. 7 (August 14, 1944), 19.

———. "The Way Home," vol. 44, no. 6 (August 7, 1944), 17.

Times-Picayune. "Concert at the Washington Armory Hall," March 27, 1846, pg. 3, col. 2.

Tolson, Melvin B. *A Gallery of Harlem Portraits*. Columbia: University of Missouri Press, 1980.

Topeka Daily Capital (Topeka, Kansas). "On Second Thought," May 27, 1915, pg. 4, col. 3.
————. "On Second Thought," June 3, 1915, pg. 4, col. 4.
Turner, Frederick Jackson. "The Significance of the Frontier in American History," *The Annual Report of the American Historical Association* (1894), 119–227.
Twain, Mark. *Adventures of Huckleberry Finn*. New York: Dover Publications, Inc., 1994.
————. *The Man That Corrupted Hadleyburg and Other Stories*. Oxford: Oxford University Press, 1996.
Untermeyer, Louis. *American Poetry since 1900*. New York: Henry Holt and Company, 1923.
Van Doren, Carl. "Contemporary American Novelists: X. The Revolt from the Village: 1920," *The Nation*, vol. 113, no. 2936 (October 21, 1921), 407–412.
Veblen, Thorstein. *Absentee Ownership and Business Enterprise in Recent Times: The Case of America*. New York: B.W. Huebsch, 1923.
Venable, W. H. *Beginnings of Literary Culture in the Ohio Valley: Historical and Biographical Sketches*. Cincinnati: Robert Clarke & Co., 1891.
Vermont Christian Messenger. "New England Villages, &c," June 11, 1847, pg. 1, cols. 1–3.
Warren, Charles. *History of the Harvard Law School and of Early Legal Conditions in America*. New York: Lewis Publishing Company, 1908.
White, William Allen. *A Certain Rich Man*. New York: Macmillan Co., 1909.
————. *The Court of Boyville*. New York: Doubleday & McClure Co., 1899.
————. *In Our Town*. New York: McClure, Phillips & Co., 1906.
————. *In the Heart of a Fool*. New York: Macmillan Co., 1918.
————. *The Old Order Changeth: A View of American Democracy*. New York: Macmillan Company, 1910.
————. "The Other Side of Main Street." *Collier's Weekly*, July 30, 1921, 7–19.
Whitman, Walt. *Leaves of Grass, 1860: The 150th Anniversary Facsimile Edition*. Jason Stacy, ed. Iowa City: University of Iowa Press, 2009.
Wilkes, George. *The Life of Helen Jewett*, New York, 1849.
Williams, Raymond. *The Country and the City*. Oxford: Oxford University Press, 1975.
Wilson, Sloan. *The Man in the Grey Flannel Suit*. London: Cassell & Co. Ltd., 1956.
The Woodstock Sentinel. "Martial Law Declared," October 1, 1862, pg. 2, col. 1.
Woolf, Virginia. *Granite and Rainbow*. New York: Harcourt, Brace and Company, 1958.
————. "Mr. Bennett and Mrs. Brown." London: Tavistock Square, 1924.
Wyler, William, et al. *The Best Years of Our Lives*. Beverly Hills, CA: MGM Home Entertainment, 2004. Original release, 1946.
The York Gazette (York, PA). "The Murder of Helen Jewett," from an article in the *Boston Morning Post*, April 26, 1836, pg. 2, cols. 3 and 4.
Zwaska, Caesar. "Modernity Exposed—And Gone One Better." *The Little Review*, vol. III, no. 5 (August 1916).

Secondary Sources

Allswang, John M. *A House for All Peoples: Ethnic Politics in Chicago, 1890–1936*. Lexington: The University Press of Kentucky, 1971.

Anderson, David D. "The Midwestern Town in Midwestern Fiction." *MidAmerica 6* (1979): 27–43.

Applebee, Arthur. "A Study of High School Literature Anthologies." Albany, NY: Center for Learning and Teaching of Literature, 1990.

———. *Teaching and Reform in the Teaching of English: A History.* Urbana, IL: National Council of the Teachers of English, 1974.

Appleby, Joyce. *Inheriting the Revolution: The First Generation of Americans.* Cambridge, MA: The Balknap Press of Harvard University Press, 2000.

Applegate, Debby. *The Most Famous Man in America: The Biography of Henry Ward Beecher.* New York: Doubleday, 2008.

Atherton, Lewis E. *Main Street on the Middle Border.* Bloomington: Indiana University Press, 1954.

———. "The Midwestern Country Town: Myth and Reality," *Agricultural History,* vol. 26, no. 3 (July 1953), 73–80.

Avădanei, Dragoș. "Wilder Masters: Recollections of Departed Souls," *Journal of Romanian Literary Studies* 15 (2018): 106–115.

Bahde, Thomas. "'Our Cause Is a Common One': Home Guards, Union Leagues, and Republican Citizenship in Illinois, 1861–1863," *Civil War History,* 56:1 (2010).

Banning, Lance. *The Jeffersonian Persuasion: Evolution of a Party Ideology.* Ithaca: Cornell University Press, 1978.

Barillas, William. *The Midwestern Pastoral: Place and Landscape in Literature of the American Heartland.* Athens: Ohio University Press, 2006.

Barker, Martin, and Roger Sabin. *The Lasting of the Mohicans: History of An American Myth.* Jackson: University Press of Mississippi, 1995.

Barrett, James R. *Work and Community in the Jungle: Chicago's Packinghouse Workers, 1894–1922.* Urbana: University of Illinois Press, 1987.

Bender, Todd, et. al. *Modernism in Literature.* New York: Holt, Rinehart, and Winston, 1977.

Berman, Art. *Preface to Modernism.* Urbana: University of Illinois Press, 1994.

Bolotin, Norman, and Christine Laing. *The World's Columbian Exposition: The Chicago World's Fair of 1893.* Washington, DC: The Preservation Press, 1992.

Boyer, Paul S., and Stephen Nissenbaum. *Salem Possessed: The Social Origins of Witchcraft.* Cambridge, MA: Harvard University Press, 1974.

Bray, Robert. *Rediscoveries: Literature and Place in Illinois.* Urbana: University of Illinois Press, 2003.

Brown, Bill. "The Popular, The Populist, and the Populace: Locating Hamlin Garland in the Politics of Culture." *Arizona Quarterly,* vol. 50, no. 3 (Autumn 1994), 89–110.

Brown, Donna, and Stephen Nissenbaum. "Changing New England: 1865–1945," in Truettner, ed., *Picturing Old New England.* New Haven: Yale University Press, 1999.

Buechsel, Mark. *Sacred Land: Sherwood Anderson, Midwestern Modernism, and the Sacramental Vision of Nature.* Kent, OH: The Kent State University Press, 2014.

Burg, David. *Chicago's White City of 1893.* Lexington: University of Kentucky Press, 1976.

Burgess, Charles E. "Ancestral Lore in *Spoon River Anthology:* Fact and Fancy," *Papers on Language & Literature* (20) 185–204. (1984).

———. "Edgar Lee Masters: The Lawyer as Writer," *The Vision of this Land: Studies of Vachel Lindsay, Edgar Lee Masters, and Carl Sandburg,* John E. Hallwas and Dennis J. Reader, ed. McComb: Western Illinois University, 1976.

———. "The Maryland-Carolina Ancestry of Edgar Lee Masters," *The Great Lakes Review,* 2(8–9) 1982, 51–80.

———. "*Spoon River:* Politics and Poetry," *Papers on Language and Literature* (23:3) 347–363. (1987).

Burnham, John, ed. *After Freud Left: A Century of Psychoanalysis in America.* Chicago: The University of Chicago Press, 2012.

Burrows, Edwin, and Mike Wallace. *Gotham: A History of New York City to 1898.* Oxford: Oxford University Press, 1998.

Campanella, Richard. *Lincoln in New Orleans: The 1828–1831 Flatboat Voyages and their Place in History.* Lafayette: University of Louisiana at Lafayette Press, 2011.

Cantwell, Robert. *When We Were Good: The Folk Revival.* Cambridge, MA: Harvard University Press, 1996.

Cayton, Andrew R. L., and Susan E. Gray, eds. *The American Midwest: Essays on Regional History.* Bloomington: Indiana University Press, 2001.

Cayton, Andrew R. L., and Peter Onuf. *The Midwest and the Nation: Rethinking the History of an American Region.* Bloomington: Indiana University Press, 1990.

Chandran, K. Narayana. "Revolt from the Grave: Spoon River Anthology by Edgar Lee Masters." *Midwest Quarterly* 29.4 (Summer 1988): 438–447.

Cohen, Lizabeth. *A Consumers' Republic: The Politics of Mass Consumption in Postwar America.* New York: Alfred A. Knopf, 2003.

Cohen, Patricia Cline, Timothy Gilfoyle, and Helen Lefkowitz Horowitz. *The Flash Press: Sporting Male Weeklies in the 1840s.* Chicago: University of Chicago Press, 2008.

Cohen, Patricia Cline. *The Murder of Helen Jewett.* New York: Knopf Doubleday Publishing Group, 1998.

Commager Henry Steele. *The American Mind: An Interpretation of America.* New Haven: Yale University Press, 1950.

Cook, Adrian. *Armies of the Streets: The New York City Draft Riots of 1863.* Lexington: University Press of Kentucky, 2014.

Costello, Matthew. "The Pilgrimage and Progress of George Bailey: Puritanism, *It's a Wonderful Life,* and the Language of Community in America," *American Studies,* vol. 40, no. 3 (Fall 1999), 31–52.

Cronon, William. *Nature's Metropolis: Chicago and the Great West.* New York: W. W. Norton & Company, 1991.

Culbert, David. "*The Best Years of Our Lives:* Social Engineering and Friedhoffer's 'Populist' Score," *Historical Journal of Film, Radio and Television,* vol. 26, no. 2, 2006, 227–233.

Davis, James Edward. *Frontier Illinois*. Bloomington: Indiana University Press, 1998.

Davies, Richard O., Joseph A. Amato, and David R. Pichaske, eds. *A Place Called Home: Writings on the Midwestern Small Town*. St. Paul: Minnesota Historical Society, 2003.

Demos, John. *A Little Commonwealth: Family Life in Plymouth Colony*. New York: Oxford University Press, 1970.

Derleth, August. *Three Literary Men: A Memoir of Sinclair Lewis, Sherwood Anderson, Edgar Lee Masters*. New York: Candlelight Press, 1963.

Dorman, Robert L. *Revolt of the Provinces: The Regionalist Movement in America, 1920–1945*. Chapel Hill: University of North Carolina Press, 1993.

Duffey, Bernard. *The Chicago Renaissance in American Letters: A Critical History*. East Lansing: The Michigan State University Press, 1954.

Eksteins, Modris. *Rites of Spring: The Great War and the Birth of the Modern Age*. Boston: Houghton Mifflin Company, 1989.

Espada, Martín. "Through Me Many Long Dumb Voices: The Poet-Lawyer." *World Literature Today* 86, no. 6 (2012): 52–58.

Etcheson, Nicole. *The Emerging Midwest: Upland Southerners and the Political Culture of the Old Northwest, 1787–1861*. Bloomington: Indiana University Press, 1996.

Everdell, William R. *The First Moderns: Profiles in the Origins of Twentieth-Century Thought*. Chicago: The University of Chicago Press, 1997.

Farrell, John. *Clarence Darrow: Attorney for the Damned*. New York: Vintage Books, 2012.

Fasick, Frank A. "On the 'Invention' of Adolescence," *Journal of Early Adolescence*, vol. 14, no. 1 (1994): 6–23.

Fay, Jennifer. "Democratic Film and the Aesthetics of Choice," *German Life and Letters*, vol. 71, no. 2 (April 2018): 169–192.

Fischler, Stan. *Long Island Rail Road*. St. Paul, MN: Voyager Press, 2007.

Flanagan, John T. *Edgar Lee Masters: The Spoon River Poet and his Critics*. Metuchen, NJ: The Scarecrow Press, 1974.

Formisano, Ronald. "The Concept of Agrarian Radicalism," *Mid-America*, 52:1 (1970).

Francaviglia, Richard. "Main Street U.S.A.: A Comparison/Contrast of Streetscapes in Disneyland and Walt Disney World," *Journal of Popular Culture*, vol. 15, no. 1. (1981): 141–156.

Goist, Park Dixon. *From Main Street to State Street: Town, City and Community in America*. Port Washington, NY: Kennikat Press, 1977.

Goodwyn, Lawrence. *The Populist Moment: A Short History of the Agrarian Revolt in America*. Oxford: Oxford University Press, 1978.

Gorn, Elliott J. *The Manly Art: Bare-Knuckle Prize Fighting in America*. Ithaca, New York: Cornell University Press, 2010.

Gross, Barry. "In Another Country: The Revolt from the Village," *MidAmerica* 4 (1977): 101–111.

———. "The Revolt that Wasn't: The Legacies of Critical Myopia," *The CEA Critic, CEA Critic* 39.2 (January 1977): 4–8.

Halper, Thomas, and Douglas Muzzio. "*It's a Wonderful Life:* Representations of the Small Town in American Movies," *European Journal of American Studies,* vol. 6, no. 1 (Spring 2011), 1–21.

Herring, Scott. "Spoon River Anthology's Heterosexual Heartland," *Literature Compass,* vol. 3, issue 3 (2006): 256–269.

Hofstadter, Richard. *The Paranoid Style in American Politics and Other Essays.* New York, NY: Vintage Books, 1967.

Gilfoyle, Timothy. *City of Eros: New York City, Prostitution, and the Commercialization of Sex, 1790–1920.* New York: W. W. Norton & Co., 1994.

Glaeser, Edward L., and Kristina Tobio. "The Rise of the Sunbelt." A. Alfred Taubman Center for State and Local Government. John F. Kennedy School of Government, Harvard University, May 2007. https://www.hks.harvard.edu/sites/default/files /centers/taubman/files/sunbelt.pdf. Accessed August 27, 2020.

Golden, Arthur. "Nine Early Whitman Letters, 1840–1841," *American Literature,* vol. 58, no. 3 (October 1986).

Grosh, Ron. "Early American Literary Realism II: The Midwestern Matrix," *MidAmerica* 16, 1989.

Greasley, Philip A. *Dictionary of Midwestern Literature: Dimensions of the Midwestern Literary Imagination.* Bloomington: Indiana University Press, 2016.

Green, James. *Death in the Haymarket: A Story of Chicago, the First Labor Movement and the Bombing that Divided Gilded Age America.* New York: Anchor Books, 2006.

Grosh, Ronald M. "Early American Realism I: The National Scene," *MidAmerica* 15 (1988), 132–144, 133.

Gross, Barry. "In Another Country: The Revolt from the Village," *MidAmerica* 4 (1977): 101–111.

———. "The Revolt That Wasn't: The Legacies of Critical Myopia." *CEA Critic* 39.2 (January 1977): 4–8.

Gustaitis, Joseph. *Chicago's Greatest Year, 1893: The White City and the Birth of a Modern Metropolis.* Carbondale: Southern Illinois University Press, 2013.

Hale, Grace Elizabeth. *A Nation of Outsiders: How the White Middle Class Fell in Love with Rebellion in Postwar America.* Oxford: Oxford University Press, 2011.

Hallwas, John. "Masters and the Pioneers: Four Epitaphs from Spoon River Anthology," *Old Northwest* (2) 389–399 [1976].

———. "Two Autobiographical Epitaphs in *Spoon River Anthology,*" *The Great Lakes Review,* 3(1) [1976].

Hallwas, John E., and Dennis J. Reader, eds. *The Vision of This Land: Studies of Vachel Lindsay, Edgar Lee Masters, and Carl Sandburg.* Macomb, IL: Western Illinois University Press, 1976.

Halper, Thomas, and Douglas Muzzio. "It's a Wonderful Life: Representations of the Small Town in American Movies," *European Journal of American Studies,* vol. 6, no. 1 (Spring 2011), 1–21.

Halttunen, Karen. *Confidence Men and Painted Women: A Study of Middle-class Culture in America, 1830–1870*. New Haven: Yale University Press, 1982.

Heerman, M. Scott. "In a State of Slavery: Black Servitude in Illinois, 1800–1830," *Early American Studies* (Winter 2016).

Herron, Ima Honaker. *The Small Town in American Literature*. New York: Pageant Books, Inc., 1959.

Hilfer, Anthony Channell. *The Revolt from the Village, 1915–1930*. Chapel Hill: The University of North Carolina Press, 1969.

Hirsch, Susan Eleanor. *After the Strike: A Century of Labor Struggle at Pullman*. Urbana: University of Illinois Press, 2003.

Hoffman, Frederick J. *The Twenties: American Writing in the Postwar Decade*. New York: Viking, 1955.

Holman, David Marion. *A Certain Slant of Light: Regionalism and the Form of Southern and Midwestern Fiction*. Baton Rouge: Louisiana State University Press, 1995.

Howe, Irving, ed. *Literary Modernism*. Greenwich, CN: Fawcett Publications, 1967.

Hurt, James. "The Sources of the Spoon: Edgar Lee Masters and *Spoon River Anthology*," *The Centennial Review*, 24 (January 1, 1980).

Hutchinson, James M. *Rise of Sinclair Lewis, 1920–1930*. University Park: The Pennsylvania State University Press, 1996.

Hynes, Samuel. "The Whole Contention between Mr. Bennett and Mrs. Woolf," *Novel: A Forum on Fiction*, vol. 1, no. 1 (Autumn 1967).

Isenberg, Alison. *Downtown America: A History of the Place and the People Who Made It*. Chicago: University of Chicago Press, 2004.

Jentz, John B., and Richard Schneirov. *Chicago in the Age of Capital: Class, Politics, and Democracy during the Civil War and Reconstruction*. Urbana: University of Illinois Press, 2012.

Johnson, Kenneth. "Demographic Trends in Rural and Small Town America," Carsey Institute, University of New Hampshire, 2006.

Jung, Patrick J. *The Black Hawk War of 1832*. Norman: University of Oklahoma Press, 2007.

Kakutani, Michiko. "Review: 'Lincoln in the Bardo' Shows a President Haunted by Grief," *New York Times*, February 7, 2017, https://www.nytimes.com/2017/02/06/books/review-george-saunders-lincoln-in-the-bardo.html. Accessed January 29, 2020.

Kasson, John F. *Rudeness & Civility: Manners in Nineteenth-Century Urban America*. New York: Hill and Wang, 1990.

Kazin, Michael. *A Godly Hero: The Life of William Jennings Bryan*. New York: Alfred A. Knopf, 2006.

———. *The Populist Persuasion: An American History*. Ithaca: Cornell University Press, 2017.

Kennedy, David. *Freedom from Fear: The American People in Depression and War, 1929–1945*. Oxford: Oxford University Press, 1999.

Kleen, Michael. "The Copperhead Threat in Illinois: Peace Democrats, Loyalty Leagues, and the Charleston Riot of 1864," *Journal of the Illinois State Historical Society* 105:1 (2012).

Klement, Frank L. *The Copperheads in the Middle West*. Glousester, MA: Peter Smith, 1972.

Knapp, James. *Ezra Pound*. Boston: Twayne Publishers, 1979.

Kohl, Lawrence Frederick. *The Politics of Individualism: Parties and the American Character in the Jacksonian Era*. Oxford: Oxford University Press, 1989.

Kosiba, Sara. "A Successful Revolt? The Redefinition of Midwestern Literary Culture in the 1920s and 1930s." Dissertation: Kent State University, 2007.

Kramer, Dale. *Chicago Renaissance: The Literary Life in the Midwest, 1900–1930*. New York: Appleton-Century, 1966.

Kundinger, Matt. "Racial Rhetoric: The Detroit Free Press and Its Part in the Detroit Race Riot of 1863," *Michigan Journal of History* 3:2 (2006).

Kryczka, Nick. "Captive Audiences: Gender, Storytelling, and the Closing of the Illinois Frontier," *Journal of the Illinois State Historical Society*, 106:1 (2013).

Lauck, Jon. *From Warm Center to Ragged Edge: The Erosion of Midwestern Literary and Historical Regionalism, 1920–1965*. Iowa City: University of Iowa Press, 2017.

———. *The Lost Region: Toward a Revival of Midwestern History*. Iowa City: University of Iowa Press, 2013.

———. "The Myth of the Midwestern 'Revolt from the Village.'" *MidAmerica* 40 (2013): 39–85.

Lears, T. J. Jackson. *No Place of Grace: Antimodernism and the Transformation of American Culture, 1880–1920*. New York: Pantheon Books, 1981.

Levenson, Michael, ed. *The Cambridge Companion to Modernism*. Cambridge: Cambridge University Press, 1999.

Lewis, Pericles. *The Cambridge Introduction to Modernism*. Cambridge: Cambridge University Press, 2007.

———. *Modernism, Nationalism, and the Novel*. Cambridge: Cambridge University Press, 2000.

Lingeman, Richard R. *Sinclair Lewis: Rebel from Main Street*. New York: Random House, 2002.

Lloyd, Joanna. "*Nebraska: A Poem* by Greg Kuzma, and: *Village Journal. Pebble #17* by Greg Kuzma, and: *Of China and of Greece* by Greg Kuzma, and: *A Turning: A Sequence* by Greg Kuzma (review)," *Western American Literature*, vol. 27, no. 4 (Winter 1993), 361–363.

Loewen, James. *Sundown Towns: A Hidden Dimension of American Racism*. New York: The New Press, 2005.

Longstreet, Stephen. *Chicago: 1860–1919*. New York: David McKay Company, Inc., 1973.

Loving, Jerome. *The Last Titan: A Life of Theodore Dreiser*. Berkeley: University of California Press, 2005.

Lutz, Tom. *Cosmopolitan Vistas: American Regionalism and Literary Value*. Ithaca: Cornell University Press, 2004.

Madison, James H. *Lynching in the Heartland: Race and Memory in America*. New York: Palgrave Macmillan, 2001.

May, Elaine Tyler. *Homeward Bound: American Families in the Cold War Era*. New York: Basic Books, 1999.

May, Henry. *The End of American Innocence*. New York: Columbia University Press, 1996.
————. "Shifting Perspectives on the 1920s," *The Mississippi Valley Historical Review* vol. 43, no. 3 (December 1956), 405–427.

May, Lary. *The Big Tomorrow: Hollywood and the Politics of the American Way*. Chicago: The University of Chicago Press, 2000.

McCue, Jim. "T. S. Eliot, Edgar Lee Masters and Glorious France." *Essays in Criticism* 64, no. 1 (2014): 45–73.

McMath, Robert C., Jr. *American Populism: A Social History, 1877–1878*. New York: Hill and Wang, 1993.

McPherson, James M. *Battle Cry of Freedom: The Civil War Era*. New York: Oxford University Press, 1988.

Medovoi, Leerom. *Rebels: Youth and the Cold War Origins of Identity*. Durham: Duke University Press, 2005.

Meer, Sarah. *Uncle Tom Mania: Slavery, Minstrelsy and Transatlantic Culture in the 1850s*. Athens: The University of Georgia Press, 2005.

Miller, John E. *Small-Town Dreams: Stories of Midwestern Boys Who Shaped America*. Lawrence: University Press of Kansas, 2014.

Miller, Laura J. "Family Togetherness and the Suburban Ideal," *Sociological Forum*, vol. 10, no. 3 (September 1995), 393–418.

Miller, Ross. *American Apocalypse: The Great Fire and the Myth of Chicago*. Chicago: The University of Chicago Press, 1990.

Mishkin, Tracy, ed. *Literary Influence and African-American Writers: Collected Essays*. New York: Routledge, 2015.

Morton, Richard. "A Victorian Tragedy: The Strange Deaths of Mayor Carter Harrison and Patrick Eugene Prendergast," *Journal of the Illinois State Historical Association*, vol. 96, no. 1 (Spring 2003).

Munich, Adrienne, and Melissa Bradshaw, eds. *Amy Lowell: American Modern*. New Brunswick, NJ: Rutgers University Press, 2004.

Neely Jr., Mark E. *Lincoln and the Democrats: The Politics of Opposition in the Civil War*. Cambridge: Cambridge University Press, 2017.

Neuman, Robert. "Disneyland's Main Street, and Its Sources in Hollywood, USA," *The Journal of American Culture*, vol. 31, no. 1 (March 2008), 83–97.

Newcomb, John Timberman. *How Did Poetry Survive? The Making of Modern American Verse*. Urbana: University of Illinois Press, 2012.

Niven, Penelope. *Carl Sandburg: A Biography*. New York: Charles Scribner's Sons, 1991.

Olson, Liesl. *Chicago Renaissance: Literature and Art in the Midwest Metropolis*. New Haven: Yale University Press, 2017.

Osborne, William. *Music in Ohio*. Kent, Ohio: Kent State University Press, 2004.

Osler, Lee. *The Ethics of Modernism: Moral Ideas in Yeats, Eliot, Joyce, Woolf, and Beckett*. Cambridge: Cambridge University Press, 2007.

Ostermeier, Benjamin. "Biography," *Borderlands: The Goshen Settlement of William Bolin Whiteside*, https://whiteside.siue.edu/omeka/biography.html. Accessed May 5, 2017.

Owens, Robert M. *Mr. Jefferson's Hammer: William Henry Harrison and the Origins of American Indian Policy.* Norman: University of Oklahoma Press, 2007.

Pacyga, Dominic A. *Chicago: A Biography.* Chicago: The University of Chicago Press, 2009.

Patterson, Anita. "The American Legacy of Prufrock," in *The T.S. Eliot Studies Annual,* John D. Morgenstern, ed. Oxford: Oxford University Press, 2017.

Perkins, Elizabeth A. *Border Life: Experience and Memory in the Revolutionary Ohio Valley.* Chapel Hill: The University of North Carolina Press, 1998.

Peterson, Mark. *The City-State of Boston: The Rise and Fall of an Atlantic Power, 1630–1865.* Princeton, NJ: Princeton University Press, 2019.

Peterson, Merrill D. *The Jefferson Image in the American Mind.* New York: Oxford University Press, 1960.

Pfeifer, Michael. *Lynching Beyond Dixie: American Mob Violence Outside the South.* Urbana: University of Illinois Press, 2013.

Poll, Ryan. *Main Street and Empire: The Fictional Small Town in the Age of Globalization.* New Brunswick, NJ: Rutgers University Press, 2012.

Postel, Charles. *The Populist Vision.* Oxford: Oxford University Press, 2007.

Price, Rachael. "Beyond 'Main Street': Small Towns in Post-'Revolt' American Literature." PhD diss. University of Arkansas, 2016, https://scholarworks.uark.edu/etd/1476 [accessed November 19, 2020].

Primeau, Ronald. *Beyond Spoon River: The Legacy of Edgar Lee Masters.* Austin: University of Texas Press, 1981.

———, ed. *Midwestern Literature: Critical Insights.* Ipswich: Salem Press, 2013.

Putzel, Max. *The Man in the Mirror: William Marion Reedy and his Magazine.* Cambridge, MA: Harvard University Press, 1963.

Ravitz, Abe C. *Clarence Darrow and the American Literary Tradition.* Cleveland: The Press of Western Reserve University, 1962.

Roberts, Cokie, Susan Stamberg, Noah Adams, John Ydstie, Renee Montagne, Ari Shapiro, and David Folkenflik. *This Is NPR: The First Forty Years.* San Francisco: Chronicle Books, 2010.

Rose, Jonathan D., and Kenneth A. Snowden. "The New Deal and the Origins of the Modern Real Estate Loan Contract," *Explorations in Economic History,* vol. 50 (2013).

Ross, Dorothy. "Freud and the Vicissitudes of Modernism in the United States, 1940–1980," *After Freud Left: A Century of Psychoanalysis in America,* John Burnham, ed. Chicago: The University of Chicago Press, 2012.

Rowe, Adam. "The Republican Rhetoric of a Frontier Controversy: Newspapers in the Illinois Slavery Debate, 1823–1824," *Journal of the Early Republic* 31 (Winter 2011).

Russell, Herbert K. *Edgar Lee Masters: A Biography.* Urbana and Chicago: University of Illinois Press, 2001.

Ryden, Kent C. "Writing the Midwest: History, Literature, and Regional Identity." *Geographical Review* 89.4 (1999): 511–532.

Sanders, Scott Russell. *Writing from the Center.* Bloomington: Indiana University Press, 1995.

Saxton, Alexander. *The Rise and Fall of the White Republic: Class Politics and Mass Culture in Nineteenth-Century America*. London: Verso, 2003.

Scheibel, Will. "Rebel Masculinities of Star/Director/Text: James Dean, Nicholas Ray, and *Rebel without a Cause*." *Journal of Gender Studies* vol. 25, no. 2 (2016), 125–140.

Schultz, Robert. "Celluloid History: Postwar Society in Postwar Popular Culture," *American Studies* vol. 31, no. 1 (Spring 1990), 41–63.

Sebastian, Jonathan. "A Divided State: The 1862 Election and the Illinois Response to Expanding Federal Authority," *Journal of the Illinois State Historical Society* 106:3/4 (2013).

Shamir, Milette. *Inexpressible Privacy: The Interior Life of Antebellum American Literature*. Philadelphia: University of Pennsylvania Press, 2008.

Shortridge, James. *The Middle West: Its Meaning in American Culture*. Lawrence: University Press of Kansas, 1989.

Skues, Richard. "Clark Revisited: Reappraising Freud in America," *After Freud Left: A Century of Psychoanalysis in America*, John Burnham, ed. Chicago: The University of Chicago Press, 2012.

Smith, Carl S. *Chicago and the Literary Imagination, 1880–1920*. Chicago: The University of Chicago Press, 1984.

Smith, Henry Nash. *Virgin Land: The American West as Symbol and Myth*. Cambridge, MA: Harvard University Press, 1950.

Smith, Page. *As a City upon a Hill: The Town in American History*. Cambridge, MA: M.I.T. Press, 1973.

Stuhr, Margaret. "The Safe Middle West: Escape from and Escape to Home." *MidAmerica* 14 (1987): 18–27.

Sugrue, Thomas J. "Crabgrass-Roots Politics: Race, Rights, and the Reaction against Liberalism in the Urban North, 1940–1964," *The Journal of American History*, vol. 82, no. 2 (September 1995).

Sullivan, Daniel J. "Sentimental Hogwash? On Capra's *It's a Wonderful Life*," *Humanitas*, vol. 18, no. 1–2 (2005), 115–140.

Sutton, Robert M. "The Illinois Central: Thoroughfare for Freedom," *Civil War History*, 7:3 (September 1961).

Thatcher Ulrich, Laurel. *A Midwife's Tale: The Life of Martha Ballard, Based on Her Diary, 1785–1812*. New York: Knopf, 1990.

Twelbeck, Kirsten. "Eden Refound(ed): Post Civil War Literary Gardening," *Rereading the Machine in the Garden: Nature and Technology in American Culture*, Eric Erbacher, Nicole Maruo-Schröder, Florian Sedlmeier, eds. Frankfurt: Campus Verlag, 2014.

Valenti, Peter. "The Theological Rhetoric of 'It's a Wonderful Life,'" *Film Criticism*, vol. 5, no. 2. (Winter 1981), 23–34.

VanWagenen, Julianne. "Masters vs. Lee Masters: The Legacy of the Spoon River Author between Illinois and Italy." *Forum Italicum: A Journal of Italian Studies* 53, no. 3 (2019): 679–698.

Watts, Edward. *An American Colony: Regionalism and the Roots of Midwestern Culture.* Athens: Ohio University Press, 2002.

Weber, Jennifer. *Copperheads: The Rise and Fall of Lincoln's Opponents in the North.* Oxford: Oxford University Press, 2006.

Weber, Ronald. *The Midwestern Ascendency in American Writing.* Bloomington: Indiana University Press, 1992.

Weller, Shane. *Modernism and Nihilism.* New York: Palgrave Macmillan, 2011.

Whitaker, Epher. *History of Southold, L.I.: Its First Century.* Southold, L.I.: Epher Whitaker, 1881.

White, Ronald C. *Lincoln: A Biography.* New York: Random House, 2009.

Wilentz, Sean. *Chants Democratic: New York City and the Rise of the American Working Class, 1788–1850.* Oxford: Oxford University Press, 1984.

———. *The Rise of American Democracy: Jefferson to Lincoln.* New York: W. W. Norton & Company, 2005.

Williams, Ellen. *Harriet Monroe and the Poetry Renaissance: The First Ten Years of Poetry, 1912–1922.* Urbana: University of Illinois Press, 1977.

Willis, Sharon. "The Politics of Disappointment: Todd Haynes Rewrites Douglas Sirk," *Camera Obscura,* vol. 18, no. 3 (2003), 131–175.

Wiltse, Charles Maurice. *The Jeffersonian Tradition in American Democracy.* New York: Hill and Wang, Inc., 1960.

Wineapple, Brenda. "The Production of Character in 'It's a Wonderful Life,'" *Film Criticism,* vol. 5, no. 2 (Winter 1981), 4–11.

Wood, Joseph S. "'Build, Therefore, Your Own World': The New England Village and Settlement Ideal," *Annals of the Association of American Geographers,* 81(1), 1991.

Wortham-Galvin, B. D. "The Fabrication of Place in America: The Fictions and Traditions of the New England," *Traditional Settlements and Dwellings Review,* vol. 21, no. 2 (2010).

Index

Jason Stacy is a professor of history and social science pedagogy at Southern Illinois University, Edwardsville. He is the author of *Walt Whitman's Multitudes: Labor Reform and Persona in Whitman's Journalism and the First* Leaves of Grass, *1840–1855* and editor of *Leaves of Grass, 1860: The 150th Anniversary Facsimile Edition.*

The University of Illinois Press
is a founding member of the
Association of University Presses.

University of Illinois Press
1325 South Oak Street
Champaign, IL 61820-6903
www.press.uillinois.edu